# Recreation
# Guide - SW

**Reed I. White**

Alta Research, Lava Hot Springs Airpark, Idaho

# Flyer's Recreation Guide - Southwest

Written by   Reed I. White

Published by   Alta Research
131 NW 4th Street #290
Corvallis, OR 97330-4702, USA
Phone 500-288-ALTA

*http://www.alta-research.com*

Printing History   First southwest edition published in 1999.
Printed in the United States of America.

Library of Congress Number   99-94694

Cataloging Data

White, Reed I.
Flyer's Recreation Guide - Southwest
Access to Adventure in the Southwestern States.
Includes index.
1. Air Pilot Guides — The Southwest.
2. Travel — Southwest (U.S.).
3. Recreation — Southwest (U.S.).
4. Southwest (U.S.). I. Title.
TL 726.W45   629.13   99-94694
ISBN 0-945549-09-1   Softcover

# About This Book

The **Flyer's Recreation Guide** is a resource of ideas and information for pilots and passengers who fly for fun and adventure. The Guide contains descriptions of southwest America's most exciting sites within convenient access of landing strips. Update bulletins at ***http://www.alta-research.com*** keep the Guide growing and current.

All sites in the Guide have been visited and researched by experienced, fun-loving pilots. Each chapter provides detailed information on a specific site to help you create your own memorable adventures. Included are tips for hikes, swimming, fishing, lodging, restaurants, and entertainment. The Guide tells how to find trailheads, hot springs, raft trips, and other items of interest. Maps and photographs help you visualize what each site has to offer.

Airport information is provided to help determine if your aircraft and skills are compatible with the destination. Aerial photographs help you locate and identify airstrips. Local services and transportation are listed. Hundreds of phone numbers are included so that you can get further information, make reservations, and verify current conditions. Also included is information that will increase the safety and enjoyment of your trip.

We encourage you to fly safely as you use this book to create your own adventures. I would love to hear about your experiences – **feedback and suggestions are always welcome!**

**Reed I. White**

*alta@alta-research.com*
*www.alta-research.com*

NANCY ROSE

## *Other sources of fly-in recreation information from Alta Research*

**Flyer's Recreation Guide - NW**,   ISBN 0-945549-08-3.

> The northwest version covers the states of Idaho, Montana, Oregon, Washington, and Wyoming.

Web site:  **http://www.alta-research.com**

> The Alta Research web site contains update information, links to other aviation sites, and ways to order publications.

# Table of Contents

## Intro-6

## California Central

| Truckee | North Lake Tahoe | **C1 - TRUC** |
| Carmel Valley | Central-western California | **C2 - CARV** |
| Columbia | Central California Sierras | **C2 - COLU** |
| Georgetown | Central California Sierras | **C2 - GEOR** |
| Harris Ranch | Central California | **C2 - HARR** |
| Healdsburg | North-western California | **C2 - HEAL** |
| Mammoth Lakes | Central California Sierras | **C2 - MAMM** |
| Markleeville | Central California Sierras | **C2 - MARK** |
| Mono Lake | Central-eastern California | **C2 - MONO** |
| Saline Valley | Central-eastern California | **C2 - SALI** |
| Tahoe | South Lake Tahoe | **C2 - TAHO** |
| Tuolumne Meadows | Central Sierras | **C2 - TUOL** |
| Yosemite Park | Central California Sierras | **C2 - YOSE** |

## California South

| Big Bear | Southern California Mountains | **C3 - BIGB** |
| Catalina Island | South-western California | **C3 - CATA** |
| Kernville | Southern California Sierras | **C3 - KERN** |
| Oceana | Southern California Coast | **C3 - OCEA** |
| Palm Springs | Southern California | **C3 - PALM** |
| Solvang | Southern California | **C3 - SOLV** |

## Colorado

| Aspen | Central Colorado Mountains | **CO - ASPE** |
| Durango | Four Corners, Colorado | **CO - DURA** |
| Glendale | Central Colorado Mountains | **CO - GLEN** |
| Mesa Verde | Four Corners, Colorado | **CO - MESA** |
| Steamboat Springs | North Colorado Mountains | **CO - STEA** |
| Telluride | Central Colorado Mountains | **CO - TELL** |

## New Mexico

| | | |
|---|---|---|
| Alamogordo | Southern Mew Mexico | **NM - ALAM** |
| Carlsbad | South-eastern New Mexico | **NM - CARL** |
| Los Alamos | Northern New Mexico | **NM - LOSA** |
| Sante Fe | Northern New Mexico | **NM - SFE** |
| Silver City | South-western New Mexico | **NM - SILV** |
| Taos | Northern New Mexico | **NM - TAOS** |

## Nevada

| | | |
|---|---|---|
| Elko | Northern Nevada | **NV - ELKO** |
| Ely | Eastern Nevada | **NV - ELY** |
| Jackpot | North-eastern Nevada | **NV - JACK** |
| Laughlin | South-eastern Nevada | **NV - LAUG** |
| Lehman Caves | Eastern Nevada | **NV - LEHM** |

## Utah

| | | |
|---|---|---|
| Bryce Canyon | Southern Utah Mountains | **UT - BRYC** |
| Escalante | Southern Utah | **UT - ESCA** |
| Fry Canyon | Utah Canyonlands | **UT - FRYC** |
| Heber City, Park City | Northern Utah | **UT - HEBE** |
| Hite | Lake Powell | **UT - HITE** |
| Mexican Mountain | Utah Canyonlands | **UT - MEXM** |
| Moab | Utah Canyonlands | **UT - MOAB** |
| Monument Valley | Four Corners, Utah | **UT - MONU** |
| Needles Outpost | Utah Canyonlands | **UT - NEED** |
| Oljato | Four Corners, Utah | **UT - OLJA** |
| Saint George | South-western Utah | **UT - SGEO** |

| | | |
|---|---|---|
| **INDEX** | Detailed Index | **XX - INDX** |

# Key

> *Boxes like this contain a quick synopsis of each chapter. The dollars at the end of the text indicate typical total cost for __two people__ to stay overnight, eat meals, and enjoy entertainment. Example: $12 - $123. Info: 500-288-2582.*

## Airport Information

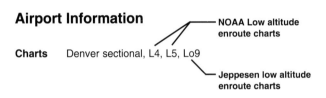

**Charts**  Denver sectional, L4, L5, Lo9

NOAA Low altitude enroute charts

Jeppesen low altitude enroute charts

## Lodging Information

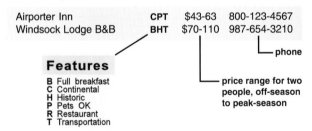

| Airporter Inn | CPT | $43-63 | 800-123-4567 |
| Windsock Lodge B&B | BHT | $70-110 | 987-654-3210 |

phone

### Features

**B** Full breakfast
**C** Continental
**H** Historic
**P** Pets OK
**R** Restaurant
**T** Transportation

price range for two people, off-season to peak-season

*__Things change!__  Prices in the Guide include taxes and are based on 1999 rates. Phone numbers for all businesses are included – use them to verify current prices and availability.*

*See __http://www.alta-research.com__ for update information.*

# DENSITY ALTITUDE CHART

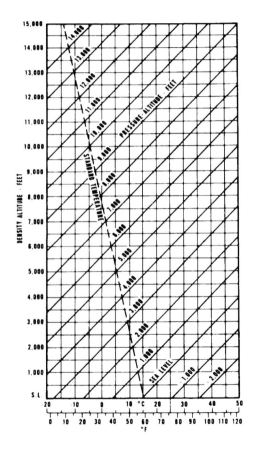

SOURCE: FEDERAL AVIATION ADMINISTRATION

# Arizona

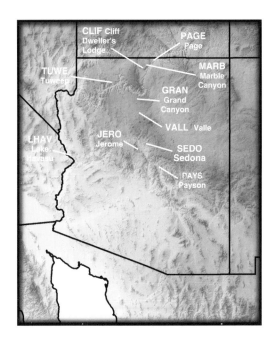

**CLIF** Cliff Dweller's Lodge
**PAGE** Page
**TUWE** Tuweep
**MARB** Marble Canyon
**GRAN** Grand Canyon
**VALL** Valle
**LHAV** Lake Havasu
**JERO** Jerome
**SEDO** Sedona
**PAYS** Payson

**Arizona Aeronautics**

**602-254-6234**

# Cliff Dweller's Lodge

## Cliff Dwellers Lodge

**Town**  Marble Canyon  **ID** AZ03
**Coord**  N-36-44.1, W-111-45.1
**Elev**  4210 feet,  SW end high
**Runway**  4 - 22,  3555 x 40' dirt
**Freq**  CTAF-122.9
**Charts**  Las Vegas sectional

> *CAUTION:* Airport information not for navigational use. Verify runway condition before landing. Watch density altitude.

> *Cliff Dwellers Lodge is a lazy desert inn, not far*
> *from the edge of the Grand Canyon.*
> *Not elegant, but serene with colorful scenery.*
> *$80-120.   Lodge: 520-355-2228.*

## Airport Description

The airport is located at the western edge of the northeastern end of the Grand Canyon.  Several miles to the west, multicolored bluffs rise 3000 feet above the airport surface.

The windsock may be bleached by the sun and difficult to differentiate from the terrain.  Look for a white, 10-foot, airplane-shaped wind-T to provide wind information.

The runway surface is uneven and sprinkled with gravel and small rocks of less than one and one-half inch diameter.  Expect a bumpy landing.  Reduce landing speed to a safe minimum before final touchdown.  Compared to other back-country strips in the area, Cliff Dwellers was acceptably safe when I last visited.  However, weather and lack of maintenance can cause dramatic changes in several months.  Call ahead for information and inspect at low altitude before landing.

Tiedown cables are stretched, but you will need your own ropes.  No tiedown fee.  Space is available for several aircraft.

## Services, Lodging, and Transportation

Airport information:  800-433-8966, Hatch Expeditions.  No fuel or services are available at the strip.  Food and lodging are provided at the Cliff Dwellers Lodge, a fifteen minute walk from the tiedown area. The lodge will pickup from the airport it you call them in advance. No other transportation is available.

## Overview

The terrain at this site is dramatically three-dimensional. The strip is within several miles of painted bluffs that tower to the west, and gaping beginnings of the Grand Canyon sink to the east. The bluffs contain a number of gorges to explore, most of which are within walking distance. A nearby dirt road provides access to a small plateau about 1000 feet higher than the strip. You will probably meet no other visitors on hikes in this area.

Cliff Dwellers Lodge and one or two other buildings are the only man-made structures in the area. Relative to Marble Can-

**Cliff Dwellers Lodge**

yon, **AZ-MARB**, the area is less populated, is more serene, and has the feeling of being less commercial.

Cliff Dwellers Lodge is a fifteen minute walk from the airport. The lodge consists of a gas station, small store, restaurant, and twenty-one sleeping units, twelve of which are new. The buildings are constructed of local rock, beautifully-colored and harmonious with the surroundings. The rooms are clean, but small and contain no phone or TV. I found their wood-paneled, Indian decor to be more to my liking than most big-city hotel rooms at double the cost. Prices have increased since the addition of the new units: now $45 to $72 for two. The owners recommend advance reservations. Write them at Cliff Dwellers Lodge, Highway 89A, Marble Canyon, AZ 86036, or call 520-355-2228. When you arrive, they will be happy to tell you about local trails.

For other Grand Canyon sites, see chapters **AZ-GRAN**, **AZ-MARB**, **AZ-TUWE**, and **AZ-VALL**.

## Canyon Raft Trips

Located less than a quarter mile from the lodge is the only other business in town, Hatch Expeditions. Hatch provides Grand Canyon **rafting expeditions**. Their standard 6.5-day trip costs $1500. Included are three "all you can eat" meals per day, hiking, swimming, and sights like beautiful fern-covered waterfalls. The $1500 also covers helicopter and fixed-wing return transportation. You will need to make reservations for June several months in advance; for other months, three to four weeks should be sufficient.

For more information, call Hatch Expeditions in Vernal at 800-433-8966. See **AZ-GRAN** for other outfitters that service the Canyonlands area.

*- RW*

# Grand Canyon

## Grand Canyon Airport

**Town** Grand Canyon **ID** GCN
**Coord** N-35-57.14, W-112-08.82
**Elev** 6606 feet, NE end high
**Runway** 3 - 21rt, 8999 x 150' asphalt
**Freq** ATIS-124.3, Apc-124.2,
Twr-119.0, lights-3x, Gnd-121.9
**Charts** Las Vegas sect., L4, L5, Lo10

> **CAUTION:** Airport information not for navigational use. Altitude restrictions. Sight-seeing traffic. NE terrain higher. Watch density altitude.

21rt

3

> **Grand Canyon airport is the main commercial airport for the Grand Canyon. A spectrum of visitor facilities and scenic activities are available. $140-300. Info: 520-638-2901.**

## Airport Description

Prior to visiting, check with Flight Service for the latest procedures and regulations for flying near the Grand Canyon. Monitor the appropriate frequency while in the vicinity of the canyon and check with ATIS for additional information. Watch for the numerous air sight-seeing flights in the area. Avoid low overflight of Grand Canyon Village.

This high-altitude runway is designed to accommodate commercial jet IFR air traffic – an easy mark for general aviation aircraft. Note that the tower closes prior to dusk and services become less available after this time.

## Services, Lodging, and Transportation

Airport office phone: 520-638-2446. FBO phone: 520-638-7117. Fuel: 100 and JetA. Grand Canyon Airlines provides fuel, tiedown, refreshments, oxygen, extensive repair service, and scenic tours. Fuel is expensive, but no tiedown fee is charged.

The following three inns pickup and are a mile from the airport, but do not allow pets: The Canyon Squire costs $60-150, 800-622-6966; the Quality Inn costs $80-200, 800-228-5151; and the Red Feather costs $80-120, 520-638-2414.

The Park Service lodges have lodging that covers a range of class and location, with prices ranging from $80-200. They do not provide airport transportation, but they do provide referral to a kennel for pet owners. Call Central Reservations, 303-297-2757, for information about prices and amenities. The local phone for the Grand Canyon Lodge system is 520-638-2631.

A Forest Service campground is located two miles from the airport and camping in the park is eight miles from the airport. See comments about the Phantom Ranch on following pages.

CASSI shuttle bus service charges $5 per person for rides between airport and park. They run hourly in summer between 8:30 and 18:00; times and frequency of service vary with the seasons. Call 520-638-2631 for taxi service or for Fred Harvey Transportation tours. As this book goes to press, there are no car rental agencies at the airport or in town.

## Overview

Flying over the Grand Canyon is an awe-inspiring experience. Though not as colorful as Bryce Canyon, **UT-BRYC**, the Grand Canyon's sheer size is overwhelming. Pilots and their passengers are among the few who can fully experience this phenomenon. Because overflight restrictions have become strict, obtain a brief of the latest from Flight Service.

Land-based views are nearly as impressive. Activities include **hiking**, **mule rides** into the canyon, staying at the Phantom Ranch on the canyon floor, **float trips** down the Colorado River, and gazing from the overlooks.

Due to the delicate canyon environment and its popularity, the National Park Service has imposed a number of restrictions: no camp fires (camp stove only), no pets, and no groups larger than

16 persons. Read carefully the information pamphlets you receive from the Information Line, 520-638-7888 (automated). You receive a topo map in the information packet. At the canyon, maps are available at either rim.

The rims are comfortable throughout the summer months. The canyon floor, on the other hand, can get very hot during the months of June, July, and August. Temperatures of 100 degrees F (38 C) are not uncommon. If you don't care for hot, desert conditions, avoid the canyon floor during the summer months.

The park's **Phantom Ranch** is located on the canyon floor. Overnight camping permits are not required for Phantom Ranch guests. Overnight mule rides, including cabin and meals, cost about $300 per person. Hikers can room in a dorm for $23 each. The trick is to secure a reservation – 23 months in advance is recommended! Contact Central Reservations at 303-297-2757.

The Park Service has a **smooth-water raft trip** for $100. A number of outfitters provide 3- to 18-day **white-water raft trips** down the Colorado River. Expect to pay $200-300 per day for motorized boat rides, and $150-250 for oar boat rides. The trips provide all-you-can-eat meals, and stop for hikes to waterfalls and petroglyphs.

Hatch River Expeditions, for example, offers 6.5-day trips for $1500 per person, 800-433-8966. Rides leave from the Marble Canyon airstrip, **AZ-MARB**. Other outfitters include: Arizona River Runners, 800-828-WEST; Arizona Raft Adventures, 800-786-RAFT; Canyonland Tours, 520-774-7343; and, Diamond River Adventures, 800-343-3121.

Also see **AZ-CLIF**, **AZ-MARB**, **AZ-TUWE**, and **AZ-VALL**.

*- RW*

# Jerome

## Cottonwood Airport

| | |
|---|---|
| **Town** | Cottonwood **ID** P52 |
| **Coord** | N-34-44.80, W-112-02.11 |
| **Elev** | 3550 feet, 1%, SW end high |
| **Runway** | 14 - 32rt, 4250 x 75' asphalt |
| **Freq** | CTAF-122.7, lights-2x3x5x |
| **Charts** | Phoenix sectional, L4, Lo10 |

**CAUTION:** *Airport information not for navigational use. 8000-foot mountains 2 miles SW.*

> **Jerome is a quaint mining town with an**
> **exceptional antique machinery museum.**
> **$100-200.   Info: 520-634-2900.**

## Airport Description

Approach and landing at Cottonwood are straightforward.
However, an airport employee suggests that during windy conditions you touch down on 14 after the large General Semiconduc-
tor building. The airport is accessible nearly 365 days per year.
Night flyers should be aware of the large mountains to the
southwest. The airport lights its beacon, dusk to dawn.

## Services, Lodging, and Transportation

Airport phone: 520-634-5635. Fuel: 100LL and JetA. Overnight tiedown fee is $3. Food is available one block from the
airport, and two local restaurants pick up from the airport. Locals claim the Whitehorse Lounge serves the best food in town.
The airport has no official campground, but camping is allowed.

The Quality Las Companas Hotel, 520-634-4207, in Cottonwood has restaurant, lodge, pool, Jacuzzi, and rooms for $60-75.
The View Motel, 634-7581, has $40-52 rooms with a view,
pool, and several nearby restaurants. Though official campsites
are not available at the airport, they can be had two miles away at
Dead Horse State Park.

Lodging in Jerome is limited, so advance
reservations are recommended. Nancy
Russel's B&B includes a full gourmet breakfast, and prefers to cater to groups of two to

**Features**

B Full breakfast
C Continental
H Historic
P Pets OK
R Restaurant
T Transportation

four. Her house is a renovated miner's home with a great view. The Connor Hotel has a few units over the bar. Jerome lodging:

| | | | |
|---|---|---|---|
| Cottage Inn | HPRT | $65 | 520-634-0701 |
| Ghost City Inn | BH | $82-104 | 520-634-4678 |
| Hillside House B&B | BHT | $83 | 520-634-5667 |
| Inn at Jerome | R | $60-95 | 520-634-5094 |
| Jerome View Inn | BHPT | $85-100 | 520-639-2824 |
| Rose Garden B&B | BHPT | $65-75 | 520-634-3270 |
| Surgeon's House | BHP | $100-135 | 520-639-1452 |

The FBO can help with rental cars, 520-634-5635. They obtain cars from Enterprise, 634-0049; or from All Red Rentals, 634-3931. Budget rents cars from a local car dealership. Call Budget at 567-3399 for airport pickup. If destined for Jerome and you want to spare the expense of a car, ask your hotel or B&B if they can arrange a pickup. Once in Jerome, most points of interest are within a 30-minute walking distance.

## Jerome

Jerome was at one time the most talked-about mining camp in America. Known as a roaring, violent town, it peaked at 15,000 people before the Great Depression. The century-old town is perched on the side of a mountain at 5245 feet, offering views of Verde Valley, the red rock of Sedona, and distant mountain peaks.

The Jerome Main Street provides hours of browsing at **galleries** and shops that specialize in copper, brass, pottery, rocks, books, jewelry, antiques, and momentos. The town has several sources of food and libations. Historic sites include: **Jerome State Historical Park** and **Douglas Mansion**, 520-634-5381, **Jerome Historical Society**; and **Gold King Mine Museum**.

Jerome's annual events include Arizona's Largest Gas Engine Show, Theme and Memorabilia Show, and music festivals.

To get to Jerome from Cottonwood, follow Highway 89A northwest for less than 10 miles. The road climbs from the valley at 3500 feet to Jerome's 5000-foot perch.

## Gold King Mine — A Working Museum

Of all the antique-machinery museums I have visited, Gold King Mine has been surpassed only by the now defunct Oscar's Dreamland in Montana. As I wandered among the old iron workhorses, sawmill, geese, goats, and buildings, the word *integrity* fixed itself in my mind. Most of the equipment on display actually works and is being used to expand the facilities. Visitors are encouraged to become involved. In a sense, it's an audience-participation theater, and you can't beat the $2-4 price!

The one-mile drive to the Gold King Mine begins at the west end of Jerome. A series of hand-hewn signs guide the way:

**Antique machinery that does real work at the Gold King Mine**

> **Where the pavement ends, the Old West begins.**
> **Gold King Museum and Campground**

> **Yup, everything you came to see is here.**
> **Nope, you can't see it from your car.**

Owner Don Robertson comments about his signs: "We feel that our road coming out here and our parking lot is what we call our *jerk filter*. All we get out here after the filter are real people."

Don and his wife Terry Ann own and run the museum. Terry Ann is an artist who sells her work at the museum and around the world. Don says, "She makes the difference between eating beans and weenies and getting to eat steak and lobster once in awhile." Don is a mechanical genius who loves to mend and play with big toys. The two seem to have found their life's calling in Jerome. I'll let Don tell his own story:

**Don and visitors pry loose a jammed log at the saw mill**

"When I was an Iowa farm boy of ten or eleven, I used to help a neighbor restore old steam engines. All I got to do the first year was scrape rust off. Somehow I cut myself and got some rust in my blood and it's just hung with me. So I love this old machinery and can't get it out of my blood.

"I ended up moving to Arizona 23 years ago and working as a diesel mechanic. Had some extra time and money, and spent my weekends buying old machinery because it's what I love. I collected stuff over a 20-year period. It got so everybody came over on weekends, brought their friends to look at [the machinery] – like it was a museum! They all told me, 'You ought to put it into a Museum.' So I heard that so many times that I got to thinking. We started traveling on weekends looking for a spot. Had to be the right place. We got the exact perfect place here!

"Anyway, I finally decided, no more bosses; I'd own my own museum and do it my way: a working museum, and it's not your typical museum with everything under glass and behind barriers. You know, it's not a plastic museum; it's the real thing.

"As it stands now, the sawmill runs, the blacksmith shop is normally working. We got the oldest trip-hammer in the world in that blacksmith shop – over 100 years old and it still works perfectly. The blacksmith's normally out there making nails and all kinds of things. We just sort of play at work. That other fella out there's a woodworker, and he'll be makin' things from wood, *our wood*, our prime wood that we milled on the saw.

"Most of the big engines, trucks, and tractors and things work – road graders, bulldozers from as far back as the Twenties. They're all in working order and we use them to plow the snow and grade the roads. Most museums are real careful not to do anything. We have to be careful not to mash too many visitors with the trucks."

RW: Do you have plans for future expansion?

"We're going to expand our museum, build a larger parking area. We're putting in a train, a 24-gauge train to move people through the museum. After that, we'll just kinda follow our nose as to what is available, what comes up for sale as a museum piece for us, for sawmill or mining."

RW: How about that huge generator?

"We have that old three-cylinder 10,000-cubic-inch gas engine. The engine runs beautifully. Someday we may hook the generator up, but we don't know what we'll do with it. Only thing comes to mind right now is to put a big searchlight up on the hill, with an eight-foot reflector. Maybe once a month on Saturday nights we'll fire it up and point it down at Sedona. I'd like to know what all those millionaires are doing over there. I think that would be fun. I don't know what else I'd do with all that electricity."

RW: Tell me about your business philosophy.

"We have more fun making a living than anybody. We're a couple, we live right here; we don't have to commute. We both do what we like to do most, and we make enough money to live comfortable. That's our home right there. I cut the logs, hauled and sawed 'em, and built the buildings and whatever.

"When it comes to people, we really strive to make every one of our customers special. I don't care what kind of lifestyle people come from. Anyone who comes and visits can work or play at the museum as long as they please. Ya'll come visit!"

For further information, call Don at 520-634-0053, or write to the Gold King Mine, P.O. Box 125, Jerome, AZ 86331.

*- RW*

**Don Robertson**

# Lake Havasu

## Lake Havasu City Airport

| | |
|---|---|
| **Town** | Lake Havasu City  **ID**  HII |
| **Coord** | N-34-34.09,  W-114-21.37 |
| **Elev** | 781 feet |
| **Runway** | 14rt - 32,  5500 x 100' asphalt |
| **Freq** | CTAF-122.7, Lights-122.7-3x7x5x |
| | AWOS-119.025, NDB-HII-364 |
| **Charts** | Phoenix sectional,  L3, Lo10 |

*CAUTION:*  *Airport information not for navigational use. Hills, banner towing, parachuting, ultralights. See nav guides for pattern (approach/depart over water). Down-drafts, both ends.*

32

14rt

*Lake Havasu, desert town on the Colorado
River, known for its imported London Bridge
and claims to be the hottest spot in the U.S.
A place for water recreation and retirement.
$60-200.   Tourism Bureau: 520-453-3444*

## Airport Description

Lake Havasu's original airport was conveniently located on
the island west of town, which is linked to the city by the
London Bridge.  Although the island airport is closed, you may
want to fly over and locate the bridge.  The new airport is six
miles north of town, a modern facility with excellent runway.
Runway 32 is the default.

As I approached the airport, I noticed the air temperature was
100 degrees at 3000 feet.  When I landed at elevation 781, the
official temperature was 108.  The tiedown-chains were too hot
to handle.  Before departure several days later, the airport temperature peaked at 115.

Fortunately, nearly every building in the area is air-conditioned.  At an open hangar, I noted an air-conditioner on wheels
pointed at a mechanic under a helicopter.  One way or another,
locals learn to live with the heat.

## Airport Services, Transportation, and Lodging

Airport phones: 520-764-3330; Century Air, 764-8000.  Fuel:
100 and JetA.  Century air has a nice air-conditioned pilot's

lounge and provides maintenance. Camping is not permitted at the airport.

Avis, 520-764-3001, has an office at the main terminal. Due partially to a significant airport tax on rentals, Avis is not competitive. Enterprise, 453-0033, has spotty coverage on weekends. Paradise Rental, 505-5277, is near the Holiday Inn and has the best prices – economy cars for as little as $20.

Many Havasu hotels provide free transportation from the airport. The Holiday Inn, for example, provides transportation and offers pilots a worthy discount. In town, the free River City Trolley stops at the hotels several times per day. Although the trolley is not practical transportation, it is an easy way to see the town.

If you can handle walking 15 minutes in the heat, a car is not necessary. The town is very friendly to visitors. Providers of services, like jet-ski or ATV (All Terrain Vehicle) rental, will pick you up at your hotel – couldn't be more convenient.

The London Bridge is the point from which all distances are measured – the focal point for Lake Havasu City. The hotels listed below are all within 15-minute walking distance of the bridge.

The expansive Nautical Inn has an attractive location on the island, and is near two golf courses. The London Bridge Resort is in the midst of action at the bridge. It has a golf course, tennis courts, swimming pools, evening entertainment, and boat rentals. The Bridgeview Motel has no amenities. Prices are lower midweek; ask for discounts.

**Features**

**B** Full breakfast
**C** Continental
**H** Historic
**P** Pets OK
**R** Restaurant
**T** Transportation

| Bridgeview Motel | P | $34-80 | 520-855-5559 |
| Holiday Inn | PRT | $44-160 | 800- HOLIDAY |
| | | | 520-855-4071 |
| Howard Johnson Lodge | C | $57-110 | 800-446-4656 |
| | | | 520-453-4656 |
| Island Inn Hotel | CPT | $54-106 | 800-243-9955 |
| London Bridge Resort | PRT | $65-300 | 888-242-8278 |
| | | | 520-855-0888 |
| Nautical Inn | RT | $44-200 | 800-892-2141 |
| Ramada Inn | PR | $50-150 | 800-528-5169 |
| Sandman | T | $33-105 | 800-835-2410 |
| Super 8 Motel | P | $50-75 | 800-800-8000 |
| | | | 520-855-8844 |
| Windsor Inn | P | $29-55 | 800-730-8300 |

If you plan to spend some time in the area, consider renting a houseboat – a terrific way to score points with family or friends. There are 45 miles of lake and 450 miles of scenic shoreline to explore. Prices range from $700 to $2,500 per week, depending upon size of boat and time of year. The following companies rent fully-equipped houseboats: H2O Houseboat Vacations, 800-242-2628; and Havasu Springs Resort, 520-667-3361. Be sure to arrange to-and-from transportation as you make the deal.

## Lake Havasu Area

After shedding my luggage at the hotel, I headed for the famous London Bridge. First impressions were, "How could anyone live in this heat, and why so many empty lots in the heart of town?" I arrive at the 160-year old London Bridge. If this once-proud bridge has a soul, it must feel like a champion weight lifter who has been relegated to a freak show. The bridge spans a fake river and is surrounded by cheaply constructed, simulated British architecture – a tacky scene, by most standards.

While those were my first impressions, I vowed not to let them ruin the stay. Clearly, many other people love the place – if they can have a good time, I reasoned, I can too! I laid down $12 for a sunset cruise on the Dixie Belle.

We departed the bridge and cruised counterclockwise around the island. On the island, there are more motor homes and trailers than the average person will see in a lifetime. That's unique. I begin downing a series of marguerites. The sky to the west turns bright orange and the air begins to cool. After my third, I think, "This is a bizarre scene; I'm beginning to like it." At that moment, the tour guide begins his tale of Lake Havasu.

Robert McCulloch of chain saw fame arrived when the site was simply desert with a dammed river. He began by creating an R&D facility that tested outboard motors on the river; but, he had a much greater vision. He was to build a paradise in the desert – a seemingly crazy idea. Over the years, he engaged in

**Dixie Belle boarding passengers before the London Bridge**

much wheeling and dealing with the government. After various land exchanges with the Forest Service, McCulloch ended up with 16,630 acres of land on a man-made lake.

He had the city designed by an expert. Still, no one in his or her right mind would buy a lot. McCulloch purchased the London Bridge for 2.46 million dollars in 1962. He had all the stones numbered and moved to Havasu. The bridge was fully reconstructed by 1971 for a total investment of over seven million. He continued his improvements on a grand scale, like purchasing a plantation of palm trees and transplanting them everywhere. He offered free transportation and lodging to anyone who would visit with the possibility of buying. He was the first person to use this scheme, and everyone thought he was nuts. He made two hundred million the first year.

I heard variations of this fable, but the basic concept holds true. At my hotel, the local singles club was having happy hour and dinner. I chatted with an eighty-year-old participant who had received a free flight from N.Y. and a weekend of fun from Mr. McCulloch in the seventy's. Pauline paid $10,000 for a lot that is now worth $30,000. She said, "McCulloch paid the government $1.00 per acre; I saw the paperwork!"

While we chatted, a wild storm raged outside the hotel. Cars in the parking lot bounced up and down like they were possessed by the devil. Later, I learned that a mild tornado had passed near town, but fortunately for me had missed the airport.

Later that evening I took a stroll. Imagine being pelted with cool raindrops propelled by a hot 25-knot wind, with a backdrop of spectacular lightning. I walked to a park; trees and limbs were down everywhere. I sat on a bench and watched two skunks checking out the storm damage as lightning illuminated their white tails.

McCulloch went to extremes to make the place more attractive. There are **free parks** and **beaches** everywhere. He graced the desert with four **golf courses**. Fees range from $13 for 9-holes of walking to $27 for 18-holes with a cart. Due to summer heat, golf is more practical in winter. When Havasu sizzles, the place to be is in or near water.

I enjoyed my first **jet-ski** experience on Lake Havasu. There are several kinds of jet-skis; they are all like riding a motor cycle on water. You can cruise at over 45 mph, a great way to keep cool while enjoying the scenery up the river. What a kick!

Listed below are a number of **boat rental** outfits. I suggest calling all of them for costs and terms. Verify if gas is included. Locals say to avoid renting from agencies under the bridge, due to inflated prices. I chose Daykation because they provided transportation from the hotel and offered the lowest 2-hour jet-ski price, $55 total. As this book goes to press, Daykation seems to have gone out of business; they come and go

| Arizona Aquatics | *jet-ski* | 520-680-4151 |
| Arizona Jet Ski | *jet-ski* | 520-453-5558 |
| Funtime Boat Rentals | *pontoon, ski* | 520-680-1003 |
| Lake Havasu Marina | *runabouts, ski* | 520-855-2159 |
| London Bridge Watercraft | *jet-ski* | 520-453-8883 |
| Palm Oasis Rentals | *boats, jet-ski* | 520-680-1131 |
| WACKO | *canoe, kayak* | 520-855-6414 |
| Water Sports Center | *boats, jet-ski* | 520-453-6212 |
| Watercraft for Rent | *jet-ski* | 520-505-7225 |
| Waterriders | *jet-ski* | 520-680-8100 |

I had so much fun on the jet-ski that I signed up with Daykation for an **ATV** trip into the mountains. An ATV (All Terrain Vehicle) is a single-person vehicle like a motor cycle, except with 3 or 4 fat tires. We took a thrilling ride into the mountains and visited a defunct mine. The morning ride cost $70. Various other **tours** and rides are listed below.

| Bluewater Charter | *jet boat to gorge* | 520-855-7171 |
| Dixie Belle | *riverboat* | 520-855-0888 |
| L.Havasu Boat Tours | *pontoon boat* | 520-855-7979 |
| Leaping Lizards Hiking | *rock climbing* | 520-855-3341 |
| London Bridge Watercraft | *jet-ski* | 520-453-8883 |
| London Jet | *Havasu to Laughlin* | 888-505-3545 |
| Lee Regnier Fishing | *fishing, golf* | 520-505-4665 |
| Off-road Adv. | *4x4 desert tours* | 520-680-6151 |
| Sandpoint Marina | *fishing* | 520-855-3413 |
| WACKO | *canoe, kayak* | 520-855-6414 |
| Water Sports Center | *parasail* | 520-453-6212 |

Leaping Lizards is actually a **rock climbing** club that does strange things like climbing a mountain on Christmas eve and lighting a 980-foot Christmas tree constructed of flares.

A $28 million fisheries improvement program was launched at the lake in 1992 – the largest freshwater fisheries program in the nation. Lake Havasu contains the following **fish**: stripers, largemouth bass, black crappie, channel catfish, bluegill, green sunfish, and rainbow trout.

You can enjoy **indoor water sports** at the Aquatic Center, 520-453-2687. The 58,000 square-foot facility is just off Route 95, south of London Bridge. Other indoor sporting activities and **massage** can be found at the fitness center at the west end of the bridge.

At some point, you should stroll the various **shops** and **bars** around the bridge. The scene at the London Bridge Resort is worth experiencing. You can visit their lounge with **live music**; or the **riverside bar**, which has disco dance music and fountain-showers for maintaining the cool. The London Arms Pub is a **microbrewery** that supports the British theme by serving fish and chips.

**The airport is north of the map area below**

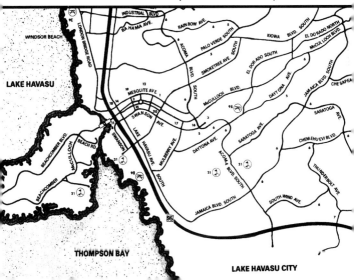

Cross the bridge, and you'll find a **fitness center** and an **air-conditioned mall**. The mall contains shops, London Bridge Brewery restaurant, and a high-end restaurant. Dozens of other restaurants and bars are sprinkled around town. Some have live music, mostly country and western.

Lake Havasu City has a surprising number of **festivals** and **events**. Some have curious names like "Mad Dog Wireless' Green Chili Association Championship," and "Meltdown - Extreme Festival Celebrating Lake Havasu's Title as America's Hottest City." Many of the activities would not be of interest to the typical visitor – "Desert Hills Fire Department Ladies Auxiliary," for example. Most events are water-related. Call the Lake Havasu Tourism Bureau at 520-453-3444 for details

In summary, Lake Havasu is not really my kind of place. What, the London Bridge in the middle of the desert! Hmmm, I wonder why I look forward to visiting this crazy place again?

**London Bridge Resort**

# Marble Canyon

## Marble Canyon Airport

| | | |
|---|---|---|
| **Town** | Marble Canyon | **ID** L41 |
| **Coord** | N-36-48.75, W-111-38.79 | |
| **Elev** | 3603 feet, NE end high | |
| **Runway** | 3 - 21, 3115 x 35' asphalt | |
| **Freq** | CTAF-122.9 | |
| **Charts** | Las Vegas sec., L5, Lo9 | |

> *CAUTION:* Airport information not for navigational use. No line of sight between runway ends. Power lines N. Watch density altitude.

NOTE: Runway paved since photo taken.

> ***Marble Canyon is the home of a remote inn
> and trading post.  A laid-back overnight.  Not
> much to do but hike, float, and fish.
> $80 - $120.  Lodge: 520-355-2225.***

## Airport Description

The airstrip is located about a quarter mile from the western
edge of the northeastern end of the Grand Canyon.  The majestic,
painted Vermillion Cliffs tower thousands of feet above and five
miles to the west.  With landmarks such as these, the runway is
relatively easy to spot.

The wind sock, located at the north end of the runway, is
difficult to see.  The north end is higher than the south end.  The
runway has been recently paved, and is somewhat smoother than
the Cliff Dwellers Lodge runway to the south.  After landing,
taxi north to tiedown your airplane.  The trading post and lodge
are a five-minute walk from the tiedown area.

## Services, Lodging, and Transportation

Phone:  520-355-2225 (at the lodge).  A shaded picnic table is
located near the tiedown area, just 1000 feet from the local
action: gas station, restaurant, trading post, and lodge.  The
trading post has a limited selection of camping gear, food, clothes,
and Indian rugs; and an excellent selection of books about the
local area.  Two other lodges are located four or more miles from
the airport, but lack of transportation make these lodges less
practical than the Marble Canyon Lodge.

## Overview

Visitors who are new to the west will be especially struck by the panorama of towering rock and color. Surrounding the lodge are cliffs of rich brown, gold, red, and orange.

A number of Native American families live in this town of less than 100 people. The settlement is nestled into an area less than 1000 feet from the tiedown bib. The "trading post" is clearly the main hub of activity in Marble Canyon. It is a good source of common supplies and specialized local books.

The **lodge** is constructed of local natural materials that blend with the countryside. It has more units than Cliff Dwellers Lodge (see **AZ-CLIF**) ten miles to the southwest. Room prices range from $55 for a room to $130 for an apartment. For reservations, write to Marble Canyon Lodge, Marble Canyon, AZ 86036, or call 520-355-2225.

**Marble Canyon Trading Post and Lodge**

You can **fish** for trout at Lee's Ferry, four miles from the lodge. Long or short **hiking** trips can be arranged with the help of the lodge. A one-day **raft trip** through Glen Canyon on the Colorado River treats you to serene, natural beauty and Native American petroglyphs.

For other Grand Canyon sites, see chapters **AZ-CLIF**, **AZ-GRAN**, **AZ-TUWE**, and **AZ-VALL**.

## Lookout Point Hike

This ten-minute hike offers a view of the canyon. It is the closest view of the Grand Canyon from a landing strip.

Walk southeast on the dirt road behind the lodge buildings for about ten minutes. The road ends at the canyon edge, Lookout Point. Adjust your expectations for a view that is less spectacular than the central Grand Canyon.

## Colorado River Hike

This hike from the lodge to the Colorado River requires three hours, round trip. Be sure to carry plenty of drinking water.

Walk north from the lodge on Highway 89A. Just after leaving the lodge, turn north on the road heading to Lee's Ferry. After about twenty minutes, you pass Cathedral Rock on the right. Ten minutes further, you encounter Cathedral Wash, a large wash that passes under the road headed for the canyon. On the left is a beautiful gorge that is also quite suitable for hiking. Follow the wash down towards the river, another 45 minutes.

The river is cold. The brave will try a quick splash. The wise will have brought the makings for a picnic. The fisherman will try to bring in an eighteen pound rainbow trout. Good luck!

*- RW*

# Page

## Page Municipal Airport

| | |
|---|---|
| **Town** | Page   **ID**   PGA |
| **Coord** | N-36-55.57,   W-111-26.90 |
| **Elev** | 4310 feet, 1.2%, S high |
| **Runway** | 15 - 33rt,   5500 x 150' asphalt |
| | 7 - 25rt,   2200 x 75' dirt |
| **Freq** | CTAF-122.8, Lights-122.8-5x |
| | VOR-PGA-117.6 |
| **Charts** | Las Vegas sectional, L5, Lo9 |

**CAUTION:**  Airport information not for navigational use.
Stacks 4 mi E.   Tour traffic over lake; monitor 122.75.

> *Page is the key access point for Lake Powell.*
> *Beautiful scenery from air, boat, or trail.*
> *Aquatic recreation, dam to visit, and night life.*
> *$100 - $250.   Chamber:   888-261-PAGE*

## Airport

The area north of Page is both amazingly beautiful by air and
seriously rugged for ground travelers.  You can see why this was
one of the last places in the U.S. to be charted.  Consider flying a
scenic diversion over the Lake Powell area before landing at Page.
If you have time, touchdown at Bullfrog Basin or Cal Black.

Page Airport is easy to locate at the south end of Lake Powell.
Fly to the on-field VOR, PGA-117.6.  Minimum altitude over the
lake is 2000 AGL.  Unicom is active with scenic flight traffic in
summer.  The airport has VOR and GPS RNAV instrument approaches.  Runway 7-25 is used only in high winds.  Runway 15-
33 and tiedown area are more than adequate for small aircraft.

## Airport Services and Transportation

Airport Phone: 520-645-2494.  Fuel: 100LL and JetA.  Page
has a modern, locked-gates style terminal that caters primarily to
scenic flight operations.  The tiedown fee for a single is $4.  The
airport is conveniently close to town.

Rental cars are available from Avis for $42 and up, 520-645-
2024 or 800-331-1212.  Lake Powell Taxi charges $5 for a trip to
town, 645-8540.   Although walking to town is a reasonable
alternative, walking is normally unnecessary, as most motels pickup

from the airport. The Wahweap lodge operates a free shuttle for guests between the airport, town, and lodge on the lake. You are considered a guest if you stay at the lodge, eat at the restaurant, or take a boat ride at the Wahweap Marina.

## Lodging and Dining

Lodging can be both difficult to find and expensive during tourist season. Super Eight motel, for example, charges double their typical fare at Page in summer. The motels that charge somewhat more than rural western prices are located on the well-traveled main streets in town. You need to hit the back streets, like 8th Avenue, in order to find friendlier accommodations. The International Hostel charges only $15 for singles. Interestingly, the Europeans seem to know how to find these places. If possible, make your reservations in advance.

| Amie Ann's B&B | CPT | $45-65 | 520-645-5505 |
|---|---|---|---|
| Antique Arbor B&B | CPT | $35-65 | 520-645-9518 |
| Bashful Bob's | PT | $32-50 | 520-645-3919 |
| Best Western – Lake | T | $43-165 | 520-645-5988 |
| Best Western Weston | PT | $58-150 | 520-645-2451 |
| Canyon Colors B&B | BPT | $45-75 | 800-536-2530 |
| Courtyard By Marriot | R | $109-200 | 520-645-5000 |
| Edie's B&B | CT | $45-85 | 520-645-2754 |
| Ramada Inn | BPRT | $50-80 | 520-645-8851 |
| Holiday Inn Express | C | $65-100 | 520-645-9000 |
| Lk.Powell Intl. Hostel | T | $24-35 | 520-645-3898 |
| Red Rock Motel | PT | $37-71 | 520-645-0062 |
| Super Eight | P | $45-84 | 520-645-2858 |
| | | | 800-800-8000 |
| Thatcher's B&B | BT | $49-69 | 800-645-6836 |
| Uncle Bill's | T | $32-77 | 520-645-1224 |
| Wahweap Lodge | PRT | $103-160 | 520-645-2433 |
| | | | 800-528-6154 |

Uncle Bill's caters primarily to pilots and Europeans. European visitors, who have interesting travel experiences to share, also dominate the economical Lake Powell International Hostel. Manager, Kate, provides guests with free rides to trailheads.

The Wahweap Lodge, a full-service lodge and marina, has a great location on the lake. Its circular dining room has a wonderful view of the lake. The cuisine is what you would expect for an inn of better caliber – quite good, but not California gourmet. They also offer a dinner cruise in a riverboat-style paddlewheeler. Public campgrounds are located a couple miles north of the lodge.

For steak meals, the place to go is Ken's Old West. They have antique western decor with western music entertainment in the evenings. Strombolli's is a fun place for New York style pizza and other Italian treats. The Marriot serves good southwestern meals.

**Courtyard by Marriot, a fine view by the golf course**

## Page and Lake Powell

The earliest known visitors, prehistoric Indians, or Paleo-Indian people, roved through the Glen Canyon area at the end of the Ice Age, 7,000 to 9,000 B.C. At about 200 B.C., their cultivation of corn sparked the beginnings of the Ancestral Puebloan Basketmakers. Commonly known as Anazasi, these "ancient ones" have left their mark throughout the Four Corners. Defiance House, near Halls Crossing, is an Anasazi cliff dwelling of 1050 A.D. that still remains.

Two young and spirited Spanish priests from Santa Fe were the first of European extraction to explore the area. They kept detailed journals and maps from their 1776 visit, and named many features in the area. John Powell, an intrepid leader who lost his arm during the Civil War, led his first expedition in 1869. At the time, this was the largest uncharted area in the continental U.S. Powell's party produced detailed journals, and his exploits provided months of vicarious pleasure for the public back east. You can find out more at the **John Wesley Powell Museum**, 520-645-9496.

Just after Powell's expedition, Mormon pioneers pushed in from the north. John D. Lee established a ferryboat service across the Colorado at Lees Ferry, south of Page and the Glen Canyon Dam. The first "tourists" floated down the river in 1896, but not until 1972 did the area become an official national recreation area.

The construction of Glen Canyon Dam began in 1957. After pouring 10 million tons of concrete and after 8 years of labor, the dam was completed. The total bill was $272,000,000, a bargain by today's standards. After completion in 1963, Lake Powell took 17 years to fill. The lake is now 200 miles in length, and has 1,960 miles of shoreline – longer than the West Coast!

Page was founded to support dam construction in the 50's. It is undoubtedly the youngest town of its size in Arizona. Today it

Petrified
Forest

Rec. Area

Village

ESCALANTE
Elev 5056

Escalante
Canyons (B.L.M.)

*Escalante Rim
Elev 7149*

29

12

SCENIC
BYWAY

*Summit
Elev 7400*

*Canaan Pk
Elev 9196*

GLEN

CANYON

Ticabo

Kaiparowits Pk
Elev 9180

STRAIGHT

KAIPAROWITS

58

Bullfrog Basin Marina

asin

Grosvenor Arch
(B.L.M.)

NATIONAL

Cottonwood Canyon
(B.L.M.)

CLIFFS

PLATEAU

RECREATION

SMOKY

AREA

No Boat
Access

Hole-in-the-Rock

MOUNTAIN

The Crossing
of the Fathers

GLEN

CANYON

RAINBOW

NAVA

89

RAINBOW BRIDGE
NATL. MON.
*Navajo Mtn.
Elev 10388*

T

BIG WATER

8

Wahweap
Marina

CLIFFS
WILDERNESS
AREA
(B.L.M.)

Glen
Canyon
Dam

PAGE

Glen Canyon
Bridge 700 Ft.
Above River
1271 Ft. Long

Lees Ferry

Bridge 467 Ft.
er 616 Ft. Long

Marble Canyon

98

NAVAJO N

34

23

36

CLIFFS

89A

13

Inscription House Ruin

Kaibito

30

White Mesa
Natural Bridge

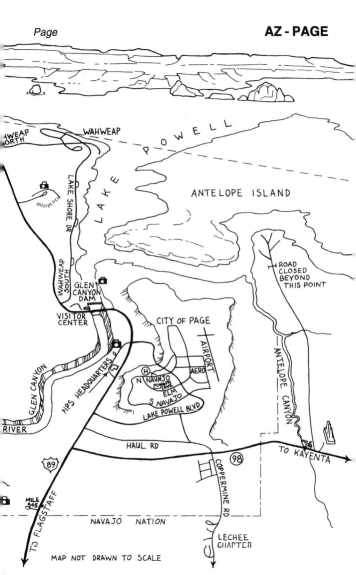

LAKE POWELL

WAHWEAP NORTH

WAHWEAP

ANTELOPE ISLAND

LAKE SHORE DR

WAHWEAP SOUTH

GLEN CANYON DAM

VISITOR CENTER

CITY OF PAGE

AIRPORT

AERO

ROAD CLOSED BEYOND THIS POINT

ANTELOPE CANYON

GLEN CANYON

NPS HEADQUARTERS

H

N NAVAJO

ELM

S NAVAJO

LAKE POWELL BLVD

RIVER

HAUL RD

TO KAYENTA

MILE

89

COPPERMINE RD

98

MILE 345

TO FLAGSTAFF

NAVAJO NATION

LECHEE CHAPTER

MAP NOT DRAWN TO SCALE

supports the three million visitors who visit the National Recreation Area (NRA). The result is an economy that makes its yearly income during the warmer months. Although Page lacks the personality of smaller sites in this book, it is well endowed with recreational options.

My first stop was the Carl Hayden Visitor's Center, 520-608-6404, a mile south of Page at the top of **Glen Canyon Dam**. The displays were fascinating. An elevator takes you down into the 710-foot dam where you see eight massive generators cranking out enough power for a town of 1,500,000 people. Don't forget to stock up on maps and visitor's information before leaving.

Next stop is the **Wahweap Lodge and Marina**, 800-528-6154, five miles north of the dam. The complex is on NRA land, requiring a $5 week's permit. You can stay at the lodge and have

Glen Canyon Dam

easy access to boating activities and various restaurants. Their shuttle provides transportation to the dam, town, and airport.

You can **rent** all sorts of **watercraft** from the marina. Various **boat tours** depart from the marina, including the Canyon King Paddlewheeler, 800-528-800. This 95-foot replica of an 1800s **riverboat** provides sight-seeing tours by day, and a 2.5-hour prime rib **dinner crusie** at sunset, $104 for two. **Rainbow Ridge**, the world's tallest arch, is a popular destination for boat tours. Call Wahweap Boat Tours at 520-645-2741 or 645-2433.

Summers bring serious heat, a perfect excuse for renting water toys. Page provides a variety of options, from **rafting** to **speed boating**, to leisurely **house boating**. Houseboats rent for $900-4200 per week, depending on size and season. **Jet-skis** rent for $100-200 per day. Conventional boats are available, as well.

**Eight mammoth generators create 1,350,000,000 watts**

| | | |
|---|---:|---|
| Antelope Travel | *jet-ski* | 520-645-3835 |
| Bubba's Prop shop | *fishing guide* | 520-645-5785 |
| Desert Service | *jet-ski* | 520-645-9164 |
| Doo Powell | *boats, jet-ski* | 800-350-1230 |
| Water World | *party barge, jet-ski* | 520-645-9323 |
| Lake Powell Charter | *fishing, ski* | 520-645-5505 |
| Old West Marine | *boats, jet-ski* | 520-645-2705 |
| Outdoor Sports | *boats, jet-ski* | 520-645-8141 |
| Red Rock Cyclery | *bikes, kayaks* | 520-645-1479 |
| Twin Fin Dive Center | *scuba* | 520-645-3114 |
| Wahweap Marina | *house, boats, jet-ski* | 520-645-1111 |
| Water World | *party barge, jet-ski* | 520-645-9323 |

Wahweap Marina benefits from a government monopoly that hinders local competition. A protective ordinance prohibits other businesses from launching boats. For better prices, make special arrangements with other renters, or rent a 4x4 with trailer hitch.

**Wahweap Marina**

Smooth- and **white-water rafting** trips generally take place on the Colorado below the dam. The following **outfitters** offer trips of several hours below the dam to many days through the Grand Canyon. Diamond River Adventures and Wilderness River Adventures are actually based in Page.

| | | |
|---|---|---|
| AZ Raft Adventures | *Grand Canyon* | 800-786- RAFT |
| Canyoneers | *river trips* | 800-525-0924 |
| Diamond River Adventures | *river trips* | 800-343-3121 |
| Grand Canyon Expeditions | *rafting* | 800-544-2691 |
| Western River Expeditions | *rafting* | 800-453-7450 |
| Wilderness River Adventures | *rafting* | 800-992-8022 |

For a list of **fishing guides**, call the Chamber of Commerce, 888-261-PAGE. **Overland tours** to Antelope Canyon are provided by: Lake Powell Jeep Tours, 520-645-5501; Photographic Tours, 801-675-9109; and Scenic Tours, 520-645-5333.

**Aerial view of Lake Powell**

Photographers should consider a $20-40 tour to **Antelope Canyon**. You walk through narrow passages of ethereal sandstone – flowing shapes and colors etched by time. The best light is at midday when the sun is overhead, creating shafts of light in the canyon.

A number of hiking opportunities can be found close to Page. Horseshoe Bend Overlook is a **short hike** with a great view. Follow Highway 89 away from the lake to marker 545. Turn west on the dirt road and park at the base of the hill. Walk less than one-half mile to the overlook. A **longer hike** follows Wireglass Canyon, a steep-sided wash that leads to the lake. Call the National Parks Service at 520-608-6404 for more information and tips.

When hiking the canyons, take care not to get caught in a flash flood. A group of Europeans died by flash flood several days before my last visit. Rather walk in a flood-free zone? Hike the trails that meander at the edge of town. Or, play a round of **golf** at First Golf, Page's well-manicured golf course, 645-2023.

Because Page is a relatively new town, it lacks old-town charm. It is, however, compact enough that you can check out the **shops** by foot. Several **gift shops** and **galleries** have authentic and simulated **Navajo art**. The town has a **movie theater**, 645-9565.

I give Page "thumb's-up" for **nightlife**. Why not make the rounds after dinner? Festooned with western doo-dads and a country feeling, Ken's Old West has country and western bands for entertainment. The Gunsmoke Saloon is the largest and most razzle-dazzle bar with live music, modern lighting systems, and high power audio gear. Windy Mesa is a small, working-class bar on North Navajo near the center of town. The band at Windy Mesa played with less precision but more feeling than the group on stage at the Gunsmoke Saloon.

*- RW*

# Payson

## Payson Municipal Airport

| | |
|---|---|
| **Town** | Payson **ID** E69 |
| **Coord** | N-34-15.41, W-111-20.36 |
| **Elev** | 5156 feet, middle low |
| **Runway** | 6rt -24, 5500 x 75' asphalt |
| **Freq** | CTAF-122.8 |
| **Charts** | Phoenix sectional, L4, Lo10 |

*CAUTION:* Airport information not for navigational use. No midfield departure. Intensive flight training.

*Payson, known for its "World's Oldest
Continuous Rodeo," is a friendly fly-in site
for scenery.  Drive the Mogollon Rim  and
stop at interesting spots along the way.
$30 - $175.  Chamber: 800-672-9766*

## Airport

Payson airport is located in a hilly area of central Arizona,
south of the prominent Mogollon Rim.  The airport's elevation
is generally at or above nearby surrounding terrain, so mountain
or rim obstruction is not a factor for operations at the airport.
Radio station KMOG on 1420 AM is an unofficial radio aid for
locating the airport.  An official NDB may be in operation by the
time you read this.  In clear weather, the runway is clearly
identifiable from ten miles.

**Airport campsite**

The airport is located at the northwest edge of town. When approaching, note the location of the pilot's campground west of mid-field. Runway 24 is the calm-wind default. Noise abatement procedures are requested. When departing Runway 6, climb runway heading to 600 feet before turning.

## Services, Transportation, and Lodging

Airport phone: 520-474-2005, pager 472-5417. Fuel: 80, 100LL, JetA. This airport has all the essentials: fuel, restaurant, rental car, and pilot's campground. The restaurant has a good view of the runway, friendly service, and serves typical small-town airport restaurant food at reasonable prices.

Although airport ambiance is tainted by extra paperwork and locked gates, it is otherwise friendly and visitor-oriented. Tiedown is $3, or free the first night if you buy fuel. The pilot's campground is beautifully developed with bathroom facilities. Don't be put off by the $10 fee; it becomes more attractive when compared to the motel rates in the area.

Quantum Car Rental provides cars at the airport for $29, up. Make reservations through the FBO, 520-474-2005. The airport also rents mountain bikes at $10 per day. There is no airport courtesy car, as erroneously listed in some flight guides.

Lodging prices are higher than the norm, even at low-end motels. A motel owner explained, "The tourist season is short, so local innkeepers must do a year's worth of business in three months." To get to town and the motels, drive east a mile on Airport Road . Turn south on Highway 87. Most of the motels are along Highways 87 and 260. Note that rooms are almost impossible to obtain during rodeo weekend in mid-August.

| | | | |
|---|---|---|---|
| Barney's Last Resort | BHPT | $86 | 520-472-7911 |
| Country Haven B&B | B | $68-120 | 520-474-5715 |
| Fountain Inn & Spa | BPT | $93-148 | 520-474-0622 |
| Holiday Inn Express | CP | $44-141 | 520-472-7484 |
| Majestic Mountain | PT | $52-165 | 800-408-2442 |
| Opal Ranch Inn B&B | BT | $50-90 | 520-472-6193 |
| Pueblo Inn | T | $54-137 | 800-888-9828 |
| Paysonglo Lodge | CP | $66-131 | 800-872-9766 |
| Inn of Payson | CP | $65-100 | 800-247-9477 |

Highway 87 passes through town. As you drive south from the airport, Highway 260 joins 87 at the center of town. The **Chamber of Commerce** is a mile further down 87 on the right at West Main, a good stop for maps and information. Amateur radio operators can obtain friendly assistance on the local repeater, 147.39+, which also has an open autopatch.

**Features**

B Full breakfast
C Continental
H Historic
P Pets OK
R Restaurant
T Transportation

Further west down Main Street are the Zane Grey Museum, Museum of the Forest, and Payson Golf Course. The Mazatzal Casino is another mile south on Highway 87. The **Zane Grey Museum** and **Counseller Art Gallery**, 520-474-6243, is a tribute to the western author Zane Grey, and shows a video about his life. The **Museum of the Forest**, contains exhibits on northern Gila County ranchers, lumbermen, Native Americans, and pioneer families.

The 18-hole **Payson Golf Course**, 520-474-2273, is two miles west of the Chamber – $30/18-holes. It includes 19th Hole and snack bar. The **Chaparral Pines Golf Course**, 520-474-1222, is a must-see for golf enthusiasts. Located northeast of town off Highway 260, Chaparral Pines is a beautiful award-

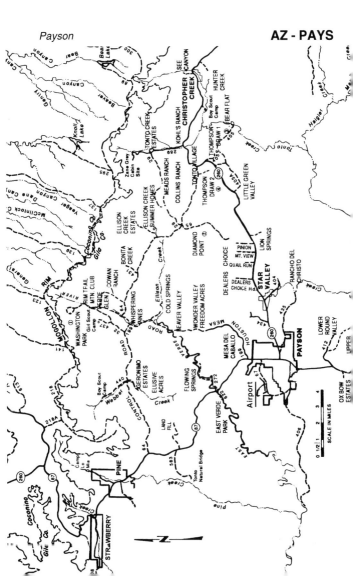

winning golf course and golf community.  Unfortunately, you can't play there unless you buy a lot.

The **Payson Zoo**, 520-474-5435, is 6.5 miles east of town. The facility also serves as a haven for orphaned and injured animals.  A number of **antique stores** can be found along Highway 87 at the Swiss Village.  The **Mazatzal Casino**, 474-6044, is the place for adults who like indoor gaming.

Most visitors come to Payson for the **scenery** - **Mogollon Rim Country**.  With the exception of the Grand Canyon, the Rim is Arizona's most impressive landform.  It follows the abrupt southern edge of the vast four-state Colorado Plateau.  To the pilot, the Rim is seen as a stretch of sheer cliffs, extending over 200 miles into New Mexico.  The middle section is now commonly known as the "Tonto Rim," simply the "Rim," or "Zane Grey Country."

**Tonto Natural Bridge**

You can **drive a loop** that takes you from Payson around the Rim. Assuming a clockwise loop, follow Highway 87 north past the Tonto Natural Bridge, Pine, and Strawberry. North of Strawberry, you follow a dirt road east along the rim. After a 40-some mile drive along the Rim, you join Highway 260 near Christopher Creek. Follow 260 west back to Payson. Bring a good map and allow for several hours of driving. Violent thunderstorms are not uncommon on summer afternoons.

There are various interesting stops along the way. Ancient history buffs will enjoy the **Shoofly Village Archeological Site**, five miles north of Payson, and east on Houston Mesa Road. Built between AD 1000 and 1250 and excavated by Arizona State University, it contains 87 rooms and courtyards accessed by an asphalt trail.

The **Tonto Natural Bridge** is a newly constructed State Park access to the Tonto Natural Bridge, eight miles north of town off Highway 87. A $5 fee entitles you to view the natural bridge. Trails go to various scenic grottos and pools. The government has tastefully developed the site. If you like this kind of thing, you can get your money's worth.

Several outfitters provide **horseback rides** and rentals into Zane Grey Country: Don Donnelly Stables, 520-478-4701; Kohl's Stables, 478-4211; and OK Corral, 476-4303. Prices range from $20 for one hour to $80 for all day.

To satisfy my soft spot for hot springs, I pointed the rental car toward the abandoned historic **Verde Hot Springs**. This proved to be an interesting several-hour adventure along treacherous roads through scenic canyons. The distance to the springs is 35.5 miles, 19 of which are on dirt roads.

Zero your trip odometer at Polson. Head north on 87 and turn left at Strawberry, mile 16.8. Follow the road west through town. After it turns to gravel, I noticed several hairy tarantula spiders crossing the road. A trail to the right (odometer reading 21.6) leads to Fossil Springs.

The road dramatically drops into the canyon at odometer reading 22.4. There are no safety rails or reflectors on this road – it would be murder at night! You reach the canyon bottom while passing a hydro plant at 26.8. The river crossing occurs at 27.9. This stretch has scenic swimming holes, a favorite getaway for local folks. At the intersection at 29.2, bear left for "Child's Power Plant" and "Verde River 6 mi." Follow the roving road and power lines to the sign "Verde River and Hot Spring Trail 1/4 mi." Park here to avoid driving on a rough road.

Walk down to the river, through the no-fee campground, and follow the trail past a mini hydro plant in the upstream direction. I noticed four groups of campers. They were friendly and represented a diverse variety of life-styles.

After the power plant, walk the trail by the river, and continue on the trail as it climbs to the dirt road above. Follow the road in the same direction until it comes back down to river level. Total walk time is 25 minutes.

Across the river, you will see two palm trees, an old person-made rock wall, and a defunct utility pole. The springs are located on the far side near where power lines with orange balls cross the river. Find a suitable upstream place to wade across, and then walk downstream to the springs on the other side.

Hot water comes from several caves that feed an outside pool and an inside pool. A cabin-sized rock building houses the pool and a small wood stove. The inside walls are covered with mural-like paintings, a cross between folk art and graffiti. In years past, this was a festive place to visit. Today, the springs host occasional visitors. Clothing may or may not be optional, depending upon cultural background of the visitors. Cleanliness is, unfortunately, marginal.

Payson's premier event is the **World's Oldest Continuous Rodeo**, which peaks in mid-August, 520-474-4515. It attracts so many enthusiasts that lodging is nearly impossible to obtain in mid-August. A second prominent event is the mid-June **Junebug Blues Festival**. Besides these, Payson sponsors a half-dozen lesser **events** each month – everything from the Zane Grey Twirler's Festival to a Doll Show and Pioneer Days Celebration. Call the Chamber for details, 800-672-9766.

**Verde Hot Springs**

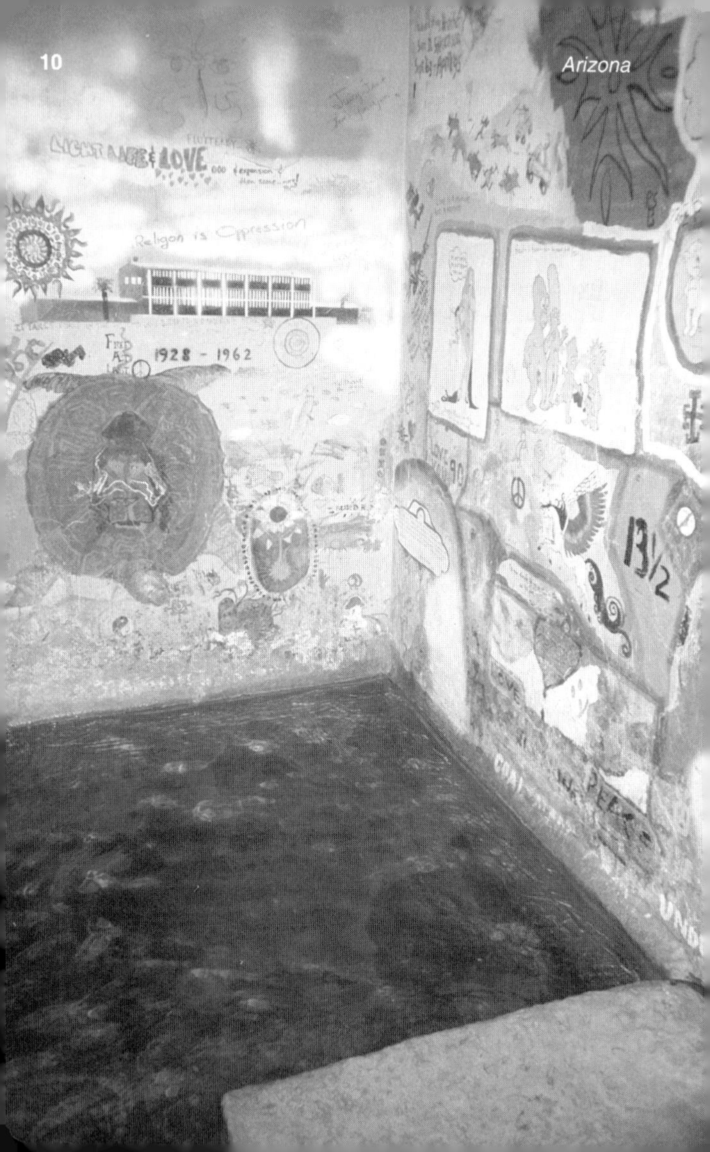
Religon is Oppression
1928 - 1962

# Sedona

## Sedona Airport

| | | | |
|---|---|---|---|
| **Town** | Sedona | **ID** | SEZ |
| **Coord** | N-34-50.92, W-111-47.31 | | |
| **Elev** | 4827 feet, 1.8%, NE end high | | |
| **Runway** | 3 - 21, 5131 x 75' asphalt | | |
| **Freq** | CTAF-122.8, lights-122.8-3x5x7x | | |
| | AWOS-118.525, 520-282-1993 | | |
| **Charts** | Phoenix sectional, L4, Lo10 | | |

> **CAUTION:** Airport information not for navigational use. Elevated runway can cause mis-judgment of approach altitudes. Up- and down-drafts. Traffic. Heavy mid-day southerly crosswinds. Deer on runway.

> *Sedona, once the favored set for classic western movies, is now the playground of wealthy retirees, art lovers, and New Agers. Lots to see and do in this little paradise. $100-300. Info: 800-288-7336.*

## Airport Description

Sedona airport is located on a 500-foot mesa that stands in a wide canyon. The city is located in the canyon at the base of the mesa, primarily to the north and east.

Because the northeast end is 92 feet higher than the other end, land on Runway 3 unless the wind favoring 21 is greater than 10 knots. Runway 21 is generally the choice for departure. Mornings are typically calm, but significant crosswinds out of the south at midday are not uncommon. The airport is said to be VFR all but a few days of the year. Sedona has several IFR approaches: GPS and RNAV, and NDB (334 KHz, if in operation).

## Airport Services and Transportation

Airport phone: 520-282-4487. Fuel: 100LL and JetA are available from Red Rock Aviation, 282-1046. Mesa Aviation provides maintenance. 282-6317. Tiedown is $5 for singles. Additional maintenance services are available at the field.

The Sedona Airport Restaurant offers fine meals and a view of the runway. The Sky Ranch Lodge is located on the mesa adjacent to the airport. It offers convenient, quality accommodations with panoramic views of the area. Discreet camping is tolerated near the airport.

Sedona's taxi services include Bob's Taxi, 282-1234; and Bell Rock, 282-4222.

Rental car agencies provide service to the airport:

| | | |
|---|---|---|
| Arizona Jeep & Car, *airport* | | 800-879-JEEP |
| Enterprise | 800-736-8222 | 800-325-8007 |
| Practical | 520-282-6702 | 800-464-8697 |

The beautiful scenery and red rock formations have fueled the local **jeep tour** industry. The tours can be more expensive than flying;  a four-person tour can cost as much as $240 for two hours. The following specialize in Sedona-area scenery:  Red Rock Tours, 520-282-6826;  Pink Jeep Tours, 282-5000.  In addition, Red Rock has tours that focus on plant life or Native American culture. Tours that visit vortex energy points are given by Red Rock and Time Expeditions.

## Lodging

The Sky Ranch at 888-708-6400 is ideally located for flyers. The facility is within walking distance of the tiedown area. The motel provides a comfortable, clean environment to weary travelers.  Prices range from $83 to $180 and advance reservations are recommended, particularly for the lower-priced units.

Other nearby motels include the Best Western Arroyo Roble, 800-773-3662; Best Western Inn, 800-292-6344; Canyon Portal, 800-542-8484; Day's Inn, 520-282-9166; and Matterhorn, 520-282-7176.

Sedona has a number of resorts that include amenities such as heated pools, Jacuzzis, saunas, massage, tanning salons, tennis, golf, health clubs, fishing by the creek, and fine dining. Some of the most picturesque are located on the creek in Oak Creek Canyon. The Junipine Resort Condo Hotel offers "creek houses" among majestic pines. Call 520-282-3375 for information and reservations. The Best Western Arroyo Roble Resort at 800-

773-3662 is geared toward the sports enthusiast. Facilities include: tennis courts, racquetball court, weight room, steam room, and sauna.     The Arroyo Roble Hotel, 800-773-3662, is located above Oak Creek Canyon, offering scenic views from many rooms. It is located within walking distance of the town center and Oak Creek.

For $58, golf players can stay at the Beaver Creek Inn Motel, 520-567-4475. It is located by the Beaver Creek Golf Course, an 18-hole championship course outside Sedona at Lake Montezuma. Poco Diablo Resort, 520-282-7333, is a full-feature resort, including golf course, that picks up from the airport.

## Sedona

Sedona was officially established in 1902 by about twenty pioneer families. Discovered by Hollywood in the 1920s, Sedona has served as a backdrop for TV serials, TV commercials, and over 50 Western movies. No longer the secret of a few, Sedona is known the world over for its red rock panoramas and scenic splendor: iron-oxide-rich soil warms the horizon with its unmistakable hue.   Red sandstone pinnacles and spires tower two thousand feet upward into the blue Arizona sky.

First-time visitors are always struck by the beauty of Sedona-country. Old-timers still say Sedona is as pretty as any place they have seen, and "the year-round climate is nearly perfect."   In recent years Sedona has received New Age notoriety for being a natural focus, or vortex, for healing energies. One such vortex is located at the airport mesa.   Nine vortices are located in the surrounding area.   Coincidentally, they are all beautiful sites worthy of a visit:  Bell Rock, Chapel of the Holy Cross, Sphinx Rocks, Schnelly Hill Road, Indian Gardens, West Fork, Coffee Pot Rock, Boynton Canyon, and Red Rock Crossing.

Other points of interest outside Sedona are: Jerome mining town (see **AZ-JERO**), Red Rock Crossing, and Oak Creek Canyon. Accessible Indian ruins include Montezuma Castle, Montezuma Well, and Tuzigoot.

Hikers will relish **scenic trails** in the area. Here are a few suggestions: the Harding Springs Trail, from Cave Springs Campground to the east rim of Oak Creek Canyon; the A.B. Young Trail, Bootlegger Campground to the west rim; and the North Wilson Mountain Trail, from Encinoso Picnic Area to the Wilson Mountain Trail. For information on trails, camping, and permits, contact the ranger station at 520-282-4119. It is located near the intersection of Highways 89A and 179. One block south of the Burger King, follow Brewer Street east. The ranger station office is located on the left across from the elementary school.

For those seeking less strenuous forms of entertainment, Sedona is a mecca for **Indian crafts** and **art** lovers. The community boasts a surprisingly wide selection of galleries. The most famous concentration of **galleries** is located at the Tlaquepaque shopping area, not far from the center of town. Local artists also show their wares at the Sedona Art Center, or "Art Barn," in Uptown Sedona.

Five **golf courses** are located within a half hour of Sedona. Kachina Riding Stables at 520-282-7252 provides **western riding** experiences in Red Rock country. See the "Transportation" section above for information on **jeep tours**. Try Great Venture Tours, 800-578-2643, for overland tours and water adventures.

The following offer **balloon rides** over red-rock country:

| | |
|---|---|
| High Country Balloon | 800-551-7597 |
| Northern Lights Balloon | 800-230-6222 |
| Redrock Balloon | 800-258-3754 |

Major Sedona events include the St. Patrick's Day parade, Easter sunrise service, Chamber Music Festival in June, Autumn Arts Festival and Jazz on the Rocks in September, Fiesta del Tlaquepaque in October, and the Festival of Lights in December. For more information, call the Chamber of Commerce at 800-288-7336.

*- RW*

**Jeep tour**

# Tuweep

## Tuweep Airport

| | |
|---|---|
| **Town** | Colorado City   **ID** L50 |
| **Coord** | N-36-18.05,  W-113-04.05 |
| **Elev** | 4682  feet, N end high |
| **Runway** | 2 - 20,  3400 x 50' ruff dirt |
| **Freq** | CTAF-122.9 |
| **Charts** | Las Vegas sectional |

> **CAUTION:** Airport information not for navigational use. Follow Grand Canyon flight rules. Verify runway condition before landing. Watch for livestock on runway. Air turbulence. Watch density altitude.

20

2

> *Tuweep is a lonely dirt strip, four miles north*
> *of the Grand Canyon. Suitable for a picnic or*
> *canyon-hike departure point. No facilities.*

## Airport Description

The strip is located in a valley between two bluffs, an estimated four miles north of the Grand Canyon's north rim. The
bluffs are sufficiently separated to allow a safe and normal
landing pattern.

The north end of the strip is higher. The windsock is located
on the west edge at midfield, and reasonably easy to spot. When
dry, the surface is loose and dusty; after a heavy rain, it could be
dangerously muddy. Bring your own stakes and tiedown-ropes.

## Services, Transportation, and Lodging

Airport information phone: 520-638-7878, Park Service, not
at airport. Aside from the shaded picnic table at the north end of
the runway, few signs of civilization are within sight of the
airport. There are no phone, lodging, or transportation available
near the airport.

## Canyon Access and Permits

The landing strip is located north of the park boundary. Permits are not required for exploration of this area. You will need a
permit if you plan to camp overnight below the canyon rim. See
**AZ-GRAN** for information on how to obtain permits. A national

Park Service ranger station is located one mile southeast. They have no phone, but can be contacted by radio from 520-638-7805.

North rim information is available from 520-638-7870. Park Service information phone 638-7888 answers with a phone menu, but eventually enables callers to speak with a real person. Call one of the following tourist information lines for a Grand Canyon information packet: 520-638-2474 or 520-638-7888.

## Overview

The Tuweep airport facilities are "unimproved." Fly in with all the water you need.

When I arrived in May, I was overwhelmed with the peaceful beauty of the valley. Colored bluffs rise on either side of the quiet valley. The ground was covered by a blanket of orange flowers. The site is simple and serene, perhaps too much so for visitors that prefer action and adventure. Access by automobile is awkward. I was the sole occupant of the valley on the day of my visit.

From the strip, you can walk the dirt road about one and one-half hours to the edge of the Grand Canyon. Though I did not hike down into the canyon, I judge this to be a tourist-free entry point. It offers one of the most **spectacular views** at the canyon. The tourist information packet provides maps and information about canyon access.

Tuweep can be a nice **picnic stop** on the way to other Grand Canyon sites. See **AZ-CLIF**, **AZ-GRAN**, **AZ-MARB**, and **AZ-VALL**.

*- RW*

# Valle

## Valle Airport

| | |
|---|---|
| **Town** | Grand Canyon  **ID**  40G (4-zero-G) |
| **Coord** | N-35-39.05,  W-112-08.78 |
| **Elev** | 6002  feet |
| **Runway** | 1- 19rt,  4200 x 45' asphalt |
| | 14rt- 32,  3785 x 71' gravel |
| **Freq** | CTAF-122.8, Lights-122.8-5x |
| **Charts** | Phoenix  sectional |

> **CAUTION:**  Airport information not for navigational use. Own Risk. Powerline S of Runway 1.

*Valle, 30 miles south of the Grand Canyon,
has an airplane museum, Flinstones theme
park, and lodging near the airport.
$30 - 150.   Chamber:  520-638-2901.*

## Airport Description

Valle is a multi-runway airport, 25 miles south of Grand
Canyon airport.  Unlike most airports at 6000 feet or above,
Valle is surrounded by flat land. The runway is being length-
ened.  Air traffic at Valle is considerably less than the Grand
Canyon National Park airport, which is often quite busy.

**Planes of Fame Air Museum**

## Services, Lodging, and Transportation

Airport phone: 520-635-5280. Fuel: 100LL and JetA. An infrequent shuttle goes to the canyon. Although rental cars are unavailable, Valle's offerings are within walking distance. Folks at the FBO have been known to drive guests 25 miles to see the canyon! If you plan to visit the Grand Canyon, the official park airport has more options for transportation.

No-frills camping is allowed at the airport. The Grand Canyon Inn, 520-635-9203, is a half mile from the airport. Rooms cost $48-83 with pickup and continental breakfast. No pets.

Camping is allowed at the nearby Bedrock City theme park for $12, 635-2600. Campers with AAA membership receive free access to the park. Although within walking distance, you will need to solicit a ride if unable to carry the camping gear. Fred [Flintstone's] Diner serves three meals per day. You can try a Chickenasaures in a Basket, or more conventional fare.

## Planes of Fame and the Flintstones

An airplane museum and Flintstones theme park seem like strange companions to find at a remote high-desert airstrip. Only in America! Though a strange juxtaposition, they offer diversity and entertainment for the family.

The **Planes of Fame Air Museum Grand Canyon**, as officially known, contains a variety of airplanes, homebuilt to military. It is a branch of the Planes of Fame Museum in Chino, California, which was established in 1957. The Grand Canyon branch is smaller, but not short in quality or variety. After a new hangar is built, the display will be significantly expanded by moving most of Chino's airplanes to Valle.

I saw civilian aircraft that ranged from a Bede BD-5V homebuilt to airworthy 1928 Curtis Robin. Military aircraft ranged from a Japanese suicide rocket to German WWII planes. Admission is $5 and less for children. Call 520-635-1000 for information.

**Bedrock City** is a theme town based on Fred Flintstone and friends, 520-635-2600. Overnight campers have access to restrooms, hot showers, grocery store, and laundry. Admission to the park is $5 for adults and less for small kids. You can tour the Bedrock shopping center and visit the Flintstone and Rubbles' houses. Kids will enjoy the cartoons and train ride through the area's only active volcano. Yabba-dabba-doo!

**Bedrock City**

# California North

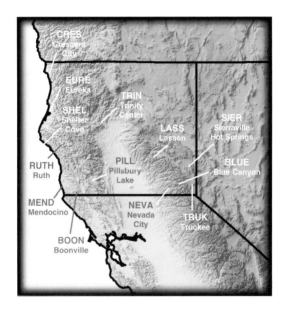

CRES
Crescent
City

EURE
Eureka

TRIN
Trinity
Center

SHEL
Shelter
Cove

LASS
Lassen

SIER
Sierraville
Hot Springs

RUTH
Ruth

PILL
Pillsbury
Lake

BLUE
Blue Canyon

MEND
Mendocino

NEVA
Nevada
City

TRUK
Truckee

BOON
Boonville

**California Aeronautics**

**916-654-4959**

# Blue Canyon

## Blue Canyon Airport

**Town**     Emigrant Gap   **ID**   BLU
**Coord**    N-39-16.49,   W-120-42.56
**Elev**      5284 feet
**Runway**   15 - 33,   3300 x 50' asphalt
**Freq**      CTAF-122.9, Lights-122.9-5x
**Charts**    San Francisco sectional

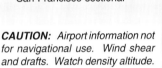

*CAUTION:* Airport information not
for navigational use. Wind shear
and drafts. Watch density altitude.

> *Blue Canyon offers a motel, astronomical*
> *observatory, unimproved camping, fishing,*
> *and a peek at a gold mine.*
> *$0-100.   Nyack Shell: 530-389-8239.*

## Airport Description

The runway is easy to locate on a mountain-side ridge.  Before landing, note wind direction and attempt to predict air flow over the varied terrain.  A trial go-around at  several hundred feet above the surface would be wise if you suspect strong down-drafts.  The airport is not plowed in winter.

## Services, Transportation, and Lodging

Phone:  530-389-8212 (unofficial, not at airport). Fuel and food are unavailable at the airport.  The only facility is a pay phone.  Tiedowns are limited, but normally not a problem.  Overnight campers are not disturbed.

Transportation is not needed for the overnight hike described below.  Conventional taxi service is unavailable.  The owner of Nyack Shell is a pilot who offers transportation to his coffee shop one mile east, 530-389-8212.  Someone at the facility may be able to drive you to a trailhead for $20 to $30.

Rancho Sierra Inn, restaurant, and bar is two miles east of the airport.  They charge $49-91 for rooms, allow pets, and pickup from the airport.  Call 530-389-8572 for reservations and pickup.

## Overview

The options a this site include visiting the Nyack Coffee Shop (half hour walk east), **hiking** and **camping**, or visiting the local **astronomical observatory**.  The observatory is open to

Sacramento Valley Astronomical Society members only, but you can become a member by calling 530-989-9281. This just may be the only airport where you'll find three serious tele- scopes available to anyone (who joins the club). A remote- control video telescope is under construction. Their big BBQ and star gazing event occurs in late June.

Trails in the area are not within a designated wilderness, and the land is not untainted by human development. However, pleasant and interesting spots are easily accessible without ex- cessive walking. The valley campsite described below is a good one-nighter. If you can handle occasional evidence of human habitation, this may be the spot for you.

The local land is mostly private, owned by corporations like PG&E and by individuals. Land marked by a fireplace or picnic table is private land. Obviously, you do not need to use these areas. I recommend finding a spot that has been unmarked by people, and that is reasonably far from any access road.

## Bear Valley Loop Hike

This loop can be a quick over-nighter or a one-day hike. You may wish to purchase the *Emigrant Gap*, California topo map, although the map is not necessary. Since trails are not marked as they would be by the U.S. Forest Service, I have provided detailed directions to a campsite near a small, scenic waterfall. The directions assume you are carrying a compass and watch.

From the landing strip, walk 10 minutes north to the inter- state highway. Follow the east off-ramp in a westerly direction. Head west for 100 feet and then cross the interstate to the westbound lane. The walk along the interstate highway takes 20 minutes. As you walk the highway, you pass vistas into the valley. On the far side of the valley, note one of your potential destinations, the old Ziebright gold mine. After the road signs

*Slippery When Wet* and *Emergency Parking Only*, turn right onto a small paved road that goes through a fence. Follow this for several hundred feet, then branch right (north) at the Y.

Follow the dirt road seven minutes from the Y, downhill to the Drum Canal.  For another seven minutes, cross the bridge over the canal, turn right, go 300 feet, and follow the small power and phone lines north and down hill.  You may continue following the small power lines down into the valley to a defunct gold mine. It's your option.  For the purpose of this narrative, we continue walking to a campsite near a small waterfall.

For the next 40 minutes, follow the newly intersected dirt road and power lines northeast. Stay with the road as it gradually leaves the power lines.  Continue on the road until the falls.  Since personal, private land is common north of the falls, I recommend camping on the PG&E land just south of the falls.

A few notes on local culture:  The night I spent at this site, I noticed some activity across the river.  Feeling in a mood to be sociable, I introduced myself to Ed and George across the stream. They owned the land on which they were camped, and were rightfully proud of it.  Several beers later, I was much the wiser about the gold mine and valley's lore.  According to George, the **fishing** is pretty good in the river.  It was a delightful evening.

The defunct **gold mine** is a 25-minute walk from your present position.  Follow the dirt road north across the river.  Shortly, it winds to the west and follows the river downstream to the mine. The gold mine has been converted into a recreational facility. Ask someone to point you toward the entrance.  It is lighted and you can walk a short distance inside.

To return to the airport from the mine, you may retrace your path, or save  several miles by following the small power lines across the valley and up to the familiar intersection with the large power lines.  From this point, return to the airport as you came.

# Boonville

## Boonville Airport

| | |
|---|---|
| **Town** | Boonville **ID** Q17 |
| **Coord** | N-39-00.76, W-123-22.97 |
| **Elev** | 371 feet, SE end high |
| **Runway** | 13 - 31rt, 3240 x 50' asphalt |
| **Freq** | CTAF-122.7 |
| **Charts** | San Francisco sectional, L2, Lo2 |

*CAUTION:* Airport information not for navigational use. High terrain and trees near 13. Possible shear in strong wind. Do not taxi on road.

> *Boonville, home of Boontling dialect, a friendly*
> *country town that accommodates fly-in visitors.*
> *Stay at a B&B and enjoy wineries, brewery,*
> *and occasional festivals.*
> *$2 - $250.   Chamber: 707-895-2379*

## Airport

Boonville Airport is located in the Anderson Valley, one mile northwest of Boonville.  The windsock is near the kiosk on the east side of the airport.  Note that the road east of and parallel to the runway is for cars; it is not a taxiway.

Due to high terrain and trees, take extra care on base and final approach to Runway 13. When the wind blows, wind shear is not uncommon.  When wind favors Runway 31, the wind can have a rolling effect close to ground.  This can be a problem for low approaches at close to stalling speed.

## Services, Transportation, and Lodging

Airport phone: 707-895-3483.  Fuel: None.  Pay the $2.00 tiedown fee at the collection box by the kiosk. The airport is a residential airpark, and has no aviation-related businesses.  Camping is allowed at the airport, with shaded picnic tables close by. When nature calls, you can use the outhouse east of the **tennis courts** in the nearby school yard.  An outside phone is located at the school, farther east.

There are no rental cars at the airport, but the walk to town requires only 15 minutes. Coast Flyers at Little River Airport is listed for car rentals, 707-937-1224. Their service, however, is for people destined for Mendocino who are unable to land at the coast. See **C1-MEND**. Local B&Bs provide transportation with prior arrangement.

The best deal for pilots is to rent a room from Jim and Jean Nickless, 707-895-2811. Their home is located approximately at midfield, 13325 Airport Road, on the northeast side of the airpark. The facilities are great, and Jim can show you his Rutan-style homebuilts. The $65 price includes fruit and light breakfast, and pets are allowed. Should you choose to stay and tour the wineries, the Nickless' may be able to give you a hand with transportation.

The Boonville Hotel, 707-895-2210, is a favorite alternate for pilots who get fogged out of Little River airport near Mendocino. The Boonville Hotel will pickup arrivals prior to 4:00 PM. The

**Guest room at the Nickless house**

hotel has been recently refurbished. The rooms tastefully done, hinting of New Mexico decor. Room prices range from $77-$220 and pets are allowed. Lunches and dinners are southwestern and tasty, served six days per week.

Additional options exist at greater distance. Anderson Creek Inn, 707-895-3091, is two miles from the airport. They will pickup from the airport and loan you a car. For $105-182, you receive breakfast and a bottle of wine. Their country facilities include pool, hot tub, and llamas. Pets are allowed.

## Boonville

Adjust your expectations – Boonville is a sleepy country town that is leisurely adding facilities to meet the needs of recreational visitors. Residents compensate for the lack of ser-

**Jim Nickless at the hangar**

vices by offering small-town hospitality, more so than the norm for California. I hope they can keep the magic.

The town's primary claim to fame seems to be a local dialect called "Boontling." Years ago when Boonville was somewhat more isolated, residents developed this unique language of their own. Initially, Boontling was used to speak privately around strangers, or just to amuse visitors.

A Chamber brochure claims, "Boontling has received world wide interest as a linguistic phenomenon. A few of the words you might see or hear while in Anderson Valley include: bahl gorms (good food), buckey walter (pay phone), pike (to walk or travel), rookie-to (quail), harp (to talk or speak), horn of zeese (cup of coffee) and Boont (Boonville)."

The town has a series of shops: deli, saloon, ice cream shop, cafés, beer supply store, grocery store, laundromat, post office,

**Buckhorn Saloon brew pub**

antique store, and shops that are art galleries in early stages of development. Take some time to stroll the town. The Anderson Valley **Historical Society Museum** is over a mile northwest.

The **Boont Dairyfarm Deli** is worth visiting. Drop in for a visual and olfactory experience: natural foods, deli counter, dining area, and blinking pinball machine in the corner. Outside, you can munch a deli sandwich at a shaded table. Zeese's Café offers country breakfast, specials, lunch, and dinner. Ice cream and Mexican food are also available in town.

The **Buckhorn Saloon** offers **microbrew** in a clean, pleasing environment. Their brewery, the **Anderson Valley Brewing Company**, has moved to a separate building. Call 707-895-3369 in advance for brewery tours and transportation from the airport.

The valley contains a dozen **wineries**, eight of which are within easy driving distance of Boonville. To visit the wineries, you need to plan ahead. Consider selecting an inn that can help solve the transportation problem.

With careful timing, you can enjoy a country festival. The **Spring Wildflower Show** is held the last Sunday and Monday of April. The **Spring Fair** is in May. The **Woolgrower's BBQ and Sheep Dog Trials** occur at the fairgrounds on the third weekend in July. Greenwood Ridge Vineyards hosts **wine tasting championships** with music on the last weekend of July. The **Mendocino County Fair and Apple Show** is an old fashioned country fair that consumes the town in mid-September.

*- RW*

# Crescent City

## McNamara Airport

| | |
|---|---|
| **Town** | Crescent City   **ID**  CEC |
| **Coord** | N-41-46.81, W-124-14.19 |
| **Elev** | 57 feet |
| **Runway** | 11 - 29, 5002 x 150', asphalt |
| | 17 - 35, 5002 x 150', asphalt |
| **Freq** | CTAF-122.8, AWOS-133.875 |
| | Lights-122.8 - 3x5x7x |
| **Charts** | Klamath Falls sectional |

*CAUTION:* Airport information not for navigational use. Birds. Helicopters. Sand dunes before 17.

> *Crescent City, a fishing village with giant*
> *redwood forest to the east, sea aquarium,*
> *cheese factory, and scenic sites to see.*
> *$100 - 200.  Chamber: 800-343-8300*

## Airport Description

The airport is close to the ocean shore and quite likely to be covered by coastal clouds, even in summer.  Weather is generally best between eleven and mid-afternoon, and pilots are often given a second chance between late afternoon and sunset.  When the clouds extend a mile or less out to sea, local pilots with coastal experience are known to slip under ceilings that would push the limits of inland pilots.

Should you arrive, only to find a patch of clouds hiding the airport, consider landing 20 miles northeast at Gasquet.  The inland skies are less likely to be covered, and you can enjoy a snack a half mile from the airport while you wait for coastal clouds to burn off.

## Services and Transportation

Airport phone: 707-465-3804.  Fuel: 100.  The FBO occasionally has a functional courtesy car for short jaunts into town, and rents older cars for $31 per day or $9 per hour.  U-Rent, 707-464-7813 or 800-308-7813, delivers newer rentals to the airport and charges $39 to $41 for the first 100 miles.  Reservations are recommended.  A ride into town costs $6-8 by taxi, 464-6030.  Low-profile **camping** is tolerated at the airport.

## Lodging and Restaurants

If weather forces you to land at Gasquet, you can stay at the historic Patrick Creek Lodge, 8 miles northeast of the airport. They will give you a ride if they can. The White Rose Inn and Fernbrook B&Bs are in Smith River, 9 miles north of Crescent City. The historic Requa Inn and restaurant is located on the river in Klamath, south of Crescent City.

The remaining listed inns are in Crescent City. The Crescent Beach Motel is the only motel on the beach. Most of the others are located close to the harbor within walking distance of seafood restaurants.

**Features**

**B** Full breakfast
**C** Continental
**H** Historic
**P** Pets OK
**R** Restaurant
**T** Transportation

| | | | |
|---|---|---|---|
| Bayview Inn | | $50-65 | 800-446-0583 |
| | | | 707-465-2050 |
| Crescent Beach Motel | | $49-70 | 707-464-5436 |
| Days Inn | CP | $47-70 | 800- DAYSINN |
| | | | 707-464-9553 |
| Fernbrook Inn B&B, *S.R.* | B | $76-95 | 707-458-3202 |
| Holiday Inn Express | B | $60-90 | 707-464-3885 |
| Motel 8 | CPT | $47-73 | 800-800-8000 |
| | | | 707-464-4111 |
| Northwoods Inn | B | $55-138 | 800-557-3396 |
| | | | 707-464-9771 |
| Pacific Motor Inn | P | $50-70 | 800-323-7917 |
| Patrick Cr. Lodge, *Gasq.* | HRT | $75-120 | 707-457-3323 |
| Royal Inn | CPT | $33-71 | 707-464-4113 |
| Requa Inn, *Klamath* | BHPR | $64-103 | 707-482-8205 |
| White Rose B&B, *S.R.* | BHT | $95-200 | 707-487-9260 |
| Travel Lodge | CR | $39 pilots | 707-464-6124 |

A number of seafood **restaurants** are located near the harbor, south of town. I enjoyed a satisfying meal at Da Lucianna Ristorante Italiano on Highway 101. Yet closer to the harbor, the Groto and Chart House are good bets.

## Crescent City Area Recreation

When arriving by air, you can't miss the crescent-shaped bay that gives Crescent City its name. The **harbor** at the east of the crescent is a good place to begin exploration. The commercial fishing boats are interesting, and you can scope the shops and restaurants for subsequent visits. For a closer look at the coast and **tide pools**, follow Enderts Beach Road, south of the harbor.

During its first 100 years as a settlement, Crescent City prospered on vast supplies of redwood, fish, and inland minerals. As resources waned, tourism became an important part of the economy. The lumber mills have all but disappeared, but you can visit the remaining protected redwoods.

The nearby **Redwoods State Parks** offer a humbling experience for those who have never experienced the quiet power of giant redwood trees. Just east of town, you can drive through the Jededih Smith Redwoods State Park and see trees over 350 feet tall with ages of 500 to 2000 years. South of town near the harbor, follow Elk Valley Road, then Howland Hill Road into the forest to Stout Grove. After strolling the trails, you can continue to Highway 199 and back to Crescent City.

On the way back to town, you pass through Hiouchi, which offers **camping**, **boating**, **hiking**, and **fishing**. For more information on the **redwood forests**, call 707-464-6101. Call 800-444-7275 for camping reservations. Tall Trees Outfitters of Orick provides tall tree **trail rides** for $30-90, 707-488-5785.

Sixteen miles south, you can get a roadside-attraction view of the trees by visiting **Trees of Mystery**, 800-638-3389. A few miles further in Klamath, you can enjoy the thrill of a **jet boat ride** up the Klamath River for $20-50, 800-887-JETS.

Speaking of roadside attractions, children will enjoy a visit to **Ocean World** in town, 707-464-3522. Don't let their tacky trinket shop put you off; the modest tour is a quality experience. They have trained seals, an unusual historic aquarium structure, and lots of slippery things to touch and feel – may be your last chance to actually pet a shark.

Plan ahead to visit the 1856 **Battery Point Lighthouse** at low tide because it is inaccessible at high tide. The lighthouse sits on a small island just west of the harbor. Near the lighthouse, you can see live seals at the **Marine Mammal Center**, or try your hand at fishing at the fishing pier, bait and rods available. The **Historical Society Museum** is further north.

Got the munchies? Here's an educational remedy – visit the **Rumiano Cheese Company** on 9$^{th}$ and E Streets. This small cheese factory, circa 1921, is the world's largest producer of Dry Monterey Jack. You can watch the manufacturing process through a viewing window while you munch on free samples.

# Eureka

## Artcata Airport

| | | | |
|---|---|---|---|
| **Town** | Arcata | **ID** | ACV |
| **Coord** | N-40-58.69, W-124-06.52 | | |
| **Elev** | 218 feet, E side high | | |
| **Runway** | 2 - 20, 4499 x 150', asphalt | | |
| | 14 - 32, 4998 x 150', asphalt | | |
| **Freq** | CTAF-123.65, FSS-122.6 | | |
| | VOR-110.2, ILS-109.5D, NDB-223 | | |
| **Charts** | Klamath Falls sectional, L2, Lo2 | | |

*CAUTION: Airport information not for navigational use. Fog. Hills SE. Birds and deer.*

> *Weather permitting, the Eureka area offers*
> *a wealth of diverse recreation. Interesting*
> *waterfront, Old Town with beautiful Victo-*
> *rian buildings, unusual museums, big trees,*
> *lumber mill to visit, boating, and more.*
> *$100 - 300.   Chamber: 707-442-3738.*

## Airport Description

Eureka has three nearby airports. **Arcata** (ACV), 25 miles
north of Eureka, is pictured on the previous page because it
offers essential services – fuel and rental cars. Arcata, with its
long dual runways and VOR (ACV 110.2) is easy to locate. It has
an IFR approach with 200-foot and ½ -mile minimums. Once on
the ground, you will discover a sizable terminal along with
decaying hangars and buildings.

The **Murray** (EKA) airport, just northeast of Eureka, was
closed for runway expansion when I visited. The **Eureka Samoa** (O33) airport, a former blimp base, is located west of Eureka
on a peninsula. It is the home of Samoa Airport B&B, nicely
refurbished from original military buildings.

The area has some 200 bad-weather days each year. Low
clouds and fog are a chronic problem in summer. Clouds tend to
linger where the sea joins the land. Local pilots have developed
skills for dealing with this weather pattern. In summer, visitors
should plan to arrive after noon.

## Airport Services and Transportation

Arcata airport phones: 707-839-5401 and 839-1502. Fuel: 100 and JetA. Even though Arcata Airport has a fine terminal, its ambiance struck me as broken. Unmaintained buildings, confusing security gates, hard-to-find fuel – a depressing entry point for fun-loving recreational pilots. Still, it has the essentials. Fuel is at the northwest end of the buildings, and the Flight Service Station and **car rental** agencies are in the terminal to the southwest. Enterprise will deliver cars to the airport.

| | |
|---|---|
| Avis, *airport* | 800-331-1212 |
| Enterprise, *Eureka* | 800-325-8007 |
| Hertz, *airport* | 800-654-3131 |
| National, *airport* | 800-CARRENT |

**Taxi** and sight-seeing services: Airporter, 707-442-9266; Coastal Cab, 839-4437; Yellow Cab, 442-4551; and Pride Enterprises for personalized tours, 445-2117. Taxis charge about $30 from Arcata airport to Eureka Old Town.

The Samoa Airport B&B (other airport) may have a vehicle you can borrow; verify in advance. Water Taxi at 443-5157 charges $30/hr for boat rides. You can travel by boat from a pier near the Samoa B&B to Eureka Old Town for $30, round trip.

## Lodging and Restaurants

**Lodging** in the area runs the gamut in character and cost. It is a buyer's market – you can have a charming room for $70-100, or clean place to crash at the south end of town on Highway 101 for $30, prices negotiable. Eureka has sixty places to stay; the more interesting sites are listed below.

**4**                                                      *California North*

The Samoa Airport B&B is an obvious alternative. The DoubleTree is the largest conventional Inn. The Eureka Inn is the largest historic inn, with two restaurants and swimming pool. They give a significant "corporate discount" to guests who are in town for business. Reservations for B&Bs can be made at 707-441-1215. Also, consider the outliers like the Victorian Inn in Ferndale.

**Features**

**B** Full breakfast
**C** Continental
**H** Historic
**P** Pets OK
**R** Restaurant
**T** Transportation

| | | | |
|---|---|---|---|
| The Daly Inn | BHT | $85-150 | 800-321-9656 |
| DoubleTree Inn | PRT | $65-162 | 800-222-8733 |
| | | | 707-445-0844 |
| Eureka Inn | HRT | $75-152 | 800-678-8946 |
| | | | 707-442-6441 |
| Grandmother's House,*Fern.* | CH | $75 | 707-786-9704 |
| Lost Whale Inn, *Trinidad* | B | $116-176 | 800-677-7859 |
| Samoa Airport B&B | BHT | $70 | 707-445-0765 |
| Scotia Inn, *Scotia* | CHPR | $65-195 | 707-764-5683 |
| Shaw House , *Ferndale* | BHT | $81-146 | 707-786-9958 |
| Southport Landing, *Loleta* | BHT | $94-130 | 707-733-5915 |
| Trinidad Bay B&B, *Trinidad* | BT | $106-166 | 707-677-0840 |
| Victorian Inn, *Ferndale* | BHPR | $82-135 | 707-786-4949 |
| A Weaver's Inn B&B | BHP | $71-137 | 707-443-8119 |

A number of fine **restaurants** can be found near the waterfront in the rectangle formed by First to Fourth Street and C to I Street. Just walk around and follow your nose. I enjoyed a memorable meal and chat with locals at the Café Waterfront Oyster Bar and Grill. Also consider the Sea Grill, Lazio's, or the Rib Room at the Eureka Inn. Want unusual? Enjoy a hearty meal at the Samoa Cookhouse, the last surviving lumber camp style eatery. See *www.humboldtdining.com*.

## Eureka Area History

**Eureka** lies on the coast in the heart of redwood country, a fertile site in 1850 for a new frontier town. Soon after founding, the nearby Trinity region introduced a catalyst that guaranteed rapid growth and prosperity – gold. Miners, loggers, and fishermen rushed in to make their mark.

After only five years, there were seven mills processing lumber and 140 lumber schooners shipping the product to other booming cities. As local stands of redwoods were cleared, railroads came to the rescue. Passenger service to San Francisco was implemented in 1914. The waterfront area became site of choice for stately Victorian homes, many of which remain today. You can still enjoy the spectacular Carson Mansion on 2nd and M Streets, built in 1885 by lumber magnate William Carson as a project to keep mill workers busy during a slow period. Across the street, a Carson "Pink Lady" is now an art museum.

**Carson Mansion, owned by the Ingomar Club, members only**

Fishing also became quickly established as an important industry.  In 1851, Salmon fisheries began to populate the Eel River.  Although salmon and whales have been mostly depleted, Humboldt Bay is  home to more than 300 fishing vessels.  Today's booty includes rockfish, Dungeness crab, salmon, shrimp, and oysters.

Eureka retains hints of her past in beautifully restored buildings by the waterfront, and in a number of interesting museums.

## What to See and Do in Eureka

**Old Town** by the waterfront is a center for **food**, **shopping**, and points of interest.  This is a good place to start.  The **Clarke Museum** on E and 3rd Streets focuses on regional history and Native American basketry regalia, 707-443-1947. **The Humbolt Bay Maritime Museum** is north at 1410 2nd Street, 444-9440. Near the museum, you will spot the splendid **Carson Mansion**

Eric Hollenbeck: traditional craftsman, artist, environmental advocate

and "Pink Lady" Victorians. You can see Old Town by foot, or enjoy a romantic carriage ride from the **Old Town Carriage Company** on the Gazebo, 2ⁿᵈ and F Streets.

At the southeast edge of Eureka, you can visit the **Fort Humboldt State Historic Park and Logging Museum**, 707-445-6567. Northeast Eureka is home to the **Sequoia Park and Zoo**. **Pride of the River Tours** takes you through Eureka to Humboldt Bay, Fort Humboldt, Victorian neighborhoods, and to lunch at the **Samoa Cookhouse**, 800-400-1849.

The Woodley Island Marina and restaurant is located across the bridge on the western edge of Humboldt Bay. Hum Boats at the foot of F rents every conceivable water vessel, from **kayak** to **sailboat**, 707-443-5157. As mentioned earlier, Hum Boat's Water Taxi provides custom **boat rides** and **tours** for $30/hr, 443-5157. Or, take a scheduled tour of the bay from Humboldt Bay Harbor Cruise for $10, 445-1910.

**Working traditional wood mill at the Blue Ox Millworks**

A top item on my list is the **Blue Ox Millworks** at the far north edge of Old Town by the foot of X Street. Here, you'll see a historic working wood-makers mill in the process of perpetual restoration. The owner, Eric Hollenbeck, has devoted his life to preserving traditional ways with wood, machinery, and pottery. His products populate the Whitehouse, and he has been recognized as being an environmental advocate by President Clinton. Eric charges $5.00 for entry and informal tour, 800-248-4259. You're guaranteed to learn something interesting.

After seeing everything this town of 30,000 has to offer, why not rest feet and quench thirst at the **Lost Coast Brewery**, 617 4th Street.

## South of Eureka

Head south on Highway 101. Your first stop is the tiny dairy farming town of Loleta, a dozen or so miles south of Eureka.

**Bizarre vehickes at the Kinetic Sculpture Museum in Ferndale**

After visiting the **Loleta Cheese factory**, 707-733-5470, continue toward nearby Ferndale.

**Ferndale** is a charming little town with an abundance of **Victorian buildings**. Don't miss the free **Kinetic Sculpture Museum** on the left as you enter. See vehicles that you could only imagine in your wildest dreams. At the other end of town, I was attracted to the Victorian Inn with its venerable "Jimmy the Piano Player." Next visit, I'll stay the night there.

Bruce Slocum, a local dairy farmer, runs his Discover Boat trip from Ferndale, 707-786-4187. Bruce provides a wonderful two-hour nature-intensive **boat ride** through the Eel River estuary for $15 per person.

Next stop, **Pacific Lumber mill** in Scotia – a personal favorite. Perhaps because I did sawmill automation in a previous life, my heart pounded with excitement when I smelled the

**Logs moving to a head rig at the Pacific Lumber mill in Scotia**

freshly cut lumber in the Pacific mill. In today's litigious society, I could not believe that Pacific Lumber actually lets people
walk through their sawmill. They provide a self-guided tour
through the mill past huge machines, belching sawdust and steam,
and a din of noise. What a treat!

To get there, you leave Highway 101 at the Scotia exit, some
30 miles south of Eureka. Part of the mill is right at the exit.
Continue a half mile south and pickup a permit at the Visitor's
Center on the left. Then drive another half mile south to the
tour. The mill shuts down 11:30 to 12:00, so plan accordingly.

Pacific Lumber literally owns the town of Scotia and has
done its part to make a pleasant community.    Workers take
pride in the town, and it shows. Consider planning to stay a
night at the pleasant Scotia Inn. Call 707-764-2222 for mill
information, and 764-5683 for the inn. This area is serviced by
the Rohnerville Airport, 8 miles north.

If you still have time and energy, keep driving south along
the **Avenue of the Giants** on 101 for a memorable tour of the
redwoods. Exit for the **Humboldt Redwoods State Park**.
Instead of returning on Highway 101, you can follow meandering Mattole Road toward the coast and back to Ferndale, a
several hour drive.

## North of Eureka

Just north of Eureka is **Arcata**. Further north at **Trinidad**,
you can enjoy a leisurely walk on the **beach**. The more ambitious will want to explore **Patrick Point State Park**. Various
**trails** take you to Wedding Rock, Sumeg Village, or the **tidepools**.
After burning all those calories, treat yourself to lunch at the
Seascape Restaurant in Trinidad.

*- RW*

# Lassen Volcanic National Park

## Chester Airport

| | |
|---|---|
| **Town** | Chester **ID** O05 (oh-zero-5) |
| **Coord** | N-40-17.24, W-121-14.33 |
| **Elev** | 4525 feet |
| **Runway** | 15 - 33rt, 5380 x 60' asphalt |
| | 5 - 23, 5320 x 120' gravel |
| **Freq** | CTAF-122.8, Lights-122.8-3x5x7x |
| **Charts** | Klamath Falls sect., L2, Lo2, Lo3 |

*CAUTION:* Airport information not for navigational use. Be alert for tanker operations in summer.

> ***Lassen Volcanic National Park has ten acres of***
> ***Yellowstone-like volcanic phenomena, diverse***
> ***hiking trails, and mountains to climb.***
> ***$35 - $150.   Chamber: 530-258-2426.***

## Airport Description

Chester airport is situated on the northwestern shore of Lake Almanor. It features a long paved runway that is kept open year-round. For noise abatement, visitors are requested to arrive on Runway 33 and depart on 15 whenever possible.

## Services, Lodging, and Transportation

Airport phone:  530-258-3616.  Fuel: 100 octane.  Tiedown fees are $2.00-3.00. Camping is permitted in the woods. Food is not served at the airport, but highway-grade meals can be had at restaurants within a mile of the airport.

Nearby lodging is available from Timberhouse, $49-72, 530-258-2729;  and, Seneca Motel, $34,  258-2815. Both pickup from the airport and allow pets.  In summer, you can rent a car from Sierra Auto Sales for $43 per day, or $25 per half day.  If requested, Sierra delivers to the airport;  call 530-258-3328.

Lassen Park is relatively easy to find. Roads are well marked, and you can obtain a free map from the U.S. Forest Service on Highway 36, just on the other side of Runway 33. You will log 60 to 100 miles to and from Lassen. Hitchhiking to Lassen is feasible, but be forewarned that hitchhiking is prohibited within park boundaries

## Overview

A sporting goods store is located one block from the Seneca Motel. Good-quality topo maps are available at the park for $4.

The variety and beauty of Lassen Park attracts hordes of people. Many of them come to view the **volcanic phenomena**. You might as well join them for a hike through Bumpass Hell. Bumpass Hell is a ten-acre micro version of Yellowstone Park. The mud pots and such are as active, if not more so, than comparable Yellowstone spectacles. It's well worth the 1.5-mile walk.

With 150 miles of **well-kept trails**, most hikers will have no problem finding a suitable scenic loop. On the other hand, your options become narrowed if your definition of "suitable" implies no people. If serenity is a priority, I recommend the Brokeoff Mountain climb.

Though permits are not required for day access, free permits are required for overnight camping. A park entrance fee is charged at the gate. Pets are not allowed on the trails. Campfires are discouraged. Park: 530-595-4444.

## Hikes in the Park

Although the **Brokeoff Mountain hike** (climb) can easily be done in one day, consider spending the night at Forest Lake on the way up. Compared to other trails at Lassen, this climb is relatively un-populated. Except on weekends, solitude is nearly guaranteed. The trail is nicely laid out, gradually sloping, and intermittently shaded for most of the ascent. Contrast this with Mount Lassen, which in some ways resembles a desert inclined at 30 degrees and teaming with hundreds of tourists.

Brokeoff Mountain trailhead is located at the southern edge of the park, a half mile before the park's toll gate. As you arrive from Chester, note the trailhead sign on the left-hand side of the road. Proceed to the toll booth to pay the park fee and pick up a camping permit. Return to the trailhead, where parking space is available.

In addition to being easy to follow, the trail is periodically marked on trees with two-inch yellow discs. After about 30 to 40 minutes, maintain a vigilant watch for Forest Lake on the right. The lake cannot be seen until after passing the most convenient access point. Backtrack, head for the lake, and pick an idyllic campsite.

The lake appears to be relatively undisturbed by man. Sitting quietly by the lake at dusk, I enjoyed watching a number of deer watering, including a mother and her spotted fawn. Meanwhile, a modest swarm of mosquitoes enjoyed me.

Before resuming the climb, I recommend stashing the overnight packs. The trail to the top is pretty and nicely graded. Seventeen hundred feet and about two hours later, you arrive at the 9235-foot peak. The view includes a broadside of Mount Lassen and a colorful panoramic view of the park.

The **Fifteen Lakes Loop** hike is a one-nighter, recommended for hikers who like lakes – lots of lakes. The trail begins at Summit Lake. Follow the trail northeast. Loop past the following lakes: Bear Lakes, Silver Lake, Feather Lake, Twin Lakes, Echo Lakes, and back to Summit Lake. The details of this loop are marked clearly on maps available at the park.

The **Corral Meadow Loop** passes by spectacular waterfalls. Pick up the east trailhead at Kings Creek Meadows. Follow the trail past Lower Meadow, Kings Creek Falls, Corral Meadow, Bench Lake, and back to the trailhead.

*- RW*

# Mendocino Area

## Little River Airport

| | |
|---|---|
| **Town** | Little River **ID** O48 (oh-48) |
| **Coord** | N-39-15.72, W-123-45.22 |
| **Elev** | 572 feet |
| **Runway** | 11 - 29, 5249 x 150' asphalt |
| **Freq** | CTAF-122.7, Lights-122.7-3x |
| **Charts** | San Francisco sectional, L2, Lo2 |

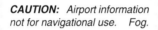

*CAUTION: Airport information not for navigational use.   Fog.*

## Airport Description

Little River Airport is located higher than the average coastal airport, and several miles inland from the ocean shore. Although this location improves the odds against coastal fog, gray stuff is not unusual at this airport. If conditions are marginal, plan on landing after noon. Consider Boonville, **C1-BOON**, as an alternate. When clouds break, the ample runway is a friendly sight. Use Runway 29 if winds are calm.

## Services and Transportation

Airport phone: 707-937-5129 and 937-1224. Fuel:100LL, sometimes closed. Fees are charged for parking and tiedown. Coastal Flyers, 937-1224, has a monopoly on rental cars. Rates begin at $36. Cars are somewhat worn and fees for mileage are significant. Mendocino Stage, 964-0167, runs regularly between the airport and Mendocino Hotel on weekends, 10:00 to 5:30. Many area inns will pickup from the airport.

## Lodging

Northern California men of taste know they can score big points by treating a spouse or special friend to a night in Mendocino. A lesser-known secret is that surrounding towns offer as much or more value at lower prices. The lodgings listed below covers the variety in Mendocino, from Albion and Little River to Fort Bragg. For help locating a B&B from 52 in the area, call Mendocino Coast Accommodations at 707-937-1913, or 800-262-7801 in California.

**Features**

**B** Full breakfast
**C** Continental
**H** Historic
**P** Pets OK
**R** Restaurant
**T** Transportation

| | | | |
|---|---|---|---|
| Agate Cove Inn, *Mendo.* | BHT | $109-274 | 800-527-3111 |
| Albion Ridge, *Albion* | BP | $140-160 | 800-482-5532 |
| Albion River Inn, *Albion* | BR | $186-286 | 800-479-7944 |
| Blanchard House, *L.R.* | BHT | $137-170 | 707-937-1627 |
| Blue Heron Inn, *Albion* | CR | $88-105 | 707-937-4323 |
| Captain's Cove Inn, *Mendo.* | BH | $166-216 | 800-780-7905 |
| Colombi Motel, *Ft.Bragg* | | $44-66 | 707-964-8015 |
| Fensalden B&B, *Albion* | BHT | $138-238 | 800-959-3850 |
| Glass Beach B&B, *F.B.* | BT | $53-151 | 707-964-6774 |
| Grey Whale Inn, *Ft.Bragg* | BH | $70-165 | 800-382-7244 |
| Heritage House, *Little Riv.* | HPRT | $105-308 | 800-235-5885 |
| Little River Inn, *Little Riv.* | HR | $77-281 | 888- INN-LOVE |
| MacCallum House Inn, *M.* | HPR | $88-210 | 800-609-0492 |
| Mendocino Village Inn | BH | $83-192 | 800-882-7029 |
| Mendocino Seaside Cott. | PT | $145-330 | 800-944-3278 |
| Reed Manor, *Mendo.* | CT | $193-385 | 707-937-5446 |
| Seabird Lodge, *Ft.Bragg* | | $66-94 | 707-964-4713 |
| Seagul Inn B&B, *Mendo.* | CH | $83-159 | 888-937-5204 |
| Stanford Inn by Sea,*Mendo.* | BPRT | $210-400 | 800-331-8884 |
| Stevenswood, *Little Riv.* | RT | $150-275 | 800-421-2810 |
| Sweetwater Inn/Spa, *M/L.R.* | HP | $61-176 | 800-300-4140 |

Mendocino's Sweetwater Inn & Spa offers cozy rooms and garden views near the Beaujolais Restaurant in Mendocino, and additional units in Little River. The decor is a visually-stimulating rustic style with commercial hippie influence. Ask about their massage specials. The Stanford Inn provides bicycles, and is totally vegetarian and nonsmoking. The Captain's Cove Inn has an oceanfront location and access to the beach. There are numerous other B&Bs in and around town.

Fort Bragg has less class, and lower prices to match. I stayed a night at the Colombi Motel. While the Colombi will not score points with a romantic associate, the rooms are clean and far less costly than the norm. I highlight the Colombi because it is a thrifty option that is not listed in tourist brochures. To get there, drive five blocks east from Highway 1 on Oak Street.

Two miles south of Mendocino, the Little River Inn with scenic **9-hole course** is a favorite for golfers. The campus includes restaurant, pro shop, and cigar and fishing store. The nearby Blanchard House is affiliated with the airport FBO; customers receive a 15% car discount. Further south, the Sweetwater Inn enjoys a scenic location, surrounded by the Van Damme State Park.

**Heritage House**

My favorite is Heritage House in Little River. They provide airport transportation, the meals are **top-notch gourmet**, and the service I received was perfect. The seaside setting is exceptionally photogenic and was used for location filming of "The Same Time Next Year" with Alan Alda.

## Mendocino Area History

Native Americans lived in the area as early as 9500 B.C. The Pomo tribe was well established and lived in peace until 1850 when a shipwreck changed their destiny. A salvage expedition led by J.B. Ford was quickly dispatched from San Francisco. By the time they arrived, the Pomo had picked the wreck clean. Disappointed but not daunted, Ford spotted valuable stands of coastal redwood that dwarfed the value of the lost cargo. By 1853, he had constructed a mill that produced 50,000 board feet per day. The Pomo were forced to relocate.

**Little River Inn**

Redwood became the mainstay for the next century. Many fine Victorian homes were built after the fire of 1870; only the Ford and Kelly homes survived from the pre-Victorian era. Mendocino prospered into the 1900s until the redwoods were depleted. The Depression finally closed the last mill. Fortunately, the town slid into obscurity and was not destroyed by improvements. Today, the whole town is on the National Register of Historic Places.

The tide turned in 1959 when artist Bill Zacha founded the Mendocino Art Center. Soon, artists and other creative individuals arrived. A coalition was formed to preserve the environment – a gift to visitors and local merchants of today. Lately, **wineries** have begun populating the county.

Fort Bragg, on the other hand, rebounded in the '40s and '50s. It became the lumber mill center for the area. A good part of Fort Bragg, from Highway 1 to the ocean shore, is occupied by a huge mill facility. However, the Skunk Train and other historic points of interest remain.

**Mendocino**

## Mendocino

The picturesque town of Mendocino sits on a body of land that juts into the ocean. Natural coastline limits growth in three directions. The town has a few shops, **galleries**, restaurants, an art center, and lots of places to stay. The **Mendocino Art Center**, 707-937-5818, is a local resource for visual and performing arts. The **Kelly House Museum** and **Ford House** are open to the public.

The best and most expensive **restaurants** in town are the 955 Ukiah and the Café Beaujolais on the east side of town – reservations advised. You can't go wrong at any of the other restaurants in town; tasty food at a reasonable price. Don't forget that excellent meals can be had at local resorts, like the Little River Inn and Heritage House (my favorite).

Mendocino has a number of events during the year, which range from the **Whale Festival** in March to the outstanding **Music Festival Concert** series in summer. Unless you happen

**Local action**

to arrive during a festival, however, there is not much to do in Mendocino. I suggest bringing a friend. Friendless and restless before sunset, I decide to stroll the town before dinner. Dark forms move on cemetery hill. Ah, the local action.

I climb the hill and join a group of young folks sitting amongst the grave stones. They confirm that there's not much to do except drink beer, and pass me a Bud. As the western sky fades, we watch the town's police car leisurely work the streets. Beats TV, I think.

If you like to see and do things, don't make the mistake of spending all your time in town. Rent a car and see the sights. Athletic visitors should check out Catch A Canoe and Bicycles Too at the Stanford Inn by the Sea, south of town, 800-320-BIKE. They offer a plethora of muscle-bending activities: **mountain biking**, river **canoeing**, ocean **kayaking**, and **outrigger** rental. This is the best way to see what the Pomo left in our care.

## Fort Bragg

Fort Bragg is known primarily for its **Skunk Train**, a descendent of the 1885 Western Railroad and Navigation Company. The Skunk Line has steam- and oil-powered train rides through the redwoods to Northspur and Willits. The cars of 1925 to 1935 are beautifully restored and maintained. Open observation cars are run in summer. Day trips cost $26, half-day trips cost $21, and kids travel for about half price. My heart pounded with excitement as the trains did their dance at the terminal.

Rather than eating at the train station, I recommend eating breakfast, or any other meal, at one of the interesting **restaurants** in the area - the Rendezvous, for example. The Mendocino County Chamber of Commerce is just two blocks east. Take some time to walk this part of town.

You pass a number of interesting **antique shops**, **art galleries**, and miscellaneous curiosities, like **tattoo parlors**. Although tattoo parlors arguably practice a form of body mutilation, the subject image is an art form. Check out the photos at one of the modern parlors. You will see unusual works, many of which seldom see direct sunlight. If you like the microbrews, save some time at 1:30 for a tour of the **North Coast Brewing Company**, 707-964-3739.

South of town, visitors can feast on the day's catch at a **Noyo Harbor** restaurant. The **World's Largest Salmon BBQ** in occurs in early July. Belle Enterprises, 964-3104, provides **smoked fish**, **scenic cruises**, **whale watching**, and **fishing** charters. Anchor Charter Boats, 964-4550, offers similar excursions.

Lumber history buffs will enjoy a visit to the **Guest House Museum** at 343 N. Main. The **Point Arena Lighthouse and**

**Museum** offers more history and a scenic view. The **Mendocino Coast Botanical Gardens** are just east of Highway 1, 3/4 mile south of Highway 20. The Ricohet Ridge Ranch, 964-PONY, is two miles north of Pudding Creek Bridge off Highway 1. They provide **horse riding** on the beach and just about any other equestrian fantasy.

Fort Bragg offers several options in theater entertainment. The **Footlighters Little Theater**, 707-964-3806, specializes in "real life Gay 1890's" comedy melodrama, complete with audience boos and cheers. The **Gloriana Opera Company**, 964-7469, has entertained locals and visitors with musical entertainment since 1977. The **Warehouse Repertory Theater**, 961-2940, provides professional comedy, drama, Shakespeare, and musicals, March to December.

**Skunk Train, ready for departure**

# Nevada City
# Grass Valley

## Grass Valley Airport

| | |
|---|---|
| **Town** | Grass Valley **ID** O17 (oh-17) |
| **Coord** | N-39-13.44, W-121-00.19 |
| **Elev** | 3150 feet, 2%, E end high |
| **Runway** | 7 - 25, 4350 x 75' asphalt |
| **Freq** | CTAF-123.0, Lights-123.0-3x5x7x |
| **Charts** | San Francisco sect.,L2, Lo2, Lo3 |

*CAUTION:* Airport information not for navigational use. Airport not for solo students. Recommend takeoff on 25. Tanker ops in summer.

> *Nevada City and Grass Valley are twin historic*
> *gold mining towns that have a variety of sights*
> *and pleasures for visitors.  $150 - 250.*
> *Nevada City: 800-655-6569,   530-265-2692.*
> *Grass Valley: 800-655-4667 CA,   530-273-4667.*

## Airport Description

The airport is easily visible, three miles east of Grass Valley.
Terrain varies in elevation around the airport.  The runway
slopes down.  Grass Valley has a VOR IFR approach, and KNCO
at 830 KHz provides an additional unofficial navigation aid.

## Services, Transportation, and Lodging

Airport phone: 530-273-3374.  Fuel: 100 and JetA.  Two FBOs
provide airplane rental and all types of small airplane maintenance
except radio repair.  Food services are not provided at the airport.

Enterprise, 530-274-7400, delivers rental cars to the airport,
except Saturday noon through Monday morning when closed.
Sierra Cab, 530-477-2424, provides transportation to Nevada City
for about $10.00.  Once in Nevada City, destinations in town are
within walking distance.

The Gold Country Stage, 530-477-0103, provides bus service
between Nevada City and Grass Valley during hours of commerce, except Sunday.  They are based at the airport and charge
$1 per ride, or $2 for an all-day pass.  The Carriage For Hire, 265-
8778, offers romantic adventure tours for $20-80 per group.

Of the two towns, Nevada City offers more entertainment and is therefore a convenient place to secure lodging. However, Grass Valley is a good backup. The National Hotel is the grand hotel of historic Nevada City. Gold Country Inn, Kendall House, and Northern Queen have heated pools. Alta Sierra Village Inn in is at the golf course. Referral lines: 800-874-7458, and 800-250-5808 or 530-477-6634.

**Features**

**B** Full breakfast
**C** Continental
**H** Historic
**P** Pets OK
**R** Restaurant
**T** Transportation

| | | | |
|---|---|---|---|
| Alta Sierra Village Inn, *GV* | T | $54-165 | 800-992-5300 |
| Deer Creek Inn B&B, *NC* | BHT | $99-154 | 800-655-0363 |
| Downey House B&B, *NC* | BHT | $83-110 | 800-258-2815 |
| Emma House B&B, *NC* | BH | $99-110 | 800-916-3662 |
| Flume's End B&B, *NC* | BH | $88-154 | 530-265-9665 |
| Golden Ore House, *GV* | BHT | $73-115 | 530-272-6872 |
| Grandmere's Inn B&B, *NC* | BH | $110-182 | 530-265-4660 |
| Holbrooke Hotel, *GV* | CH | $61-165 | 530-273-1353 |
| Kendall House B&B, *NC* | BHT | $108-216 | 530-265-0405 |
| Miner's Inn Motel, *NC* | CHP | $50-154 | 800-977-8884 |
| Murphy's Inn B&B, *GV* | BHT | $110-170 | 530-273-6873 |
| National Hotel, *NC* | HR | $75-124 | 530-265-4551 |
| Northern Queen Inn, *NC* | R | $66-110 | 800-226-3090 |
| The Parsonage B&B, *NC* | BHPT | $77-150 | 530-265-9478 |
| Piety Hill Inn B&B, *NC* | B | $88-165 | 530-265-2245 |
| Red Castle Inn, *NC* | BH | $70-140 | 800-761-4766 |
| Swann-Levine House, *GV* | BHPT | $88-105 | 530-272-1873 |

## Nevada City

Nevada City was founded in 1849 on the banks of Deer Creek by Gold Rush pioneers. Early reports told of miners who pulled a pound of gold per day from the creek. Overnight, the area became honeycombed with mines. Lore has it that the town's curi-

ous pattern of streets follows the early mule trails to and from the
mines.  Downtown Nevada City is still alive with the spirit of its

founders.  The Victorian architectural look and feel has been preserved and the streets are still lit by gas lamps.

One can easily spend a day wandering through shops and
points of interest.  Nevada City is a hot spot for **art**.  Along Broad
Street, the New York Hotel has been converted into a mall of
shops and galleries.  On Sundays, **art auctions** are often held by
local celebrated artists.  The mall's Truffle Shop has the best
**truffles** this chocoholic has ever experienced, and claims to be a
direct supplier to the Pope.  Nineteen restaurants, many of which
are excellent, are sprinkled throughout town.  Locating a restaurant is easy – just follow your nose around the next corner.

On weekends, live **music** is available at half of the two dozen
restaurants and bars.  The Foothill Theater Company, 530-265-
TKTS, presents seven different plays per year.  The Magic Theater, 265-8262, shows the best in American and foreign **classic**

**films**.  The **Miners Foundry Historic Cultural Center** at 265-
5040 on 325 Spring Street sponsors over 200 events per year,
everything from teddy bear conventions to music concerts.  Just
down the street is the **Nevada City Winery** and tasting room.

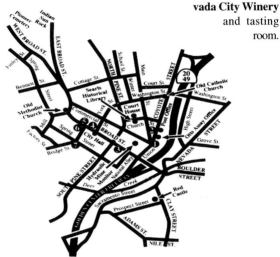

Nevada City has a number of **mining historical sites.**   You
can visit historical markers, walk the Deer Creek Miner's Trail,
visit the Malakoff Diggins State Historical Park, and explore the
Firehouse Museum, 530-265-5468.   **Gold panning tours** are
offered at outlying areas, 432-2546, 265-2740, and 273-3884.

## Grass Valley

Although second to Nevada City in entertainment, Grass Valley is an interesting town in its own right.  Having became the
richest mining town in California with one billion dollars in gold

extracted from its mines, Grass Valley owes its heritage to the mining industry. Today, you can still experience artifacts of the Gold Rush era. **Museums**, **renovated mine ruins**, and Victorian architecture bring back memories of the town's colorful past.

The Holbrooke Hotel, circa 1851, contains the oldest continuously operating saloon in the state. The hotel and a number of B&B establishments have been renovated to contemporary standards. **Gourmet dining** is available at the Main Street Cafe.

The **Empire Mine** State Park, 530-273-8522, is located east of town, off Colfax Highway (Highway 174). This 748-acre park allows you to view workshops, mine shafts, and a collection of old mining equipment. You can walk the park's trails and visit managers' and workers' quarters. The Empire Mine, operated from 1850-1956, was the richest hardrock gold mine in California. Six million ounces of gold were hauled through 367 miles of underground tunnels before the mine was retired from use.

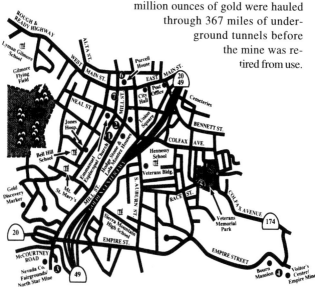

More relics can be seen at the Gold Mine and Pelton Wheel Museum at Allison Ranch and McCourtney Roads. The **North Star Mining Museum and Pelton Wheel Exhibit**, 530-273-4255, has a 30-foot Pelton wheel, assay room, blacksmith shop, stamp mill, and other historic exhibits.

Located at the center of Memorial Park, the new **Video History Museum** catalogs and maintains footage of mining, logging, and transportation. Several tapes are available for viewing, 274-1126

## Festivals

Nevada City (*NC*) and Grass Valley (*GV*) are socially active communities. Their Living History Days and Music in the Mountains events occur throughout the summer. A partial list of annual events follows:

| | | | |
|---|---|---|---|
| Apr, end | Good Old Days Car Show | *GV* | 530-272-8315 |
| May, mid | Living History Days | *GV* | 530-273-8522 |
| May, end | Sierra Festival of Arts | *GV* | 530-272-8315 |
| Jun, mid | California Bluegrass Fest. | *GV* | 530-273-4667 |
| Jun, mid | NC Classic Bicycle Race | *NC* | 530-265-2692 |
| Jun, mid | Early Day Gas Engines | *GV* | 530-432-1502 |
| Jun, end | Music in the Mountains | *GV* | 530-265-6124 |
| Jul,begin | Music in the Mountains | *GV* | 530-265-6124 |
| July, mid | World Music Festival | *GV* | 530-891-4081 |
| Jul, end | World mtn. Bluegrass Fest. | *GV* | 408-425-2270 |
| Aug, all | Living History Days | *GV* | 530-273-8522 |
| Aug, end | Music in Mtns. Brewfest | *GV* | 800-218-2188 |
| Sep, mid | Music in the Mountains | *GV* | 530-265-6214 |
| Sep, end | Draft Horse Classic Faire | *GV* | 530-273-6217 |
| Oct, mid | Chili Cookoff, $25K prize | *GV* | 530-272-4320 |
| Oct, mid | Gem & Mineral Show | *GV* | 530-477-6825 |
| Nov, end | various festivals | *NC&GV* | 530-265-5804 |
| Dec, all | Victorian Christmas | *NC* | 530-265-2692 |
| Dec, all | Chornish Christmas | *GV* | 530-272-8315 |

**Nevada City Fire House**

# Pillsburry Lake

## Gravelly Valley Airport

| | | | |
|---|---|---|---|
| **Town** | Upper Lake | **ID** | 1Q5 |
| **Coord** | N-39-26.99, W-122-57.32 | | |
| **Elev** | 1900 feet, 1.5%, N end high | | |
| **Runway** | 1 - 19, 4050 x 175' gravel | | |
| **Freq** | CTAF-122.9 | | |
| **Charts** | San Francisco sectional | | |

*CAUTION:* Airport information not for navigational use. Hills to the north. Do not land S of road. Watch for hang gliders.

> *Pillsbury Lake offers water activities, hiking,*
> *camping, and resort facilities. It is off the beaten*
> *path and suitable for a picnic or overnight.*
> *$0 - 100. Resort: 707-743-1581.*

## Airport Description

The north end of the runway is marked with an X, probably because it butts up against the base of Hull Mountain. This encourages landings on Runway 1 only. However, 20-knot winds that favor Runway 19 are not uncommon. Use your judgment. Because the valley is surrounded by mountains, keep in mind that clouds below 6000 feet will make arrivals and departures difficult.

## Services, Lodging, and Transportation

Airport phone: 707-275-2361 (not at airstrip). Tiedown space is available at the south end of the strip, between the road and the lake. There were no tiedown ropes when I visited.

The Lake Pillsbury Resort is located on the western edge of the lake. Campsites are $16.50, and rustic cabins rent for $52-60 per day, but only by the week in summer months. The resort has a store and marina with facilities to provide **boating**, **swimming**, **fishing**, and **water skiing**. I have not had an opportunity to visit and review the resort.

Except for the pickup service provided by Lake Pillsbury Resort, transportation is unavailable. Although you can easily walk to Oak Flat Campground, a fold-up bicycle would be useful for exploring the perimeter of the lake.

## Overview

The key feature at this site is easy access to a **camping** and **swimming** area on the lake. Other options include **climbing** Hull Mountain and **hiking** up a nearby river valley.

The campgrounds are more idyllic and less crowded than most in California, probably due to 18 miles of bad road that keep the tourists at bay. Add to this the fact that the nearest power is almost twenty miles away. Except for several homes in Pillsbury Lake Ranch and a resort, civilization has been kept reasonably in check in this basin.

Camping permits are not required in the area, but open campfires are generally not permitted except in designated areas.

## Pillsbury Lake

**Oak Flat Campground** sits at lake edge near the airport. Follow the road that crosses the runway, east. After walking about 15 minutes, you arrive at the entrance to the Mendocino National Forest campground. This campground is free.

**Swimming** is available at the campground, but the water recedes during summer months. Water temperature in mid-June is just right. Mosquitoes are occasionally present, but are not a serious threat to sanity. In the evening, gas lanterns draw gnats.

**Pogie Point Campground** is one mile to the west and becomes farther from the lake as water recedes. **Sunset Campground** is one mile to the east and has the best access to the lake. **Lake Pillsbury Resort** (mentioned earlier) also has campsites.

## Hull Mountain Climb

Hull Mountain peaks at 6873 feet. It has become a popular departure point for **hang gliders**. From airport to peak, the climb is 4973 feet. Trails up the mountain begin at the north end of the airport. These trails have been etched into the mountain ridges by dirt bikes, and are clearly visible from the air.

To locate the trailhead, walk to the north end of the runway. This seems to be a heavily used **target practice area**. Turn right and walk a short distance east to the trail that heads straight up the mountain. It's all good, healthy exercise from this point on.

The climb up the mountain is long and steep. Water is unavailable for the duration of the climb, so carry your own. Due to southern exposure and summer heat, this climb is more pleasant in spring or fall. If you have what it takes to reach the top, the reward is a lookout station and a beautiful view.

## River Route Hike

While circling to land, carefully observe the two rivers from the northwest that feed Pillsbury Lake. Note that the northern-most river is most easily accessible from the north end of the runway. This river is available to the backpacker.

The other river, beautiful though it may be, passes directly through Lake Pillsbury Ranch. The ranch does not take kindly to visitors. To make their point, they have surrounded their land by an eight-foot fence, and have posted a 24-hour gate keeper at the ranch's only entrance.

The northernmost river is just north of Lake Pillsbury Ranch property. You can reach it by walking to the north end of the runway and turning left. Walk about ten minutes west until you intersect the river. During the dry season the river bed may be totally dry. Follow it northwest and you eventually encounter a steady flow of water. During the summer, water level is quite low, making the valley reasonably accessible by foot. Evidence indicates that during winter and spring, water levels can be high enough to inhibit travel around the streams.

*- RW*

# Ruth

## Ruth Airport

| | | | |
|---|---|---|---|
| **Town** | Ruth | **ID** | Q95 |
| **Coord** | N-40-12.68, | W-123-17.85 | |
| **Elev** | 2781 feet | | |
| **Runway** | 13 - 31, 3170 x 50' asphalt | | |
| **Freq** | CTAF-122.8 unmonitored | | |
| **Charts** | Klamath Falls sectional | | |

*CAUTION:* Airport information not for navigational use. Mountains surround. Drafts. Trees.

13

31

> *Ruth offers quick access to scenic, unim-*
> *proved, riverside campsites. The Flying AA*
> *Ranch at the airport is closed as this goes to*
> *press. Marina and lodging are available at*
> *Ruth Lake, 707-574-6441.        $2 - $175.*

## Airport Description

The strip is located in a valley between two mountain ridges.
The peaks rise one to two thousand feet above the valley floor.
Prevailing winds favor Runway 31. Either way, a nonstandard
approach is necessary. Make a long final approach, following the
river. Winds permitting, turn base over the lumber mill and make
your long final over the river for Runway 13.

As you fly in over the river for landing on 31, glance down for
a view of the site of the river hike, described below. Final approach
may be bumpy and wind direction may shift by the time you land.

Ample tiedown space is available. The county tiedown fee is
$2.00, which you can deposit in a box.

## Services, Lodging, and Transportation

Phone: 916-623-1635 (not at airport). Fuel: none. At the time
of this writing, the adjacent Flying AA Ranch is closed and up for
sale. Consequently, until it is purchased and reopened, services are
unavailable at the airport.

Journey's Inn Resort, 707-574-6441, is another alternative. It
is located 17 miles away on Ruth Lake. They charge $10 each way
for transportation, and rent rooms for $46-80. Pets are an addi-

tional $5. The facility includes a restaurant with full bar. A nearby marina **rents boats** and provides a **fishing guide service**.

## Flying AA Ranch

When the Flying AA was open for business, its owners liked to describe the resort as "a working cattle ranch" that caters primarily to fly-in guests. The ranch was comfortably rustic with medium-luxury accommodations. It provided a lodge environment for those who prefer to relax and game; as well as activities for the serious outdoorsman.

Activities included: **tennis**, **swimming** in a heated pool, assorted **ball games**, **hiking**, **fishing** in lake (wide mouth bass) or

**Flying AA Ranch, currently closed and up for sale**

river, good deer **hunting**, **trap shoot**, **bike riding**, **hayrides** on
Fridays, and **horseback riding**. Overnight trail rides took guests
on rides through 100,000 acres of mountain country.

Before closure, rates were $41 to $44 for a cabin, or $21 for a
tent-house with shower available. Three a-la-carte meals were
served each day. Dinners featured barbecue ribs and chicken,
steak, lobster, and prime rib. They operated a bar, but prohibited
guests from bringing their own to the resort. Live country and
western bands entertained on some evenings.

It's a shame to see the Flying AA close. I hope a reader will fall
in love with this opportunity and bring it back to life. It can all be
yours; call Coldwell Bankers at 800-776-4458.

## Mad River Hike and Campsites

This hike follows the Mad River upstream from the airport.
You encounter suitable campsites less than ten minutes from the
airport. Topo map and compass are not required. The hike is easy;
no special footwear is needed. Be prepared for freezing temperatures on clear nights in spring or fall.

Walk from the airport to the entrance of the Flying AA Ranch.
From the entrance, follow the paved road southeast several hundred feet to the pump house on the left side of the road. Intersect
and follow a narrow horse trail that heads upstream. You pass a
skeet range and eventually meander into the bed of the river.
Continue following the trail upstream as it parallels the river. As
you walk, you will see inviting sites to pitch your tent on either side
of the trail.

This area is refreshingly free of trash and campfire rings. Find
a nice place for the tent and take some time to cool your feet in the
river.

*- RW*

# Shelter Cove

## Shelter Cove Airport

| | |
|---|---|
| **Town** | Shelter Cove   **ID**  0Q5 |
| **Coord** | N-40-01.66, W-124-04.40 |
| **Elev** | 69 feet |
| **Runway** | 12rt - 30, 3400 x 75' asphalt |
| **Freq** | CTAF-122.9 |
| **Charts** | Klamath Falls sectional, L2, Lo2 |

*CAUTION:* Airport information not for navigational use. No night operations. Hills to the east. Down-drafts at both ends.

> ***Shelter Cove is a small ocean-side community
> that caters to fishermen, hikers, and beach
> dabblers. Sea-view from campsite or motel.
> $0 -200. Mario's: 707-986-7432.***

## Airport Description

Shelter Cove's runway is aligned parallel to the coast, dominating a peninsula that juts into the Pacific Ocean. Weather for arrivals and departures is best between noon and dusk. Airport lighting is not provided, and night operations are prohibited. No-fee tiedown is available at either end.

## Services and Transportation

Airport phone: 707-986-7361, 986-7415. Fuel: none. The airport is not attended, but food, lodging, and recreation are available within easy walking distance.

Most destinations are within walking distance. The Shelter Cove Ocean Inn has bicycles available for their guests.

## Lodging and Restaurants

You can camp by your airplane for free, or at the official campground for $15 per day. Facilities include 105 sites, picnic tables, showers, mini-laundromat, deli, and grocery store, 707-986-7474. Leashed pets are allowed.

Lodging is available at both ends of the airport. Before picking a place to stay, consider that there is a cultural difference between the north and south ends. The north end attracts people who are looking for a quiet, romantic weekend, and perhaps a round of golf. The south end is for fishermen and folks who like to get down and mingle.

At the north end, the Shelter Cove Motor Inn provides a quiet ocean-view environment. Prices range from $80-160, and AOPA members get a 10% discount. Bicycles are available for guests. Call 707-986-7521 for reservations.

The Shelter Cove Ocean Inn B&B, 707-986-7161, is two blocks north of the northern tiedown. The newly-renovated rooms cost $71-115. Continental breakfast is included; lunch and dinner can be provided on request.

**View from the Shelter Cove Ocean Inn B&B**

Mario's Marina Motel is located at the south end near the community's center of activity. The $54-62 rooms are clean and modern, and can be reserved via 707-986-7595 or 986-7432. Mario's also rents a number of mobile home units with kitchen facilities. Funky on the outside and clean on the inside, these $70-80 units are often fully rented in advance. The mobile home units are the only rentals at Shelter Cove that allow pets.

Located on a rise above the south end is the six-unit Shelter Cove Beachcomber Inn. Units cost $50-83; call 707-986-7733.

Mario's Restaurant sits on a bluff with ocean view at the south end of the airport. Mario's provides three family-style meals per day, May through Labor Day. A fish-and-chips deli is located close to the campground.

Cove Landing Restaurant is located in an A-frame building at the north end of the runway. This restaurant has by far the best food, but is typically closed Monday through Wednesday. Further, seating is limited, so call 707-986-7793 for reservations.

## Recreation

The big draw at Shelter Cove is **fishing**. Fisherman are attracted by outstanding deep sea salmon fishing. Ling/rock cod, red/black snapper, abalone, crab, and shellfish are also abundant in local waters.

Walt Mitchell runs the boating operation at the south end. If not at the Marina, look for Walt on a farm-style tractor, hauling boats to or from the beach. He provides **small-craft charters** for $55 per person per four-hour trip, April through September. Walt can help you arrange diving, surfing, and **whale watching** trips as well. Gray whales can be seen on their 6000-mile migration in early spring and late fall. Because resources are limited, call Walt at 707-986-7624 for reservations.

The marina provides **fishing supplies** for the fisherman and **fresh catch** for retail sales. You will find a small general store and gift shop located near the marina at the southern end.

Compliance with fishing regulations is closely monitored. I watched an incoming fisherman get pinched. His plead of ignorance bought no slack. Take care.

**Horse shoe pits** and **pool table** are located at Mario's Restaurant. **Golf Links** at the north end charges $ 10 for a round of golf. Their bar also includes a pool table.

**While parents fish, kids play serious pool at Mario's**

The surrounding countryside offers **hikes** ranging from a twenty-minute peek at **tidal pools**, to all-day beach and **cliff-climbing** excursions.  To visit the nearby tidal pools, head west from the marina towards the ocean.  Continue walking through Mal Coombs Park and follow the wooden stairway down the cliff to the rock and tide pools below.

Serious hikers will enjoy walking to the **black sand beach** up the coast from Shelter Cove.  Ask at the marina about trails that wind through local terrain.  The area provides alternatives for a vigorous afternoon hike or overnight adventure.  Avid climbers should consider following the trail to **Kings Peak**.  At 4086 feet, Kings Peak is the highest point on the U.S. Pacific coastline.

Through the efforts of local realtors, Shelter Cove has become settled by a mix of retired professionals, fishermen, artists, and writers.  Lots near the airport are available for purchase.

*- RW*

# Sierraville Hot Springs

## Sierraville Dearwater

| | |
|---|---|
| **Town** | Sierraville **ID** O79 (oh-79) |
| **Coord** | N-39-34.86, W-120-21.26 |
| **Elev** | 4984 ft, SW end high, 1% |
| **Runway** | 3 - 21rt, 3260 x 50' asphalt |
| **Freq** | CTAF-122.9 |
| **Charts** | San Francisco sect., L2, L7, Lo2 |

*CAUTION:* *Airport information not for navigational use. Mountains. The runway is relatively short for this altitude. Watch density altitude. Livestock.*

> *Sierra Hot Springs is a "new age" resort,*
> *walking distance from the airport.  Natural*
> *food, rustic facilities, and open-air hot-pools.*
> *Good for quick soak or overnight.*
> *$24-85.  Lodge:  530-994-3773.*

## Airport Description

The runway is easy to spot on the flat valley floor at the edge of forested hills.  In good weather during daytime, the surrounding mountains are not a threat for aircraft operations.  The runway has been recently maintained.  Unfortunately, the airport is at risk for closure; verify in advance.

## Services, Lodging, and Transportation

Airport phone:  530-289-3201 (in town).  The airport is unattended, with no services provided at the strip.  However, food and lodging are within walking distance.  Sierraville is located about a mile northwest of the airport; Sierraville Hot Springs is located one-half mile east.  Groceries are available in Sierraville and meals are available at either location.

Rooms at the lodge cost $50-70.  Before you can stay, you must be a member, which costs $15 per year or $3 for a one-month trial membership.  Three vegetarian meals are served per day on weekends only.  Camping costs $14-18 <u>per person</u>.  Overnight visitors receive free access to the hot springs.  Day visitors pay $10.00 per person, or $7.00 for three hours.  The organization also owns a hotel in town.  Verify availability and costs in advance by calling the resort, 530-994-3773.

Those who wish to camp without paying $14-18 per person may do so on U.S. Forest Service land, south-southeast of the airport. However, you are still obligated to pay for access to the springs.

Transportation is unavailable at Sierraville airport. Fortunately, walking from airport to lodge takes 15 minutes.

## Overview

This site offers a **lodge** and **hot springs** with **new age ambiance**. The facilities are somewhat run down, but are in the process of being restored by new management. As an alternative, you can enjoy unstructured **hiking** and **camping**, with the option to soak in a rustic, **spring-fed hot tub** at the end of your hike. Due to logging and fires decades ago, the terrain is relatively easy to cross. Though the land has been altered by man, I found the extra space and visibility to be a refreshing change from the dense wilderness areas.

Water is scarce. Jogging shoes are adequate footwear. A topo map is not necessary for the hike described below.

## Sierra Hot Springs

Sierra Hot Springs is located a half-mile east of the airport. Look for a large white building. To its left is a smaller building with *Welcome* on its roof. The facility includes a lodge and a number of baths fed by hot springs. It is located on 680 wooded acres at the southern end of a peaceful valley.

In years past under the name Campbell Hot Springs, the facility served as a training center for **rebirthing**. Rebirthing is a practice, like yoga, for improving one's life experience. Casual visitors were invited to experience rebirthing, but there was no additional pressure to become involved. Many folks visited simply for the springs and mountain serenity.

Life-style at Campbell was very casual. Typical attire at the baths was none. Children were well received. In my book, Campbell Hot Springs scored a near ten in the placid category.

In 1992, the New Age Church of Being leased the land and changed the name to Sierra Hot Springs. Management style and price structures have changed somewhat since the old regime. In the past, bargaining and negotiating prices were a part of the culture. The new management seems more conventional. They are working to renovate the rundown lodge, and have tackled an old hotel in town as well.

**Two hot springs soaking units at Sierra Hot Springs**

The New Age Church of Being is a spiritual community that is dedicated to promoting well being of the planet and  spirituality in all forms.  Alcohol and drugs are prohibited on the premises.  Smoking is allowed in one designated area, only.  Clothing is optional at the springs.

Improvements are being made at a leisurely pace.  New soaking facilities are planned, which may be functional by the time you read this.

## Southeast U.S. Forest Loop Hike

This hiking loop takes you southeast, beyond Sierraville Hot Springs property.  The terrain is gentle and unobstructed;  tennis shoes and shorts are adequate protection.  You can walk the loop in two or three hours.  Extensions and variations are possible without the aid of a topo map, assuming proper use of a compass.  Carry a good supply of water in summer.

The National Forest area is easily reached from the southeast end of the runway. Follow the barbed wire fence south.  In early summer, the subtle shades of green vegetation in this area are very pleasing.  Continue walking along the grassy area until you reach the base of the hill to the south.  At this point, about a mile from the runway, you may duck under the wire and follow a trail up the hill.

This area was burned or logged perhaps thirty to fifty years ago.  It supports a population of deer who are frequently visible. The foliage and terrain allow pleasant cross-country travel.  If you lose track of the trail, simply continue southeast until you reach the top of the ridge, which is less than three miles from the airport. Relax for a moment and enjoy the view.  If you are carrying sufficient water, you may find this to be an attractive campsite.

Follow the ridge southeast.  Eventually you connect with the remnants of an old 4x4 trail.  Continue following the trail southeast.  After about twenty to thirty minutes on the ridge, the terrain becomes nearly treeless.

As you would expect, water is unavailable on the ridge.  For a campsite with water, turn right and head cross-country, south-west down the ridge.  Shortly, you will encounter a paved road.  Cross over the road and descend the bank on the other side.  Five minutes below is a stream.  Make your way upstream until you find nice site to camp.

To return to the valley, retrace your footsteps back to the trail on the ridge.  Follow the ridge-trail east for about five minutes until it bends right toward the southeast.  At this point, leave the trail walking north (left) toward the shallow ravine.  Follow it northwest all the way into the valley.

Eventually, you emerge into the valley on the edge of the Sierra Hot Springs property.  To orient yourself, note that the runway is visible about one mile due northwest.  Walk roughly west, passing some stables and cabins on the way to the lodge.

Consider soaking in the cool pool or hot springs at the end of your hike.  The cool pool is located to the left of the lodge.  The hot tubs are located west, near the numbers for Runway 3.  Ask the first person you see for directions.

*- RW*

# Trinity Center

## Trinity Center Airport

**Town**    Trinity Center **ID** O86 (oh-86)
**Coord**   N-40-58.99, W-122-41.65
**Elev**    2390 feet
**Runway**  14 - 32rt, 3200 x 50' asphalt
**Freq**    CTAF-122.8
**Charts**  Klamath Falls sect., L2, Lo2

*CAUTION:* Airport information not for navigational use. Mountains nearby. Balloons, ultralights, gyrocopters, aerobatics.

> ***Trinity Center** is the gateway to the beautiful
> **Trinity Alps**. Lakeside resorts and rugged
> backpacking are the main draw. $20-170.
> Wyntoon Park Resort: 800-715-3337.*

## Airport Description

Landing at Trinity is safe and straightforward in good VFR
weather. Avoid the bluffs at the northeast end of Runway 14.
Because the airport is located in a basin surrounded by mountains, low cloud cover can inhibit arrivals and departures.

The runway is plowed in winter after all county roads have
been plowed.

## Services, Lodging, and Transportation

Airport phone: 530-266-3350 (not at airport). No fuel. The
airport is unattended. Ample tiedown area is available for a $2
fee. Rest rooms and pay phone are at the south end.

A restaurant, bar, and motel, called the Airporter Inn is located
at the north end of the strip. The Airporter caters to pilots and has a
loaner car available for pilot use in summer. New owners plan to
add tennis courts, Jaccuzis, and a swimming pool. Rooms cost
about $50, and pets are OK. Call 530-266-3223 and ask about their
special package deals for pilots.

The Wyntoon Park Resort, 800-715-3337, is located one mile
north of the airport on Mountain Road. The resort has **camping**,
marina, **boat rentals**, store, and snack bar. They pickup from
the airport and pets are allowed. Tents cost $22 and cabins cost
$84-124. Pets cost an additional $8.

Transportation options are limited, but the walk into town takes less than ten minutes. Since most back-road traffic is hikers or fishermen, hitchhiking can be a practical mode of transportation. However, success is highly dependent on luck, since traffic to the trailheads is often light.

Gerry Gray's On the Fly Guide Service provides a variety of services: **jeep tours**, **fishing**, **gold panning**, **trailhead drops**, and more. Call 888-286-7250 or 530-266-3542 for details.

Most businesses in the area are willing to help with transportation. The Airporter Inn is adjacent to the airport and in summer has a car that pilots can use. The Wyntoon Park Resort provides free transportation to overnight customers. Just one-half mile south of the airport, Trinity Center Marina at 530-266-3432 provides free pick-up to boat rental customers. They also rent houseboats for $750-1450 per week.

## Overview

Several activities are located within a ten minute walk of the airport. The town is west from the airport. The **Scott Museum**, 530-266-3378, has items on display from pioneer days. It is open in the afternoons. When the lake is full, the **swimming** area is a five-minute walk northeast of the airport. **Boat rental** is available from Trinity Center Marina, a half mile south. Options expand as you increase your radius from the airport. The Wyntoon Park Resort has a number of activities, including **camping** and **boat rentals**.

The Salmon Trinity Wilderness area offers beauty and challenge for the **mountain backpacker**. Unless snow camping is your objective, visit in summer or fall. Trails typically fall within the 5000- to 8000-foot levels, and are generally easy to follow. Wildlife is plentiful and frequently visible to those who are quiet and patient.

Backpacking permits are required. Although permits cannot be conveniently obtained near the airport, they can be obtained via mail from the Forest Service at Shasta-Trinity National Forest, P.O. Box 1190, Weaverville, CA 96093, 530-623-2131.

Hikers should purchase the following California topo maps: *Schell Mountain*, *Trinity Dam*, and *Coffee Creek*; or purchase a map from the Forest Service, 530-623-2131. These three maps are a must in the Trinity Wilderness Area. They will tempt your imagination with a number of interesting and varied possibilities. Select an interesting loop and go for it.

## Swift / Steer / Granite Creeks Trailhead

A likely trailhead for fly-in visitors at Trinity Center is located at the west end of Swift Creek.

Leave the airport, heading west on the road that accesses the northwest end of the airport. Walk a half-mile through the little town of Trinity Center. Near the end of this segment you can buy food. You may be able to purchase a ride from someone in town. At the intersection with the main highway, turn right and cross over Swift Creek. After crossing the bridge, turn left on the dirt road that heads west, paralleling Swift Creek.

The distance to the trailhead is seven or eight miles. If you have not acquired a ride, try hitchhiking as you walk. The topo map shows the road going half this distance. Actually, the road has been extended to the junction of Swift, Steer, and Granite Creeks. At the trailhead, options include heading southwest toward Granite Lake and north along Steer Creek.

*- RW*

# Truckee

## Truckee Airport

| | | | |
|---|---|---|---|
| **Town** | Truckee | **ID** | TRK |
| **Coord** | N-39-19.20, W-120-08.37 | | |
| **Elev** | 5900 feet | | |
| **Runway** | 10 - 28, 7000 x 100' asphalt | | |
| | 1 - 19rt, 4650 x 75' asphalt | | |
| **Freq** | CTAF-122.8, AWOS-118.0 | | |
| | Lights-122.8-5x | | |
| **Charts** | San Francisco sect., L2, L7, Lo2 | | |

*CAUTION:* Airport information not for navigational use. Watch for ballooning, gliders, and ultralights. Mountainous terrain. Drafts. Density altitude in the summer can exceed 9000 feet.

> *Truckee and Tahoe City, gateways to northern*
> *Lake Tahoe and alpine hiking trails. Outdoor*
> *activities in summer and winter. $120 - $350.*
> *Chamber: 530-587-2757, www.truckee.com*

## Airport Description

With care and acceptable weather, Truckee is a safe airport for most aircraft. UNICOM is responsive and helpful. Snow removal is said to be exceptional. The local FBO estimated that the airport is open to VFR traffic during more than 80% of the winter. During the summer, it is almost always open.

The airport supports a number of aerial activities: ultralights, helicopters, banner-towing, balloons, and gliders. Watch for such traffic and note the airport's published noise abatement procedures.

## Airport Services, Lodging, and Transportation

Airport phone: 530-587-4119, -2717. Todd Aero, 587-4465; Regent Air, 582-1102. All fuel. Tiedown is ample and costs $3.00 per evening. Snacks are available at the airport.

The Truckee Tahoe Inn is one mile from the airport. Donner Country Inn, Donner Lake Village, and Loch Leven Lodge are on Donner Lake. Northstar-at-Tahoe is a 2500-acre resort, complete with marina. The Resort at Squaw Creek is a golf-oriented up-scale resort.

Call 800-548-8388 or 800-824-6348 for Truckee-area central reservations.

**Features**

B Full breakfast
C Continental
H Historic
P Pets OK
R Restaurant
T Transportation

| | | | |
|---|---|---|---|
| 10064 River Rd. B&B | BT | $95-121 | 530-582-1923 |
| Alpine Village | P | $42-64 | 800-933-1787 |
| Donner Country Inn | B | $116 | 530-587-5574 |
| Donner Lake Village | | $80-250 | 800-621-6664 |
| Hanna's B&B Inn | BHT | $105-150 | 888-600-3735 |
| Loch Leven Lodge | | $84-163 | 530-587-3773 |
| Northstar-at-Tahoe | R | $100-160 | 800-466-6784 |
| Richardson House | BHT | $93-165 | 888-229-0365 |
| Resort at Squaw Creek | R | $190-2K | 800-327-3353 |
| Super 8 Lodge | CP | $82-90 | 530-587-8888 |
| | | | 800-800-8000 |
| Truckee Hotel | CH | $94-138 | 800-659-6921 |
| Truckee-Tahoe Inn | CR | $85-112 | 800-824-6385 |

Taxi service is provided by Yellow Cab, 530-587-0600; Truckee Taxi, 583-8294; and, Royal Limousine Service, 800-660-4546.

Except for Enterprise, the following car rental agencies have offices at the airport. Enterprise is closed on weekends.

| | | | |
|---|---|---|---|
| Airport Auto Rental | $41-73 | 800-660-4546 | 530-587-2688 |
| Enterprise | $42 | 800-325-8007 | 530-550-1550 |
| Lakeside | $66 | | 530-587-6000 |
| Tod Arrow | $43 | | 530-587-4465 |

To get to Truckee, leave the airport and turn right on the main highway, California 267. Drive 2.1 miles until the intersection of Highways 89 and 267. The Chamber of Commerce is one block to the right. The U.S. Forest Service, 530-587-3558, is one mile to the right, just after Highway 80. Topo maps may be obtained from Alpenglow and Mountain Hardware. U.S. Forest Service and Truckee maps are available at the Chamber. Alpenglow is one block from the intersection of 89 and 267. Mountain Hardware is one mile to the left of the intersection.

## Truckee and Tahoe City Area

If you are simply passing through and are without car, you can enjoy a historic walking tour of town. Truckee's buildings date back to 1863. Along the way, you can enjoy an ice cream treat at Bud's Sporting Goods, or a satisfying meal at one of Truckee's better restaurants.

Truckee's roots date back to the mid 1800s when pioneers were pushing west. One such group of pioneers decided to take a shortcut through the area in 1846. Due to unfortunate decisions and bad weather, the train of 20 wagons got snowed in for the winter near Donner Pass. They ran out of food, and some members resorted to cannibalism. Only 47 of the 89 members survived the ordeal. You can get the whole story at the **Memorial State Park** and museum, west of town.

Somewhat before the Donner Party tragedy, the railroads began a survey to find the best route through the mountains. Finally in 1863, Central Pacific Railroad took the challenge, and thousands of Chinese workers were brought in to do the labor. They built 15 tunnels, the longest measuring 1,600 feet. Due to chronic problems with snow, Central Pacific built a 37-mile roof over the tracks. The peaked-roof snowsheds required 65 million feet of timber and 900 tons of bolts and spikes!

Later in the 1900s, promoters turned the abundance of snow into an asset by creating 14 **downhill ski areas.** Tahoe City has become the north lake ski center. Squaw Valley, eight miles northwest, was the site of the 1960 winter Olympics and is the largest facility in the area. **Cross-country skiers** will enjoy the Tahoe Nordic Ski Area, 2.5 miles northeast of Tahoe City. Other cross-country ski areas can be found in the mountains, west of Truckee. You can rent **snowmobiles** from the Tahoe City Recreation Area, 530-583-1516, in the heart of town.

Tahoe City, ten miles due south of the airport, is the outdoor recreation hub of north Lake Tahoe. Its beaches attract swimmers and sun bathers. Marinas offer **cruises**, **sailing**, **boating**, **water-skiing**, and **fishing**. You'll find **bicycle paths**, **hiking** trails, **campgrounds**, and **golf** facilities. To get to Tahoe City, follow Highway 267 southeast from the airport for ten miles. When you arrive at Lake Tahoe, follow Highway 28 southwest along the lake's edge, ten additional miles to Tahoe City.

All types of **boat rental** and **water ski instruction** are provided by High Sierras, 530-525-1214 and 583-7417. Jet-skis, for example, rent for $70/hr. An **aerial tram** is located at the Squaw Valley Ski Center, 530-583-6985. They also have an **Olympic Ice Pavilion**, **swimming lagoon**, and 40-person **hot tub**. **Horseback riding** is available from Alpine Meadows Stables, 583-3905. **Golf** is available at the following:

| | |
|---|---|
| Biju, 9-holes | 530-542-6097 |
| Edgewood Tahoe Championship | 702-588-3566 |
| Glenbrook, 9-holes | 702-749-5201 |
| Incline Village | 702-832-1144 |
| Incline Village Mountain | 702-832-1150 |
| Lake Tahoe | 530-577-0788 |
| Northstar-at-Tahoe | 530-562-1010 |
| Old Brockway, 9-holes | 530-546-9909 |
| Ponderosa, 9-holes | 530-587-3501 |
| Resort at Squaw Creek | 530-581-6637 |
| Tahoe City Golf Course | 530-583-1516 |
| Tahoe Donner | 530-587-9440 |

The land in the vicinity of Truckee and Lake Tahoe offers some of the most appealing **hiking** opportunities our country has to offer. The effort required to get to a mountain peak is rewarded by spectacular views. The areas of North Tahoe appear to be less populated with hikers than the nearby Desolation Wilderness Area, probably because the Truckee trails are less well known. Trails are often difficult to follow, and sometimes disappear entirely. Expect a good deal of cross-country hiking, even if the topo indicates the presence of a trail.

Due to the occasional steep cross-country gradients, smart and light packing is highly recommended. Avoid jogging shoes, and wear broken-in hiking boots. The traction of a good sole is needed for crossing inclined banks of snow. Other key items are compass, topo, and potent insect repellent. Locating filterable water in this area is not a problem.

The mountains surrounding Truckee are accessible for normal hiking from early summer until mid-fall. Call the U.S. Forest Service at 530-587-3558 for further information.

## Events

Truckee has up to a dozen events per month in summer months.  Major events are listed below.  For more information, contact the Chamber of Commerce at 530-587-2757.

| | | |
|---|---|---|
| Apr, begin | *Contests, music, and more...* | 530-526-9000 |
| May, mid | West Shore Jazz Festival | 800-824-6348 |
| Jun, mid | Valhalla Renaissance Festival | 530-542-6550 |
| Jun, mid | Beer Festival at Northstar | 530-562-1010 |
| Jun,end | Young Eagles Flight Rally | 530-562-0617 |
| Jun, end | Lake Tahoe Summer Music Fest. | 530-583-3101 |
| Jul, mid | Cannibal Cruise, *antique cars* | 530-587-7576 |
| Jul, end | Concert on the Green, *classical* | 530-587-9404 |
| Jul, end | World Champ. Motorcycle Trials | 530-426-3635 |
| Jul, end | Old Highway 40, *antique cars* | 530-582-1214 |
| Aug, all | Shakespeare Festival | 800-747-4697 |
| Aug,begin | Art Music and Wine Fest | 530-587-7576 |
| Aug,begin | Truckee Championship Rodeo | 530-582-9852 |
| Aug,begin | Lake Tahoe Summer Music Fest. | 530-583-3101 |
| Sep,begin | Labor Day Music Festival | 800-747-4697 |
| Sep, end | Railroad Days Celebration | 530-550-9005 |
| Oct, mid | Oktoberfest, *food and beer* | 530-583-3494 |
| Oct, mid | Annual Chocolate Festival | 530-546-7804 |

## Paradise Lake Loop Hike

The **Donner** topo map is required for the beautiful Paradise Lake Loop.  Access should be carefully selected since the public land is surrounded by private property.

Private property in the mountains often belongs to large corporations, and access is typically no problem.  In some cases, however, finding a new and interesting place to hike can be like playing the horses:  One plays to win, but must be prepared to lose.  The following is an example of one such loss:

The first time I spotted Paradise Lake from the air, I knew I had to get there. The logical point of access seemed to be Carpenter Valley, directly between the airport and Paradise Lake. After gathering information from the Forest Service and folks around town, I determined that Carpenter Valley was private property, but that access should be no problem. Local customs supposedly allow hikers to follow dirt roads across private property, and even across locked gates.

A locked gate guarded the entrance to Carpenter Valley. Parked by the gate were several vehicles, generally an indication of good access. Posted near the gate were several *No Trespassing* signs, and a comforting sign that read *Access Only, Next 2 Miles, No Stopping*. This confirmed my belief that hikers could just walk on through.

**Paradise Lake is the upper lake, barely visible in this photo**

Twenty minutes past the gate, an old man emerged from an isolated cabin and told me unequivocally to "git out." I tried to make friendly conversation, but finally acknowledged failure when he said, "As fer as I'm concerned, you can take all dem goddam cars down by the gate and tow 'em all away."

So much for how *not* to get to Paradise Lake. Here's how to experience Paradise Lake and beautiful views from Basin and Castle Peaks. But first, a few words of warning. This loop involves cross-country travel and a demanding climb. Though definitely worth the effort for persons in reasonably good shape, it is not recommended for inexperienced backpackers.

When you arrive at Truckee from the airport, turn left at the intersection of Highways 89 and 267. Travel through town and in less than one mile take Highway 80 heading west. Drive ten miles on Highway 80 to the exit labeled *Castle Peak, Boreal Ridge*. After leaving Highway 80, turn right, drive a half-mile, and park at the trailhead where you'll see a sign that says *Basin Peak Via Trail 6 Miles*. Note that Highway 80 is not yet on the topo map. The trailhead is near the last "e" in "Andesite Ridge."

The next couple of miles are a 4x4 trail that passes northwest through Castle Valley. Though not labeled as such, this is part of the Pacific Crest Trail. You can see a green grass valley, patches of snow (in early summer), and the rock outcroppings of Castle Peak. After 40 minutes, the 4x4 trail ends. A sign marks the hikers trail: *North Creek 6 Miles, White Rock Lake, Peter Grub Hut 1 Mile*. Follow the trail up to nearby Castle Pass. Memorize this location, because it is the point at which the loop will rejoin.

Continue down the other side toward Peter Grub Hut. Wild flowers are varied and plentiful, and trees are short and sparse enough to allow continuous views of the surrounding mountains. Soon you will find yourself in the valley at the Peter Grub Hut, approximately one hour from the trailhead.

Those who arrive at the airport late Friday afternoon will find the Peter Grub Hut to be a convenient place to spend the night. The hut is maintained by the Sierra Club, and is available for use during the summer without reservation. In winter, reservations are required. Of architectural interest is the hut's accompanying twenty-foot-high outhouse. This provides a clue as to the depth of winter snows in Round Valley. Observe the ridge to the east between Basin and Castle peaks; this will be your return route.

Continue northwest toward Paradise Valley. The trail becomes difficult to follow, and often impossible to read when covered with patches of snow. Prepare to travel cross-country until reaching Paradise Valley. Cross-country travel on this terrain is of medium difficulty. As you approach Paradise Valley, you discover why mosquito repellent was on the list of required items. Other than the mosquitoes, the valley central can be easily identified by North Creek. Follow the trail or creek east to Paradise Lake. Sections of the Paradise Valley are uniquely beautiful. Hiking time from hut to lake can take as long as three hours.

Paradise Lake is an absolutely beautiful alpine lake, situated more than 7700 feet above sea level. It is surrounded by a table of rock formations that seem to be designed especially for sunbathers. I believe this paradise would be teaming with humanity were it not for the inconvenient access. A campsite can be selected from any number of choice locations around the lake. The lake appears to be stocked with lake trout. Due to the thin population of trees, wood is scarce. As a courtesy to future visitors, please burn wood conservatively.

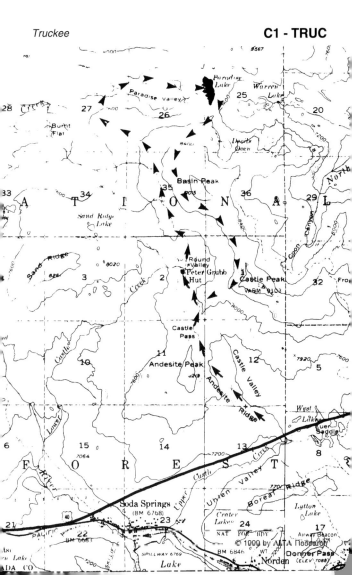

When you finally *must* leave, walk around to the rock table at the east edge of the lake.  Look straight up the rocky ridge that heads roughly toward Devil's Oven, and start climbing straight up.  After climbing about one third the total distance, bear right.  Though relatively steep, this climb is safe if you choose your path wisely.  If you encounter a cul de sac, simply backtrack and try again.  Including time for breathers and picture-taking, the ascent to the ridge above the lake takes less than one hour.

At the top of the ridge, head southwest.  The objective is to circle around the west side of Basin Peak.  When you encounter a horse trail, follow it until it heads down the mountain.  At this point, leave the trail, staying above the 8500-foot contour.  On the southern side of Basin Peak, follow the ridge leading to the top of Castle Peak.  The view from the ridge is fantastic.  On a clear day, you can see the Diablo and coastal mountain ranges.

Several hundred feet before reaching Castle Peak, begin following the southwest ridge down toward Castle Pass.  Approximately two and one-half hours will have elapsed since leaving Paradise Lake.  Attempt to follow the trail that wanders down the ridge.  Take care not to lose your footing in the dust and loose rock.

At Castle Pass, turn left when you intersect the familiar trail that heads south, back to the trailhead.  Total time from Paradise Lake to trailhead is three to four hours.

Of course, there is no compelling reason to follow my footsteps.  With compass and chart, you can pick an alluring destination and find your own special paradise.

*- RW*

# California  Central

GEOR
Georgetown

TAHO  Lake Tahoe

MARK  Markleeville

COLU
Columbia

TUOL  Tuolumne
Meadows

HEAL
Healdsburg

MONO
Mono Lake

MAMM
Mammoth

CARV
Carmel
Valley

YOSE
Yosemite
Park

HARR
Harris
Ranch

SALI
Saline Valley
Hot Springs

**California Aeronautics**

**916-654-4959**

# Carmel Valley
## Ventana Wilderness

### Carmel Valley Airport

| | |
|---|---|
| **Town** | Carmel Valley **ID** O62 (oh-62) |
| **Coord** | N-36-28.91, W-121-43.81 |
| **Elev** | 450 feet |
| **Runway** | 11rt - 29, 2475 x 45' oiled gravel |
| **Freq** | CTAF-122.9 |
| **Charts** | San Francisco sectional |

*CAUTION: Airport information not for navigational use. No night ops. Mountains. Powerlines rwy 11. Watch out for people, animals, and cars on the runway.*

> *Carmel Valley is a pleasant lunch and shop stop. Enjoy a day or two at a luxurious golf resort or backpack the Ventana Wilderness. $100 - $1000. Chamber: 408-659-4000.*

## Airport Description

Carmel Valley airport is located literally in the center of town. Naturally, noise abatement is an issue. No touch and goes or night operations are allowed. Pay attention to the power lines at the end of Runway 11 and the mountains to the northeast.

When departing on Runway 29, take a straight-out departure, turn left 20 degrees, and make no major turns below 1000 feet. When departing 11, turn right 20 degrees as soon as possible.

## Services, Lodging, and Transportation

Airport phone: 408-659-0860 (in town). The airport is unattended and without fuel or services. Space is available for tiedown, but existing ropes appear to be used by local residents. If you want to attach your bird to the earth, bring your own.

A grocery store and a number of pleasant restaurants and  are located within several blocks of the airport. The quality and diversity of dining has improved significantly since my first visit. To get to the center of town, head due southwest from where you parked your plane, down an in-cline at the edge of the runway, and follow the street two blocks to the main highway.

Blue Sky Lodge and Valley Lodge are within walking distance of the airport.

**Features**

B  Full breakfast
C  Continental
H  Historic
P  Pets OK
R  Restaurant
T  Transportation

| | | | |
|---|---|---|---|
| Acacia Lodge | C | $70-170 | 800-367-3336 |
| Blue Sky Lodge | P | $60-130 | 408-659-2256 |
| Carmel Valley Ranch | BHPRT | $250-700 | 800-4CARMEL |
| Hidden Valley Inn | C | $120-250 | 800-367-3336 |
| Los Laureles Lodge | HR | $100-500 | 408-659-2233 |
| Quail Lodge | | $210-400 | 408-624-1581 |
| Robles del Rio Lodge | CHRT | $100-210 | 408-659-3705 |
| Stonepine Estate Resort | CHRT | $300-800 | 408-659-2245 |
| Valley Lodge | BPT | $110-300 | 800-641-4646 |

Most of the above have at least one swimming pool; some have Jacuzzis. Outside of town, Carmel Valley Ranch Resort is a place of quiet elegance – five-star quality with golf course, tennis courts, and pools. The 330-acre Stonepine resort has the oldest **equestrian center** west of the Mississippi.

Food and shops are located within easy walking distance of the airport. If you need a rental car, land at Monterey, instead. The Los Padres Dam destination described below is not within practical walking distance. Due to lack of transportation, I have resorted to hitchhiking and bicycling.

## Overview

The town of Carmel Valley is a good fly-in destination for a casual day of visiting **shops**, **restaurants**, **crafts stores**, and **boutiques**. **Golf** enthusiasts have a choice of three championship golf courses: Rancho Canada, Quail Lodge Resort, and Carmel Valley Ranch Resort. Two resorts have tennis courts. Several wineries have tasting rooms within striking distance.

Nearby, the peaks of the Santa Lucia Mountain Range tempt area visitors. The upper ranges of this preserve offer hikers and horseback riders sweeping valley and coastal views. To the south, Zen monks provide a retreat at Tassajara Hot Springs.

Out of the 27 wilderness areas in California, **Ventana Wilderness Area** is one of the few near the coast. Compared to Sierra sites, elevations are lower; trails seldom run above 4000 feet. (Most other parks start at 3000, and go up from there.) A benefit of this relatively low elevation is the park's year-round accessibility.

In summer, some areas can become uncomfortably hot. Be careful not to spend too much time on southern exposures without a hat and adequate water. The streams at the lower elevations offer a wonderful retreat from afternoon heat. They are warm enough for swimming in late spring through fall.

Established trails provide the easiest way to get around. Cross-country travel on southern mountain sides is difficult due to heat, wiry vegetation, and poison oak. On a positive note, southern-exposure chaparral has a variety of delightful fragrances. A cross-country technique that worked for me was to follow the streams while wearing a pair of running shoes. At first you try to avoid getting your feet wet, but once you do, walking in the stream feels great.

The Ventana Wilderness Area has a wealth of wildlife, perhaps nine on a ten-point scale compared to other California wilderness areas. You will see lots of birds. Visitors who are still and patient will observe a number of small mammals. Deer leave their signs everywhere. Local frogs perform a masterclass symphony every evening – their rhythm section is worthy of critical acclaim.

The insects are relatively friendly. The mosquitoes, though present, showed little interest in me. Local flies occasionally bite, but they are much slower than domestic flies, which man has bred for speed. I found the use of repellent to be unnecessary, but carry some just to be safe.

## Camping Permits

From the Carmel Valley side of the Ventana Wilderness Area, you experience beautiful country before penetrating the park. If you expect to camp in the wilderness area, a permit is recommended.

As is often the case, a ranger station is not easily accessible from the airport. The rangers will, however, send you a permit through the mail if you tell them where you plan to camp. Tell them where you plan to enter the park and ask them to recommend a good campsite. Request copies of their maps. The maps are hand-drawn and useful when combined with a topo map. Contact the Forest Service at Los Padres National Forest, 406 S. Mildred, King City, CA 93930, phone 408-385-5434.

## Los Padres Dam Entry

Clearly marked on your sectional, the Los Padres Dam is located adjacent to the north corner of the wilderness area. The distance from the airport exceeds that which one might ordinarily care to walk. I turned this obstacle into an opportunity to create a hybrid bicycle/wilderness experience.

Should you opt to bicycle to the dam, I offer two recommendations: Because there are uphill grades, the trip will be more pleasant with a bicycle that has gears. And, travel light (no portable TV or dual-burner Coleman on this trip). Although you may not care to follow my example, I lived out of a ten-pound daypack on my first overnight visit to the park.

The airport is located very close to a restaurant and shops in town. Coast your bicycle several blocks into town. Follow main highway G16 in a southeasterly direction out of town, and go four miles to Chachagua Road. At this intersection, you will see a sign indicating a right turn for Los Padres Dam. Unless you like steep hills, do not follow Chachagua Road to the dam as the sign suggests. Continue on G16, a longer but friendlier route.

Continue following G16 six and one-half miles to Tassajara. This portion becomes ranch country, less shady and windy than the first segment. Except for the last mile, which is steeper, the first five and one-half can be done in second and third gears on a three-speed bike. Total time from airport to Tassajara Road is somewhat less than two hours.

The trip is nearly all downhill from this intersection. Turn right on Tassajara Road, following it downhill about one mile to Chachagua. Turn right again, following Chachagua along a stream about three miles to Nason Road. If a beer sounds good, you can satisfy your thirst at the campgrounds bar about a half-mile before the Nason intersection. You will see a sign pointing left on Nason to the dam. Follow Nason a half-mile to the dam parking lot.

From the parking lot, walk a half-mile to the dam. Follow a path that heads toward the right side of the dam. Safe drinking water is available from a spring about halfway to the dam. After reaching the dam, follow the dirt road around the right side of the lake. Several roads and paths branch off to the right and left. To avoid making a wrong turn, remember always to bear right. Eventually the road turns into a trail. Shortly down the trail is a sign that indicates directions and distances to various Ventana Wilderness Area destinations. You are now patched into the Forest Service trail system.

*- RW*

# Columbia

## Columbia Airport

| | |
|---|---|
| **Town** | Columbia **ID** O22 (oh-22) |
| **Coord** | N-38-01.83, W-120-24.87 |
| **Elev** | 2118 feet, N end high |
| **Runway** | 17rt - 35, 4060 x 75' asphalt |
| | 11 - 29, 2600 x 100 turf |
| **Freq** | CTAF-123.05, AWOS-124.65 |
| | Lights-123.05-3x-5x-7x |
| **Charts** | San Francisco sectional, L2, Lo3 |

*CAUTION:* Airport information not for navigational use. Wind variable. Ultralights. Tanker activity in summer. Deer. No line of sight between 17-35 ends.

*Columbia is an "operating" historical mining town — nearly the whole town is a state-run museum-park with a variety of activities. Fun for kids from 2 to 80. $25 - $175. Chamber: 209-536-1672, Park: 532-0150.*

## Airport Description

Columbia airport is a well-maintained airport with GPS IFR approach (which replaces the original NDB approach). UNICOM is active and helpful. Pay attention to surrounding hills when operating in the area. Watch for ultralights and deer on the runway. Utilize noise abatement procedures.

Tiedown fees are $3.00 for singles and $6.00 for twins. Tiedown space is nearly unlimited, due to Columbia's turf overflow area on Runway 11-29.

## Services and Lodging

Airport office phone: 209-533-5685. Bald Eagle Aviation, 533-4616; Courtney Aviation, 532-2345. Fuel: 80, 100, and JetA. Powerplant and avionics repairs can be performed on site. Ten aviation-related businesses are located at the field.

Camping facilities and nearby tiedown are available to pilots for a fee of $6.00. The camping area is pleasantly shaded and comes complete with toilet and shower facilities. Turf tiedown is available adjacent to the camping area.

Fallon House, 209-532-1470, includes breakfast in their fee of $64-114. The City Hotel, 532-1479, also serves breakfast for

$92-114. The latter two are period-decorated, historical buildings. Both require 72 hours cancellation notice. Reservations two months in advance are recommended for weekend visits.

The following inns pickup from the airport. Columbia Inn Motel, 209-533-0446, charges $39-82; Blue Nile Inn B&B, 532-8041, charges $98-130; and the Harlan House B&B, 533-4862, charges $92-145. None of the above allow pets.

## Transportation

Transportation is not required if you travel light and spend all your time in Columbia State Park. For a taxi, call Vintage Cab at 209-532-5466 or Courtesy Cabs at 536-6222. Enterprise delivers rental cars to the airport, 533-0500. Beware that they provide no service between Saturday afternoons and Monday.

## Overview

Now an official state park, Columbia is interesting, alive, and tastefully done. During the summer season, unusual special events occur almost every day. Columbia can provide the basis for an enjoyable family outing. Although the town can be fully enjoyed in one day without staying overnight, consider staying over for a pleasant meal and evening at the theater. For general information, including coming events, call the Chamber of Commerce at 209-536-1672, or the park at 532-0150.

The trail to Columbia holds the record for the shortest and easiest backpacking experience reported in this book. The trail is a one-half mile "nature trail" that leads from the airport to the restored gold mining town of Columbia. With a rental car, you can extend your range to the back roads of gold country, or drive to the Melones Reservoir for a refreshing dip.

## Town of Columbia

Columbia sprang to existence in 1850 soon after a party of transient prospectors discovered gold. Within weeks, Columbia was a bustling tent city; within two years the population peaked at 5000. By 1860, the gold was gone and the town lost the vitality for which it was known.

The walk to Columbia begins at the nature trail behind the terminal buildings. Follow the trail northeast toward town. You meander past specimens of local vegetation and curious rock piles from gold mining days, emerging in ten short minutes at the elementary school parking lot. Walk through the parking lot and turn left onto the main road. Even though the park boundary is still ahead, building architecture is noticeably pre-twentieth century. You walk past the Columbia Inn Motel on the left-hand side of the road. After about seven minutes from the parking lot, turn right before the red brick building labeled "Masonic Hall." You are entering the park proper.

You can visit an operating **old-time newspaper** and a **theater** at the Fallon House. The Columbia Actors Repertory presents nine different plays per year, call 209-532-4644. The Fallon House and City Hotels offer a number of package deals including theater, meals, and lodging. Prices range from $12 for a ticket to $150 for an overnight package for two. Both hotels are fully restored and decorated with period antiques.

Further into town are a number of shops, some of which are operating, and some of which are **still-life museums**. I found the two fire houses with their beautiful antique pumpers particularly interesting. All shop operators are dressed in authentic period garb. They seem to enjoy their roles and are effective at helping to transport you 100 years into the past.

One fellow played the part of a still-life. He looked exactly like a mannequin, except that his eyes followed me as I walked past. A crowd started to form. Someone dropped a quarter in his tin cup, and the fun began – some of the best mime I have seen. This remarkable man entertained us in style with appropriate period comedy.

Adults will enjoy the **old-time saloons**. There are homemade soft drinks for the pilot and plenty of cold beer for the lucky passengers. When I visited, entertainment was provided by musicians who looked like prospectors of gold-rush days. The songs they sang and stories they told were filled with amusing local lore. Food is available in a wide range of sophistication, from pushcarts to a white tablecloth meal at the hotel.

Family entertainment is available for a fee. Kids can enjoy riding the **stage coach** or a **pony ride**. Or, try your luck at

**Try your hand at panning for gold, or visit a mine**

**panning for gold** at The Columbia Supply Store. The store also offers a one-hour tour of a local working **gold mine**. Children, students, and seniors receive discounts on this one. Everything mentioned thus far is within easy walking distance.

Ahwahnee Adventures, 800-359-9790, is a **whitewater rafting** outfit whose main office is located in Columbia. They offer one, two, or three-day rafting trips on the Tuolumne River. The Ahwahnee guys will probably suggest that you fly 20 miles southeast for pickup at Pine Mountain Lake Airport.

## Melones Reservoir

On a hot day, the nearby Melones Reservoir can offer refreshing relief. To reach the reservoir from Columbia central, follow Highway E18 north. I was able to hitch a ride to the reservoir for a cooling swim. On foot, the walk requires about an hour and ten minutes to get to the road that branches off to the right toward the water's edge.

In late spring, the water was surprisingly warm and clear. Conditions may vary with the seasons and water level. Due to the lake's young age, trees still exist below the water line. Camping is not allowed at this site.

Do not expect to find the wilderness experience on this lake. It is clearly artificial, and you will be in the company of speedboats filled with people enjoying their kind of fun. But, when the mercury peaks at 100F, who cares!

*- RW*

# Georgetown

## Georgetown Airport

| | |
|---|---|
| **Town** | Georgetown **ID** Q61 |
| **Coord** | N-38-55.27, W-120-51.89 |
| **Elev** | 2623 feet, ends high |
| **Runway** | 16 - 34, 2920 x 50' asphalt |
| **Freq** | CTAF-123.05, Lights-123.05-5x |
| **Charts** | San Francisco sectional, L2, Lo3 |

*CAUTION:* Airport information not for navigational use. Occasional parachuting. Trees at each end.

Photo, courtesy of Friends of Georgetown Airport

> *Georgetown is located in Sierra gold country,*
> *a low-key stop for a meal, hike or overnight*
> *camping. Whitewater rafting in nearby*
> *Coloma. Home of jeepers' jamborees.*
> *$0 - $150. Skyways: 530-333-0810.*

## Airport Description

The airport is on a ridge, just south of the American River. The middle of the runway is ten feet lower than either end; keep this in mind if you want to make a smooth touchdown.

## Services, Lodging, and Transportation

Phone: county office, 530-622-0459. Skyways Flying Service, 333-0810; and Treiber Enterprises, 333-2607. Fuel: 100 octane. Skyways serves snacks and sells camping supplies. There are no rental car agencies in Georgetown, but Skyways provides courtesy rides to and from town, and has plans to provide rental cars in the future. Tiedown costs $3.

A pleasant, shaded camping area is available for airport visitors. It is located adjacent to and west of the runway. The camping area has toilet facilities, running water, fire pits, and picnic tables. Donations are appreciated.

The historic Georgetown Hotel, 530-333-2848, has a bar, Mexican restaurant, and rooms for $45-55. The American River Inn B&B, 333-4499, allows pets and provides breakfast, wine, and cheese. Rooms cost $90-110. The Pine View Motel, 333-4359, rents rooms for $44-61 and conditionally allows small pets. Hilltop Motel, 333-4141, charges $44-66 but does not pickup from the airport.

Town is located two miles to the southeast. If Skyways Flying Service is unable to provide a ride, hitchhiking sometimes works, and walking is a reasonable alternative if all else fails. Walk out the airport gate and turn left onto Spanish Dry Diggins. Follow the road less than two miles to Georgetown.

## Overview

Georgetown is located in the heart of **Sierra gold country**. Not high in elevation, this area should be clear of snow and pleasant to visit in spring and fall. The terrain is wooded, hilly, and endowed with a high density of creeks and rivers.

Nearby Georgetown is alive and well on weekends. At least one picturesque **old-time bar**, the Georgetown Hotel, is likely to have a lively band, suitable for dancing. Walls and ceiling are decorated with curious turn-of-the-century antiques. In particular, the ceiling is hung with conspicuous quantities of old boots. Figuring there must be a good story behind the boots, I asked the bartender for an explanation. "Nothin' special," he said. "Some places put customers' business cards on the wall. We put their boots on the ceiling.

Considering its rural location, Georgetown has a number of fine **restaurants**. Korner Kitchen serves breakfast and lunch. Buckeye Lodge is a good evening dining establishment. Try the Royal Dragon for Chinese, and Papa's for pizza.

Georgetown Airport has four major **events** during the year. In mid-June, they have their Moonlight Dance and Fly-in. On Labor day, tail-draggers amass for the Tail-draggers and Swine Tasting event. Cessna 120/140 owners have a fly-in in September. The Fly-in Chili Cook-off occurs in mid-October.

Georgetown is a center for 4x4 events, the largest of which is the Jeepers' Jamboree, 530-333-4771. On the last weekend of

July, the town of 1600 doubles in size as 450 four-wheel-drive vehicles prepare for a bumpy trek across back mountain trails to Lake Tahoe. The festivities last for three days. Other 4x4 events are coordinated by Mark Smith, 333-4777.

Just seven miles from Georgetown, Coloma is a popular gold-country town to visit. In addition to historic sites, Coloma hosts **whitewater rafting** on the American River and **ballooning**. Skyways can provide details and arrange transportation.

Camping permits are not required, but according to local lore, camping in many areas has been officially banned. Camping was outlawed as a deterrent to chronic wild and noisy parties thrown by bikers. However, sources claim that quiet campers are not harassed by locals or the authorities. You will be in harmony with Georgetown if you are discreet, stay clear of inhabited property, and don't build any fires.

## Local River Campsite

This **hike** takes you to a choice of isolated campsites within a one-hour walk of the airport.

Walk south on the runway for about ten minutes. Just outside the airport fence, turn right onto the small paved road. Follow it downhill for about 25 minutes until the first intersection. Turn right onto Starlight Drive. You will note a small pond on the right. Follow Starlight 500 feet to a horse trail on the left, located before a second, larger pond. Follow the horse trail northwest along a little creek.

After ten minutes, the trail crosses the creek. You may camp here, or bear right and continue toward a larger river site. As you continue for another fifteen minutes, the creek evolves into a roaring river. Eventually, the trail joins the river and provides easy access to river campsites.

*- RW*

# Harris Ranch

## Harris Ranch Airport

| | |
|---|---|
| **Town** | Coalinga   **ID** 3O8 (3-oh-8) |
| **Coord** | N-36-14.88, W-120-14.26 |
| **Elev** | 470 feet |
| **Runway** | 14rt - 32, 2820 x 30' asphalt |
| **Freq** | CTAF-122.9 |
| **Charts** | San Francisco sectional, Lo3 |

*CAUTION:* Airport information not for navigational use. Pole near Runway 14, powerline 32.

14rt

32

> *Harris Ranch, a travelers' oasis in the San Joaquin valley. Known as a stop-over for steak meals and quality overnight facilities. $100 - $200. Harris Ranch: 800-942-2333*

## Airport

The airport is easy to spot, parallel to Interstate 5. The owners request conventional landing patterns, with right traffic on 14, and no straight-in or base approaches.

Phone: 209-935-0717. Fuel: 100LL, days. Order fuel by direct phone near the tiedown. Pay at the Texaco station. Fuel is somewhat more costly than the norm. Restaurant and lodging are within short walking distance.

## Harris Ranch

Since 1937, Harris Ranch has been an oasis in central California's San Joaquin Valley, an agricultural area that travelers consider hot and boring. By car or plane, this is one of the best places for a meal stop between Sacramento and Bakersfield.

Its well-deserved claim to fame is steaks, **big juicy steaks**. After spending a night in the bush, I remember walking hot and dusty into the cool adobe complex – what a relief! Civilization has its merits.

I sat at the counter and ordered a massive steak and eggs breakfast. Arrival of the meal was slow, but the attentive wait-

ress kept me plied with a dozen bottomless Dr. Peppers. Although not a gourmet presentation, the meal was generous and satisfying. Expect to pay about $15 - $30 per person.

The various **dining areas** and **bars** are expertly decorated in Mexican/Western decor, quite pleasing to the eye. Lodging is upscale. The 123-room motel facility is built around an **Olympic-style pool**, which is surrounded by manicured landscaping. Prices for two range from $92 to $225. Remember to ask for a 10% AAA or AARP discount. Pets are allowed.

If you stay the night, plan on rolling your own entertainment. Live music is limited to Karaoke on weekends. However, you can eat, drink, soak in cool water, and explore the following: Fountain Court Dining Room, Ranch Kitchen, Jockey Club, Bar and Lounge, **spas**, **fitness facility**, and Country Store. Not surprisingly, the store sells big red steaks.

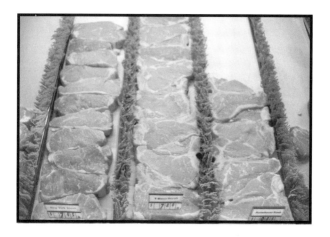

# Healdsburg

## Healdsburg Airport

| | |
|---|---|
| **Town** | Healdsburg  **ID** O31 (oh-31) |
| **Coord** | N-38-39.21,  W-122-53.97 |
| **Elev** | 278  feet |
| **Runway** | 13rt - 31,  2707 x 60' asphalt |
| **Freq** | CTAF-122.8 |
| **Charts** | San Francisco sectional,  L2, Lo3 |

*CAUTION:*  *Airport information not for navigational use. Ultralights and balloons. Down-drafts at both ends.*

> *Healdsburg, center of Sonoma Valley wine*
> *country, a pleasant small town with over 50*
> *wineries within easy striking distance.  Many*
> *good restaurants and antique shops to visit.*
> *$150-300.   Chamber: 800-648-9922.*

## Airport

Healdsburg Airport sits in rolling hills above Dry Creek Valley, three miles northwest of Healdsburg.  Vinyards surround in nearly all quadrants.  Due to land topography,  a bumpy final with downdrafts is possible, especially at the southeast end. Santa Rosa Airport, 10 miles southeast,  is the logical alternative for visitors who need IFR approach or more services.

## Services, Transportation, Lodging, Restaurants

Airport phones: 707-433-8540, 431-3306.  Fuel : 80, 100LL, automated and inexpensive.  Healdsburg is a sleepy airport with seemingly part-time aviation businesses and an aircraft upholster who has been around for years.  Healdsburg Aviation has comprehensive maintenance and repair, 433-8540.

There are no rental cars at Healdsburg Airport;  make arrangements with your inn or land at Santa Rosa.  At Santa Rosa, Avis, 571-0465, and Hertz, 528-0834, are on the field; and Enterprise, 545-2888, will deliver to the airport on weekdays.

Healdsburg has a number of fine B&Bs within walking distance of the town square.  Madrona Manor, just west of town, has

the most elegant restaurant in town. The Grapeleaf Inn B&B
includes free tasting of seven to eight local wines every evening.

Two single units at River Rose on the Russian River offer swimming and canoeing. Up the Lazy River is associated with Camp Rose Theater. River Rose is a cabin for four, with canoe and kayak.

## Features

| | |
|---|---|
| **B** | Full breakfast |
| **C** | Continental |
| **H** | Historic |
| **P** | Pets OK |
| **R** | Restaurant |
| **T** | Transportation |

| | | | |
|---|---|---|---|
| Belle De Jour Inn | BT | $148-269 | 707-431-9777 |
| Calderwood B&B | BH | $135-202 | 707-431-1110 |
| Camellia Inn B&B | BHT | $82-170 | 800-727-8182 |
| Dry Creek Inn | CR | $100-150 | 707-433-0300 |
| Frampton House B&B | BH | $77-99 | 707-433-5084 |
| Geyserville Inn | | $50-90 | 707-857-4745 |
| Grape Leaf Inn | BH | $104-181 | 707-433-8140 |
| Haydon Street Inn | BH | $104-181 | 707-433-5228 |
| Healdsburg Inn on Plaza | BH | $93-269 | 800-431-8663 |
| Honor Mansion B&B | BHT | $131-240 | 800-554-4667 |
| Madrona Manor | CHPR | $169-278 | 800-258-4003 |
| River Rose | H | $90-110 | 707-433-4305 |
| Up the Lazy River | HT | $85 | 707-431-1325 |
| Vineyard Valley Motel | C | $50-98 | 800-499-0103 |

Healdsburg has nearly three dozen **restaurants**. Madrona Manor serves the best and most expensive dinners. The Chateau Soverain is at a winery, north near Geyserville off Highway 101. It serves lunch and dinners Friday and on weekends, and is the most picturesque. Near the Square, try: Healdsburg Restaurant Charcuterie, Mangia Bene (Italian), Ravenous Café, or CK House (Chinese). Whenever I visit Healdsburg, I enjoy breakfast at the Singletree Inn, and a traditional Italian meal at Giorgio's, southeast of town on Healdsburg Avenue.

## Healdsburg

Except during the Depression when many farmers resorted to growing prunes, Healdsburg has been a premier spot for vineyards for as long as anyone can remember. Today, Healdsburg is surrounded by over fifty wineries, and the industry is still expanding.

Most visitors come to visit the **wineries**. There are three regions within a ten-mile radius of Healdsburg: the Russian River Region, Dry Creek Valley, and Alexander Valley. These three valleys produce internationally renowned wines that, in my opinion, are the best in California.

Nearly all the wineries have tasting rooms. Though wines are less expensive at the Healdsburg Safeway, you can taste before you buy at the wineries. Visiting the tasting rooms is a great tradition. You learn wine trivia, enjoy a wide selection of wines, and meet interesting people along the way.

**Hop Kiln Winery on Westside Road, a popular stop for photographers**

With fifty wineries in the area, it is hard to know where to start. Frankly, you can't go wrong with a random selection. At the risk of biasing your decision, I will share some of my favorites: Clos Du Bois, Dry Creek Vineyard, Hop Kiln Winery, Foppiano Winery, Mill Creek Vineyards, J. Pedroncelli Winery, Trentadue Winery, and Jordan by appointment. **Wine country tours** are offered by J. Shaw & Co., 707-433-1145, and Tour de Wine, 431-1388. Expect to pay $50-175 per person.

For historical information about winemaking in the valley, visit the **Healdsburg Museum**, 707-431-3325, or the **Sonoma Country Wine Library**, 433-3772. The Chamber of Commerce at 217 Healdsburg Avenue has excellent maps for visiting the wineries. Ask for their Russian River Wine Road brochure.

In summer, Healdsburg can get hot. For a quick fix, visit the **Bear Republic Brewing Company** on Healdsburg Avenue,

**Tasters sample Hop Kiln wines before a backdrop of ribbons**

707-433-2337.  You can **swim** at various points in the Russian River at access points off Fitch Mountain Road, Healdsburg Avenue, and at a number of unmarked spots downstream.  Ask the locals how to find a river access that meets your needs.  W.C. Trowbridge provides canoes and shuttle service for **canoe trips** down the Russian River, 800-640-1386.  They arrange **bike trips**, as well.

Lake Sonoma, 15 minutes northwest, is a 2,700-acre reservoir that is used for **fishing**, **skiing**, and other water sports.  A Visitor's Center and **fish hatchery** are open to the public, 707-433-1625.  Back on the east side of town, you can play a 9-hole game of golf at the municipal **golf course**, 707-433-4275.  For around $175 per person, you can enjoy a morning **balloon ride** from Aerostat, 800-579-0183, or from Air Flamboyant Hot Air Balloon Excursions, 800-456-4711.

**Antiques range from the beautiful . . .**

Backroads Tours, 800-GO-ACTIVE, is a nationwide **bicycle tour** organizer that offers a bicycle tour of the area. The tour departs Healdsburg, heads toward the coast, and follows the Russian River back to Healdsburg. Yes, it stops at wineries.

Healdsburg is an attractive town with over a dozen **galleries** and **antique shops** to visit. You can start north of the square and work your way south to the antique shops. Most are located on Healdsburg Avenue and at the Main Street Antique Mall.

At night, **music** is a likely happening at one of the restaurants or bars. Molly Malone's is a likely spot. On summer weekends, the town often has **free concerts** in the square. The Raven **movie theater** has expanded to five screens, and they have maintained their tradition of showing unusual films, now and again. **Camp Rose Theater** on Fitch Mountain Road by the

. . . to the unique

Russian River occasionally provides small theatrical productions, 707-431-8942. A list of weekend festivals follows:

| | | |
|---|---|---|
| Jan, mid | Winter Wineland, *wine tasting* | 800-723-6336 |
| Mar, early | Barrel Tasting, *wine tasting* | 800-723-6336 |
| Apr, end | Passport to Dry Cr., *wine tasting* | 707-433-1944 |
| May, begin | Round Robin Tasting, *wine tasting* | 433-1944 |
| May, mid | Healdsburg County Fair, *fair, parade* | 431-7644 |
| May, end | Memorial Day Weekend Antique Fair | 433-4315 |
| June, mid | Chili in the Plaza, *cook-off, music* | 431-PARK |
| July, begin | Fourth of July Weekend Antique Fair | 433-4315 |
| Aug, begin | Jazz Festival at Geyser Peak | 525-5993 |
| Aug, end | Healdsburg Guitar Festival | 433-1823 |
| Aug, mid | Harvest Time in Alexander Valley | 431-2894 |

*-RW*

**Healdsburg town square, the place for concerts on weekends**

# Mammoth

## Mammoth-June Lakes Airport

| | |
|---|---|
| **Town** | Mammoth Lakes  **ID** MMH |
| **Coord** | N-37-37.44,  W-118-50.32 |
| **Elev** | 7128  feet,  W end high |
| **Runway** | 9 - 27rt, 7000 x 100' asphalt |
| **Freq** | CTAF-122.8, AWOS-118.05 |
| | Lights-122.8-3x5x7x |
| **Charts** | San Francisco sectional, L5, Lo3 |

> **CAUTION:**   Airport information not for navigational use. Due to high terrain, avoid night operations unless familiar with the area. Watch density altitude. Turbulence and shear when wind above 10 knots.

27rt

9

> *Mammoth offers scenic alpine hiking in sum-
> mer, and all modes of snow sports in winter.
> Hot springs, just north of the airport.
> $20 - $350.   Visitor Info: 800-367-6572.
> Chamber:  760-934-3068.*

## Airport Description

Landing at Mammoth is straightforward during daytime in good weather.   Sometimes, however, Mammoth experiences hazardous crosswinds in excess of 20 knots.  UNICOM is active, and the FBO provides useful landing advisories.   Since the airport serves two small airlines, the runway is kept clear of snow year round.

Mammoth is one of the highest airports reported in this book. Carefully check density altitude before departing.  Prior to departing across the Sierras under questionable weather conditions, you may be able to arrange for a radio weather update from one of the commercial carriers that routinely cross the mountains.

## Services and Lodging

Airport office phones:  760-934-3813.  Sky Trek Aviation: 924-2221.  Fuel:  100 and JetA.  Tiedown is ample, but expensive – $10 for a single.  No restaurants are located at the airport. No car rental agencies are represented full time at the airport.

Lodging is not available close to the field, but numerous motels and condos populate the Mammoth Lakes area.  Winter rates are higher than summer rates.  A sampling of the 80 local

### Features

**B** Full breakfast
**C** Continental
**H** Historic
**P** Pets OK
**R** Restaurant
**T** Transportation

inns follows. Hot Creek Ranch is for serious fly fishermen who are willing to book far in advance. For further information and reservations, call the Mammoth Visitor's Center, 800-367-6572.

| | | | |
|---|---|---|---|
| Hot Creek Ranch , *fly fishing* | | $137-146 | 800-924-5637 |
| Mammoth Mountain Inn | RT | $110-300 | 800-228-4947 |
| Royal Pines | PT | $65-105 | 760-934-2306 |
| Shilo Inn | CPT | $109-150 | 800-222-2244 |
| Swiss Chalet | T | $54-94 | 760-934-2403 |
| Travel Lodge, Thrift Lodge | T | $60-150 | 800-255-3050 |
| | | | 760-934-8576 |

## Transportation

Town is 7 miles west. Mammoth Shuttle, 760-934-3030, charges $21 to drive two people to town; Sierra Express, 924-8294, asks $18. Sierra Rent-A-Car, 760-935-4471, charges $50-75 per day. Watch for hidden add-ons from Sierra. Mammoth Rental, 934-8111, charges $33-60. Both deliver to the airport.

Convict Lake and its campsites are located two miles south of the airport, a feasible walk. The Laurel Lake / Convict Lake loop described below is close enough to reach by foot, but the several-mile walk is unshaded and boring.

## Overview

Numerous scenic points of interest are located within twenty-five miles of the airport: Devil's Postpile, Hot Creek hot springs, Crystal Crag, and eight major lakes. **Hiking** and **mountain biking** opportunities are nearly limitless; several options are listed below. For further information, try the Forest Service Visitors Center at 760-934-2505.

A permit is required for entering Mammoth wilderness areas. Due to population pressure, overnight access of numerous trails is regulated by a strict quota system. Reservations <u>must</u> be made in advance through Wilderness Reservation Service, 888-374-3773. For $3, they efficiently mail you a permit. Sadly, this reasonable fee sets the precedent for further charges to Americans for access to our public lands. The local Forest Service can be reached at 760-934-2505. Once you manage to get connected to a real person, they will answer questions about their area.

The Mammoth area is well known for winter recreation. Mammoth Mountain offers some of the best **downhill** and **cross country skiing** in the state, 760-934-2571. It has 23 lifts and 3100 vertical feet of skiing. One of Mammoth's more unusual winter offerings is **dog sledding**. Call Dog Sled Adventures at 934-6270 to arrange a ride, $85 per person per hour. Or, try your hand at **bobsledding**, Bob Sledz International, 934-7533.

Not surprisingly, **snowmobiling** is popular in the area. Rent from or ride with one of the following: DJ's Snowmobile Adventures, 935-4480; Mammoth Snowmobiles, 934-9645; or, Senterfeet Snowmobiles, 934-6888.

In summer, the mountain country near Mammoth is an alpine **hikers paradise**. Mountain trails in the area are all at high elevation, generally 7500 to 12,000 feet. The trails are usually well maintained and adequately marked. Be forewarned that some trails are not represented accurately on the topo maps. You will occasionally need to practice orientiering skills.

Water in the area requires purification. Trees are sometimes sparse, so come prepared to protect yourself from excessive sun. Mosquitoes can be a serious problem, so don't forget the repellent. I found jogging shoes to be adequate footwear, but most Mammoth hikers wear hiking boots. Of course, carry whatever you need for a safe, high-country backpacking trip.

## Sherwin and Valentine Lakes Hike

This day-hike is a top choice for early- and late-season hikers. Fall colors peak in October. The 820-foot climb to Sherwin Lakes is steep, but short enough to qualify as a medium-length hike. The **fishing** at Sherwin is said to be good. More energetic hikers may climb an additional thousand feet to Valentine Lake. A permit is required for Valentine, but not for Sherwin Lakes.

The trailhead begins just off the unpaved Sherwin Creek Road, 2.5 miles south of Mammoth. It begins in forest and climbs to open slopes with exquisite views to the north and east. The distance to Sherwin Lakes is only two miles, and an additional three to Valentine Lakes.

## Hot Springs Loop Hike

This flat-lands loop takes you by Hot Creek, **fumaroles**, **geysers**, and several **hot springs**. I have not yet taken this hike, but include the following for those who like to visit hot springs. The hike travels approximately ten miles over barren land.

The trail begins at the northwest end of the runway. Follow the road one mile north to Hot Creek Hatchery, California's first

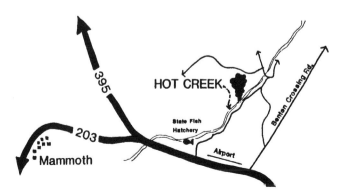

**warm water trout hatchery**, 760-934-2664.  **Hot springs** and other volcanic phenomena are located approximately one mile north of the hatchery on the other side of Hot Creek.  Prolonged immersion in the hot springs is not recommended due to arsenic and other chemicals.  Camping is not permitted at the springs.

The trail continues north-northwest, parallel to Hot Creek. Follow it several miles until it intersects a branch to the south. Continue south past Little Alkali Lake to the road at Whitmore Hot Springs,  several miles after Hot Creek.  Follow the road one mile southwest to Highway 395 and walk another 1.5 miles back to the airport.  (Verify details with local residents and Forest Service before taking this hike.)

## Laurel Lakes / Convict Lake Loop Hike

The loop begins at a jeep trail several miles southwest of the airport, follows a trail between Bloody and Laurel mountains, and emerges at Convict Lake, a couple miles south of the airport.  The trail passes by seven scenic lakes, most of which have campsites. Trail elevation ranges from 7500 to 11,000 feet.  Estimated length from taxi drop-off to pick-up is 15 miles.  The hike can be done with one overnight, but plan on two if you like extra time for leisure and local hikes.

A permit is required, but there is no quota.  If you take the hike in reverse, you may still be able to get a permit from the self-service station at Convict Lake.  You will need the *Mt. Morrison*  15-minute topo map and a compass.

At the airport, ask the taxi driver to take you to Laurel Road (on the north side of Laurel mountain).  Obtain a permit from the ranger station on the way.  The taxi will be able to take you one half mile up Laurel Road until it becomes a 4x4 trail.  You begin the climb at 7500 feet, walking south up the mountain.

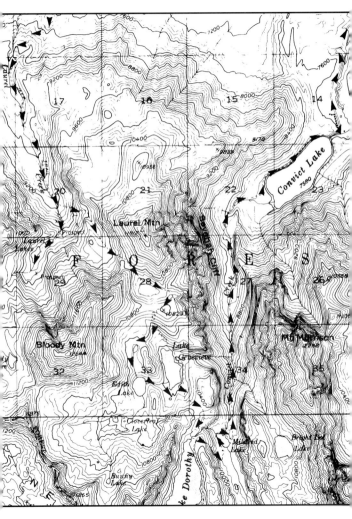

After a little over an hour, you pass a small meadow at 8400 feet on the right. If the sun is less than two hours from the horizon, this is a good place to camp.

Three hours from the taxi-drop, you encounter a split in the trail. My altimeter indicated 9700 feet. A sign saying *Genevieve Trail and Edith Lake* marks the trail that branches off to the left. If you have sufficient energy and daylight to continue for another three hours, follow this trail. Otherwise, bear right and follow the 4x4 trail 20 minutes up the hill and down to a campsite at the edge of Laurel Lakes. Note that actual trails do not match trail positions marked on the topo map in this area.

The south end of the lakes has several good campsites. Check out the stream and small waterfall at the southern tip. When I visited, I saw small furry animals and an occasional fly, but no mosquitoes – savor this luxury while you can!

Back at the intersection, follow the trail toward Lake Genevieve. The trail is a footpath with numerous switchbacks. It is ordinarily easy to follow, but would be difficult to locate in snow. After an hour of hard labor, you reach the pass between Bloody and Laurel mountains at close to 11,000 feet. Forty minutes later, you cross a second ridge.

As the trail descends to Lake Genevieve, its direction occasionally becomes ambiguous. You can see the lake, so there is no danger of getting lost. I chose the scenic route, following the trace of a trail southwest by a small lake down to Edith Lake. I noted several pleasant campsites on the way.

Cross the creek that exits the east side of Edith Lake and join the trail that follows the creek down to Lake Genevieve. This trail is pleasing to the eye and easy to follow, but is not marked on the topo map. Soon, you arrive at the south end of Lake Genevieve, altitude 10,000 feet. Hiking time from the intersection near Laurel Lakes is about three hours.

You can find attractive campsites where the creek enters Lake Genevieve. The only major flaw is vicious mosquitoes that work the area.

Locate the trail that heads south at the south end of the lake. Follow it up over a 10,400 foot ridge to Lake Dorothy. Time from lake to lake is less than one hour. Lake Dorothy also has attractive campsites, but the basin can get windy.

From Lake Dorothy, the return leg is practically all down hill. Follow the trail north down to Convict Lake. Time from Lake Dorothy to the store at the northeast end of Convict Lake is a little over three hours. You can return to the airport by walking the roads north for one hour, or by calling a taxi.

*- RW*

Photo: Mammoth Chamber

# Markleeville

## Alpine County Airport

**Town**    Markleeville  **ID**   Q82
**Coord**   N-38-44.16, W-119-45.98
**Elev**    5867  feet, 1%, N end high
**Runway**  17 - 35rt, 4440 x 50' asphalt
**Freq**    CTAF-122.9
**Charts**  San Francisco sect., L5, Lo3

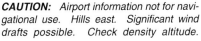

> *CAUTION:* Airport information not for navigational use. Hills east. Significant wind drafts possible. Check density altitude.

> *Markleeville, an isolated burg on the eastern*
> *edge of the Sierras. Resorts, hot springs, and*
> *whitewater rafting. Hike from the airstrip to a*
> *placid campsite on the East Carson River.*
> *$0 - 250. Chamber: 530-694-2475*

## Airport, Services, Lodging, and Transportation

Markleeville Alpine County Airport is located in the eastern hills of the Sierra Nevada Mountains, away from all but remnants of civilization. It is closed in winter due to snow. The runway was repaved in 1992.

Airport phone (not at airport): 530-694-2140. The airport has no services, no phone, and is unattended. The tiedown area is paved and equipped with sturdy tiedown chains. A camping area, located just south of the tiedown apron, is partially shaded, but has no water or toilet facilities.

Family Mountain Shuttle, 530-694-2966, charges $15 per party for rides into town, or $20 round trip. The owner drives hikers to trailheads and can tell you about local land and lore. The inns and rafting companies are pilot-friendly and will generally pickup by prior arrangement. Because there is <u>no phone</u> at the airport, advance planning is a must.

The following lodging is located in Markleeville (*M*) or Woodfords (*W*). Most of the inns are on the river with fishing less than 100 yards away. The Bed, Bike, & Bagel has four mountain bikes available to guests at no extra charge. Grandma's Home is a complete house. East Fork Resort is a focal point for rafting trips.

### Features

**B** Full breakfast
**C** Continental
**H** Historic
**P** Pets OK
**R** Restaurant
**T** Transportation

Curiously, whenever I called East Fork Resort, I was only able to talk to an answering machine, and no one returned my calls.

| Bed, Bike, & Bagel, *M* | **CHPT** | $125 | 530-694-9337 |
|---|---|---|---|
| Grandma's House, *M* | **HT** | $220 | 530-694-2253 |
| J. Marklee Toll Station, *M* | **CPRT** | $50 | 530-694-2507 |
| Mountain & Garden, *W* | **BPT** | $71-121 | 530-694-0012 |
| Sorenson's Resort, *W* | **R** | $77-440 | 800-423-9949 |
| Woodford's Inn, *W* | **T** | $49-65 | 530-694-2410 |

## Markleeville Area

Alpine County has less than 1500 year-round residents. Markleeville is a vortex in Alpine's isolation, at risk for becoming a fashionable getaway. Its lodging is diverse, and some units are still attractively priced. Even though ground transportation is less than convenient, pilots have already discovered the authentic **Zillagili Italian Restaurant**.

As witnessed by the **Alpine County Museum**, the county is not short on a colorful past. Many of the town's structures ooze of history; they all have their story. The **Alpine Hotel** (no longer a hotel) was once a serious biker's saloon. Today, the bar is festooned with bras that hang from the ceiling. The Alpine is a good place for a drink or a meal.

**Grover Hot Springs**, 530-694-2248, is a state-owned facility 4.5 miles south of town in a wooded mountain valley. Water flows from several sources at 147F. The soaking pool is 102-105F and the swimming pool is 70-80F. Clothing is required at the springs. You can pitch a tent at the campground for $16 and enjoy day-hikes in the mountains. Bring your own food.

**Whitewater raft trips** begin and end at Hangman's Bridge, two miles east of Markleeville. The upper section (south) fea-

tures 7.3 miles of Class III rapids.  The lower stretch (north) has
20 miles of fast Class II river with gentle rapids and a 104F hot
spring along the way.  On the longer trips, there's a good chance
you will see mule deer, Canada geese, and traces of beaver,
which are plentiful on the East Fork of the Carson.

Of the four rafting companies that work the river; the following two pickup from the airport.  Sunshine River Adventures,
800-359-9790, charges $69/half-day, $98/day, and $249/two-
days.  Ahwahnee Adventures, 800-359-9790, charges $75/half-
day, $120/day, and $245/two-days.

## Carson River Hike and Campsite

Note the position of the lake, river, and trails while in the
landing pattern.  The lake is located just west of the airport, and
the East Fork of the Carson River runs parallel to, and a half-mile
east of the runway.  Aside from the runway and a road, there are
no man-made structures for miles around.

The land surrounding the airstrip is suitable for cross-country
**hiking**.  Tree population is just dense enough to be interesting,
yet sparse enough for good hiking visibility.  Topo maps are
unnecessary for the hike below.  For more ambitious ventures,
consider purchasing the *Freel Peak* and *Mt. Siegel* quadrangles.
For additional coverage to the south, add the *Markleeville* and
*Topaz Lake* quadrangles.

The East Fork of the Carson River is only a thirty-minute hike
from the airport.  The trails are easy to follow; here's how:

Walk 500 feet southwest of the tiedown apron.  Follow the
dirt 4x4 road that heads south-southwest down toward a ravine.
After about fifteen minutes, you intersect the ravine.  Follow the
trail down the ravine to the east. Fifteen minutes after joining the

# MARKLEEVILLE QUADRANGLE
## CALIFORNIA – ALPINE CO.
### 15 MINUTE SERIES (TOPOGRAPHIC)

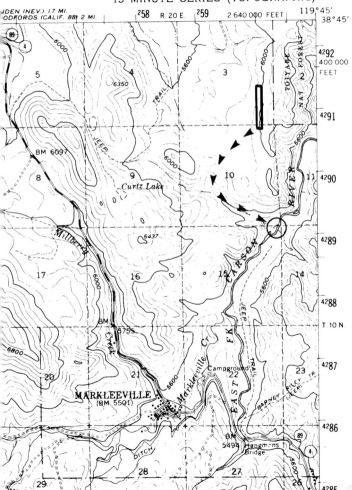

ravine, you should reach the river, the route that J. C. Fremont and Kit Carson followed in their 1843-44 exploration.

When I visited in late June, there was a gentle wind and the air temperature  was pleasant.  The river was 30 to 40 feet wide with a water temperature that was about right for a quick, refreshing dip.  Pick from a variety of campsites by the river.

Given sufficient time, you can try returning to the airport by following the river north and looping back to the airport north of the bluffs.  (I went back the easy way.)

*- RW*

# Mono Lake

## Lee Vining Airport

| | |
|---|---|
| **Town** | Lee Vining **ID** O24 (oh-24) |
| **Coord** | N-37-57.50, W-119-06.39 |
| **Elev** | 6802 feet |
| **Runway** | 14 - 32rt, 4090 x 50' asphalt |
| **Freq** | CTAF-122.9, Lights-122.9 |
| **Charts** | San Francisco sectional, L5, Lo3 |

*CAUTION: Airport information not for navigational use. Serious crosswinds in afternoon. Check density altitude.*

> *Mono Lake, a desert lake with ghostly tufa*
> *formations; walking distance from airstrip.*
> *A three-hour sight-seeing hike or overnight.*
> *$0 - $100.  Forest Service: 760-647-3044,*
> *Mono Lake Committee: 760-647-6386.*

## Airport Description

The airport is located just east of Lee Vining and east of the prominent Sierra mountains.  Though the mountains are safely clear of the landing pattern, note their close proximity when landing in marginal weather.  The nearby mountain peaks can stir up surprisingly hazardous winds, most probable from mid-morning to early evening.  Since the windsock has faded to match the color of the land, it is difficult to spot.

If density altitude is a problem, consider departing on Runway 32 toward Mono Lake.  The land drops off a couple hundred feet between the north end of the runway and the lake.  This provides an extra margin of safety, should you have difficulty gaining altitude.

## Service, Lodging, and Transportation

Phone (not at airport):  760-932-5252, 932-7549.  The airport is unattended, without food, fuel, or telephone.  Six tiedowns are located at the south end – an adequate supply for this location.  You can camp at the airport or stay at a motel.  Nearby Lee Vining has food, lodging, several gas stations, and limited supplies.  The best restaurant in town is Yosemite's Trail Inn.

The motels are located close together in the small town of Lee Vining – a 25-minute walk from the airport. Follow the airport access road toward the mountains. Turn right at the main highway and walk into town. A small Visitor's Center is located in town, next to Nicelys restaurant.

**Features**

B Full breakfast
C Continental
H Historic
P Pets OK
R Restaurant
T Transportation

| | | | |
|---|---|---|---|
| Blue Sky Motel | **PR** | $60 | 760-647-6440 |
| Best Western Lakeview Lodge | | $53-114 | 760-647-6543 |
| Gateway Motel | **T** | $50-91 | 760-647-6467 |
| Murphy's Motel | **P** | $42-96 | 760-647-6316 |

The hike to Mono Lake does not require transportation. The "trail" begins at the airport, as described later in this chapter. However, if you plan to take a Forest Service or Mono Lake Committee tour, you will need to solicit a ride from a tour guide or visitor.

At this airport, I received an involuntary lesson in high-altitude airplane maintenance. The morning of my departure, I was unable to start my engine. I deduced correctly that the combination of fouled plugs and thin air were preventing ignition.

At a gas station in town, I explained my dilemma: "In order to minimize load for mountain flying, I left my tools at home." The owner retorted, "Well, SHAME ON YOU . . . I never loan my tools." A local resident overhearing the conversation took pity. He graciously rounded up some tools and provided transportation to and from the airport. The gas station owner regained favor by sandblasting the plugs without charge. I now carry a plug wrench with me at all times.

## Overview

The town is named after a prospector named Leroy Vining. He came to the area in 1853, made his fortune by mining and operating a saw mill, and then accidentally shot himself dead in a saloon in nearby Aurora, Nevada. The main attractions here are: Mono Lake, the dove-colored Mono Craters, the sinister glass structures of Obsidian Dome, and the ghost town of Bodie. Mono Lake is the easiest of the four to visit without land transportation.

The color of Lake Mono is a striking sapphire blue. But its beauty is slowly dying as its waters are diverted to quench the thirsts of Los Angeles. As evidenced by concentric white rings around the lake, its level is dropping at the average rate of 18 inches per year. This has exposed the interesting white tufa

**Hiking path from landing strip to Mono Lake tufa formations**

formations that were created by the flow of mineral-rich springs. Most of the formations now stand on dry land, and the area has been reclaimed by vegetation and wildlife.

**Bird watchers** will want to visit during the months of April through October. Avocets, gulls, plovers, sandpipers, and snipe nest here; phalaropes and grebes migrate through by the thousands. The volcano vents in the middle of Mono were once major breeding grounds of California gulls. The dropping water level allowed the coyotes to gain access to the breeding grounds and feed on the eggs and chicks. The gulls have moved to smaller islands to nest.

Permits are not required. **Camping** is legal in the Mono Lake area, but is not actively encouraged by the Forest Service. Fires are not permitted. Tours are conducted daily by personnel from

**Tufa formations at the edge of Mono Lake**

the Forest Service Visitor's Center, 760-647-3044.  By calling
them in advance and exercising some diplomacy, you may be
able to hitch a ride from the center to the starting point of the
tour.  In summer, the Mono Lake Committee offers **hiking and
canoe tours**, 647-6386.  Tours leave from the South Tufa parking lot at the south shore several times per day.

## Mono Lake South Shore Hike

From the tiedown area, walk ten minutes northwest on the
runway.  Not far after passing the runway's midpoint, leave the
runway and walk north toward the volcano cones in the middle
of Mono Lake.  At the runway's edge you encounter the hike's
most difficult obstacle, a barbed wire fence.  Carefully climb
over it and continue toward the lake.

The terrain allows easy cross-country travel, and gradually
slopes down toward the lake.  When I visited in May, the desert
flowers were just beginning to bloom.  Many of the shrubs were
producing pink and yellow flowers. Soon you will see the white
tufa formations at the lake's edge, roughly in line with the
volcano cones in the middle of the lake.  Keep walking toward
the formations.  Cross the first dirt road, but use the second dirt
road you encounter to take you closer to the tufa formations.
Elapsed time from runway to destination should be less than 40
minutes.

After you have explored the area, you can return to the airport
by the same route.

*- RW*

# Saline Valley

## Saline Valley Airstrips

| | |
|---|---|
| **Town** | Saline Valley Hot Springs |
| **Coord** | N-36-48.45, W-117-46.92 |
| **Elev** | 1250' approx, N ends high |
| **Runway** | W: 16 - 34, 1400' dark gravel |
| | E: 3x - 21x, 1100' CLOSED |
| **Freq** | CTAF-122.9 announce intentions |
| **Charts** | Las Vegas sectional (not shown) |

*CAUTION:* Airport information not for navigational use. The E strip is closed. The W strip ends in a hill, making last-minute go-arounds dangerous. Low-flying military jets. Watch density altitude.

*Saline Valley is a primitive, desert hot spring paradise, with daily military low-altitude air shows. Camping only. Cost per day is the cost of food you fly in. Comfortable in spring and fall.*

## Airport Description

Saline Valley Hot Springs has two landing strips within 0.7 miles of each other, east and west. The east strip has been closed by the U.S. Forest Service, but may not be properly marked as closed. Neither runway is marked on the sectional. "Saline Valley" is labeled on the sectional, 15 miles northeast of Lone Pine.

The east runway, known as the "Hero Strip," is the original of the two. Located just east of the lower hot springs, it is the easiest to spot from the air. The runway surface is bumpy and uneven, but contains no potholes. Before closure by the USFS, it was used by STOL and semi-STOL aircraft.

The west strip (sometimes called "Chicken Strip") is difficult to spot because its dark surface blends with surrounding terrain. Its perimeter is marked with white rocks that are difficult to see from a distance. Look for a white circle around a windsock at the edge of the field. Note the hill to the north. The fine gravel surface is smoother than the east strip, but loose particles will take a minor toll from your prop. Land on Runway 34 and depart from 16. Several tiedowns are located at the north end. They provide essential protection from surprise desert winds.

A sign at the west strip says "Chicken Strip, 1360." My altimeter indicated the elevation to be closer to 1250 feet.

## Airport Services, Transportation, and Camping

Neither airport services nor supplies of any kind are available in the valley. Telephone service is likewise unavailable. The manager at Saline Valley has emergency radio communication capability on a government frequency.

With luck, someone from the hot springs area will drive to the tiedown area and offer you a ride. Otherwise, walk 15 minutes cross-country southeast to the lower springs. To get to the upper hot springs, follow the road north 15 minutes from lower springs. Visitors are very friendly and will help with transportation if you ask.

You may camp anywhere within reason. Camping is free, but everyone pitches in to keep the area clean and habitable.

**Upper Springs**

Photo: Skip Russie

## Hot Springs

The valley and its society of visitors are unique – a functional departure from worldwide trends of control and pressure. Where else can you live for free, savor the sensuous gifts of nature, and enjoy a daily air show from low-flying military jets? The springs are a melting pot where people from all walks of life can slip into soothing waters and safely share thoughts and humor. On my first visit to Saline Valley, I don't believe the smile ever left my face.

Although pleasant desert weather is the norm, I learned that nature can deal serious blows from her bag of tricks. Wind and sandstorms can be oppressive; and, they quickly lose their novelty. Be prepared with secure tiedown and a robust tent. Spring and fall are the most popular seasons to visit. Once on site, you need to decide where to pitch your tent, upper or lower springs. Coordinates of the hot spots follow:

| | |
|---|---|
| Chicken Strip, *west strip* | N-36-48.445, W-117-46.921 |
| Hero Strip, *east strip* | N-36-48.182, W-117-46.370 |
| Lower hot springs, *oasis* | N-36-48.345, W-117-46.396 |
| Upper hot springs | N-36-48.789, W-117-45.978 |

The lower spring is an oasis with grass, trees, picnic tables, open-air library, and soaking pool. This vortex is the social site, inhabited by soakers who swap yarns for hours. Musical instruments are a hit at either site. Clothing is the exception at both.

The upper spring is located about 0.7 miles north. It lies in open desert where shade is scarce. The upper facilities are more primitive and typically less crowded than at the lower spring. Campfires are allowed, but wood is not easy to find nearby. Although visitors tend to be less social and isolate in separated campsites, they freely commune in the pools. A central source

**Visitors need minimal skin protection at the lower springs oasis**

feeds two tubs. The east tub is the hottest. The west tub's temperature is perfect for multi-hour soaking.

Though officially now under the auspices of the National Park Service, the springs are casually managed by a non-uniformed, civilian volunteer. "There are really no rules," commented one manager, "except common courtesy." There are guidelines, however, such as: Do not walk in the hot springs source pool. Wash dishes in designated areas only. Clean the tubs daily, etc. Such information is available from other people at the springs and is passed from person to person like sacred rituals.

Visitors pay close attention to maintaining good hygiene. Daily rituals include emptying the tubs and scrubbing every square inch with bleach. Always wash your feet before entering a tub. Be sure to ask where to wash your dishes and where to bathe with soap.

As though freedom were forbidden fruit, the Park Service gradually increases control.

They have closed a runway, reduced the maximum days of stay, and have added signs and parking zones. Uniformed rangers visit more frequently. Though this trend is a concern for regular visitors, nature's pagentry helps us forget.

**Western "Barnacle Tub" at the Upper Springs**

## Greater Saline Valley

Saline Valley offers a number of activities, most of which require a 4x4 vehicle. Make friends with your neighbors. Perhaps you can exchange a plane ride for a land-based excursion. Mountain canyons offer shaded **hikes**, a welcome relief from desert sun. Some canyons have fern-lined water falls and ponds. The cool water offers stimulating contrast to the lazy hot springs.

Visit the salt flats, but do not drive a vehicle on the seemingly solid crusts of salt. We learned the hard way that even a 4x4 is not immune to a fate that awaits naive adventurers. Eight to fourteen inches below the salt lurks a sea of mud. Should your wheels break through, you find yourself in deep yogurt.

Near the salt flats, you will see remnants of an **old salt mining operation**. Early miners hatched a plan like the tree harvesting

**4x4 stuck in Saline Valley salt flat**

scheme of Zorba the Greek. Their plan was to haul chunks of salt over the mountains by aerial cable. Unfortunately, the completed engineering success proved to be a financial failure.

Many visitors are content to play within walking distance of the tubs. They soak several times per day. Time between soaks is leisurely filled by walks in the desert, cooking, eating, and making music. Airplane buffs thrill to the low-altitude maneuvers and dogfights performed by military jets. The young military pilots seem to delight at putting on a show for the tubbers. Imagine the thunder as a jet passes 200 feet over your tub, kicks in its after burner, and shoots almost straight up!

Saline Valley is a remarkable blending of natural serenity and military might, intellectuals and rednecks, beautiful sunsets and fierce sandstorms. Unlike the world we see on the Six O'clock News, dichotomies work at Saline Valley.

**Photo from the Desert Photography Workshop**

photographer wishes to remain anonymous

# South Lake Tahoe
## and Desolation Wilderness

## Lake Tahoe Airport

| | |
|---|---|
| **Town** | S. Lake Tahoe **ID** TVL |
| **Coord** | N-38-53.63, W-119-59.72 |
| **Elev** | 6264 feet, 1.5%, S end high |
| **Runway** | 18 - 36rt, 8544 x 150' asphalt |
| **Freq** | Twr-118.4, Lights-3x5x7x, APC-128.8E,127.95W, Gnd-121.9 |
| **Charts** | San Francisco sect, L2, L5, Lo3 |

*CAUTION: Airport information not for navigational use. Mountains all quadrants. Watch density altitude, turbulence, and cul de sac to the south. All southern terrain is higher than airport. Tower cannot see all of traffic pattern.*

36rt

18

*South Lake Tahoe, a bustling mountain enter-
tainment center with year round outdoor activities and frisky night life. Enjoy beautiful scenery
by day and good entertainment at night. Spectacular backpacking close to town. $50-300.
Chamber: 530-541-5255, www.tahoeinfo.com.*

## Airport Description

The runway is a high-altitude paved surface of adequate quality for commercial IFR traffic. Check noise abatement procedures. When arriving, if wind is greater than 25 knots from the
south, be cautious of down-drafts at either end of the runway.
When departing, check density altitude and loading. Gain adequate altitude before leaving the basin. When leaving to the
south under a low ceiling, you will find yourself in a cul de sac if
you miss Luther Pass (a.k.a. Johnson Pass or Echo Summit).

In winter, keep close tabs on current weather. Call 530-541-
3302 for current Tahoe basin weather during tower hours. Weather
in the basin can change dramatically in ten minutes. Beware of
icing conditions.

## Services, Lodging, and Transportation

Airport phone: 530-5541-2110. Fuel: 100LL and JetA. FBO
service is good, but the $10 tiedown fee and high fuel costs have
been known to offend. (At this elevation, it is prudent to consider departing with half-full tanks, anyway.)

South Lake Tahoe offers over one hundred options for lodging. Call the following reservation services for help finding lodging: Lake Tahoe Accommodations, 800-228-6921; Lake Tahoe Reservations, 800-288-2463; and Lake Tahoe Visitor Services, 888-544-7050.

**Features**

**B** Full breakfast
**C** Continental
**H** Historic
**P** Pets OK
**R** Restaurant
**T** Transportation

| | | | |
|---|---|---|---|
| 7 Seas Motel | | $38-100 | 800-800-7327 |
| Alpen Rose Inn | CP | $33-150 | 800-370-4049 |
| Harrah's Lake Tahoe | PR | $100-290 | 800-427-7247 |
| Horizon Casino Resort | R | $130-500 | 800-648-3322 |
| Inn at Heavenly B&B | CP | $83-150 | 800-692-2246 |
| Inn by the Lake | CR | $108-350 | 800-877-1466 |
| Motel 6 | P | $42-80 | 530-542-1400 |
| Station House Inn | BR | $98-160 | 800-822-5953 |

Call 530-542-6077 for "pool-van" taxi service , which charges $5 per person for a ride to the casino area. The Casino Express, 800-446-6128, charges $17 per person. Once at the casinos, casino courtesy vans will take you where you want to go. Call 530-542-6077 for municipal bus information.

Rental cars are available at the airport. On weekends, holidays, and in the summer, be sure to reserve the car in advance.

| | | |
|---|---|---|
| Avis, *State Line* | 800-331-1212 | 755-588-4450 |
| Hertz, *State Line* | 800-654-2200 | 775-586-0041 |
| National, *closest* | 800-CARRENT | 530-541-7994 |

You can rent bicycles from a number of shops:

| | |
|---|---|
| Anderson's | 530-541-0500 |
| Country Scooter | 530-544-9814 |
| Lakeview Sports | 530-544-0183 |
| Camp Richardson's Resort | 800-544-1801 |

## Overview

Lake Tahoe has a 72-mile shoreline with interesting stops and beautiful scenery every mile. Consider taking several hours to drive around the lake.

Lake Tahoe's marinas offer a wide selection of aquatic activities: **jet-ski rental**, **boat rental**, **fishing**, **water-skiing**, and **sailing**, plus a variety of **sight-seeing cruises**.

| | | |
|---|---|---|
| Anchorage Marina | *power, sail, jet...* | 530-541-1777 |
| H2O Sports | *jet-ski* | 775-588-3055 |
| Lakeview Sports | *jet-ski* | 530-544-0138 |
| Lakeside Marina | *power and other* | 530-541-6626 |
| Ski Run Boat Company | *jet-ski* | 530-544-0200 |
| Tahoe Keys Marina | *power, sail, other* | 530-541-2155 |
| Timber Cove Marina | *power, sail, other* | 530-544-2942 |
| Watersports | *parasail, jet-ski* | 530-544-JETS |
| Zephyr Cove Marina | *power and other* | 775-588-3833 |

Camp Richardson Resort, 800-544-1801, specializes in aquatics. They rent everything from kayaks to jet-skis. Their **water ski school** teaches people of all ages and abilities how to nearly walk on water. The following also provide water ski instruction: Lake Tahoe Water Ski School, 530-577-7928; and Werley's Water Ski School, 530-544-5099.

The following specialize in **sport fishing**: Dennis's Fishing Charters, 530-577-6834; Blue Ribbon Fishing Charters, 530-541-8801; Tahoe Fly Fishing Outfitters, 530-541-8202; and, Tahoe Sportsfishing, 800-696-7797.

M.S. Dixie, 775-588-3508, takes you on a 350-passenger **paddlewheeler** with music and dancing. Day-cruise prices start at $68. The Tahoe Queen is a second alternative, 530-541-3364. Woodwind, 888-867-6394, specializes in **sailing cruises**. Their

boat has a full bar and can carry 30 people. How about a quiet
**champagne cruise** in the evening?

You can rent a **4-wheel ATV** from Ride the Rubicon and ride
the Rubicon Trail. Prices begin at $69 for a half day and go up to
$495 for a three-day experience. Call 530-541-5875 for details.
Lake Tahoe Adventures is another alternative, 530-577-2940.
Tahoe has a number of **balloon ride** providers:

| | | |
|---|---|---|
| Aero Vision Balloons | 800-468-2476 | 775-265-5177 |
| Alpine Adventures Aloft | 800-332-9997 | 775-782-7239 |
| Balloons Over Lake Tahoe | | 530-544-7008 |
| Dream Weavers | 800FUNALOFT | 775-265-1271 |
| Lake Tahoe Balloons | 800-827-9294 | 530-544-1221 |
| Mountain High Balloons | 800-231-6922 | 530-587-6922 |

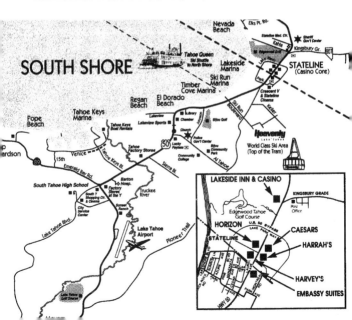

Scenic, wooded riding trails network the Tahoe area. The following stables offer **horse rental** by hour or day: Camp Richardson's Corral, 530-541-3113; Cascade Stables, 530-541-2055; Sunset Ranch, 530-541-9001; and, Zephyr Cove Stables, 775-588-5664.

Over a dozen **golf courses** are sprinkled around the lake. Four **golf courses** are near South Tahoe: Bijou Municipal, 530-542-6097; Edgewood Tahoe, 775-588-3566; Lake Tahoe Country Club, 530-577-0788; and, Tahoe Paradise, 530-577-2121.

An all-season **aerial tram** is located at Hidden Valley Ski Resort, two miles south of town via Ski Run Boulevard on Saddle Road. Dining is featured at the top. Call 775-586-7000 for information or 530-544-6263 for dinner reservations.

South Tahoe has the perfect remedy for foul weather. For $20 per hour, couples can rent luxury **hot tubs** at Nephele's Restaurant, 530-544-8130. Imagine, a restaurant and bar with hot tubs! Casinos on the Nevada side of town provide **gambling** and **nightclub entertainment**, another alternative for uncooperative weather.

The following outfitters specialize in **whitewater rafting**:

| | |
|---|---|
| Ahwahnee Whitewater | 800-359-9790 |
| Emerald Bay Rafting | 530-541-1801 |
| Rapid Descent Adventures | 530-642-2370 |
| Tributary Whitewater Tours | 800-672-3846 |
| Whitewater Connection | 800-336-7238 |

The Desolation Wilderness Area is one of the most picturesque **backpacking** areas in the country. It attracts a proportionately large number of visitors each year. Trails are easy to follow when not covered by snow. Cross-country routes are easy to negotiate, and offer the benefit of fewer people. The terrain is

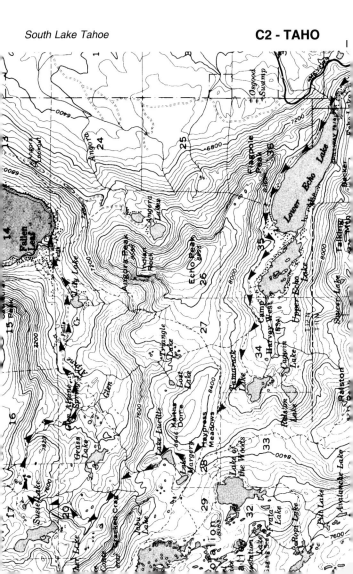

endowed with visible landmarks;  with a good map, compass, and pilot's savvy, you will find it difficult to get lost.

Permits are required for access to the Desolation Wilderness. Call the Forest Service at 530-573-2600 or 573-2674 in advance for information.  Normally, permits must be picked up in person. However, if you courteously explain that you are arriving by small airplane, they will mail you the permit.  Make reservations at least 3 weeks in advance by calling 530-644-6048.

The U.S. Forest Service is located 2.0 miles north of the airport. Follow Highway 50 north until it turns right. Head straight through the intersection.  The Forest Service is located shortly thereafter in Plaza 89 on the left.

## Lower Echo Lake / Fallen Leaf Lake Loop Hike

Take a taxi to the trailhead at Lower Echo Lake.  From the airport, go 5.5 miles south on Highway 50 and 89.  Before the uphill passing lane begins, turn right onto an unmarked road that heads up to Lower Echo Lake.  Follow signs to the lake, traveling another 5.5 miles to the boat dock.  At the dock there is a store from which you can get supplies and free daytime hiking permits.  (More than one daytime permit can be acquired, but they do not cover overnight camping.)  At this location, a boat-taxi can be hired at $3.50 per person for passage to the other end of the lake.  Otherwise, the trail begins here.

For this loop, use the *Fallen Leaf Lake* topo map.  Follow the marked trail along Lower Echo Lake, up to high country, and eventually to Lake Lucille. This scenic lake is a potential campsite. Proceed cross-country from Lake Lucille through a valley to a beautiful 200-foot falls that is probably fed by Susie Lake.  The cross-country trek is straightforward except for crossing the stream down the center of the valley.  I was lucky and found a good, solid snow bridge.  Be creative (and careful). Man-made bridges are not the rule when traveling cross country, yet I managed to find ways to cross all streams. A useful trick is to use a walking stick for stability while you hop stones.

This beautiful valley contains waterfalls and Grass Lake. If you choose to camp here, carefully select a site that is well sheltered from wind. Total time recorded from the trailhead to the falls is approximately four hours.

From my campsite at the base of the falls, I climbed north beside the falls until I intercepted a well-kept trail above the falls. Following the trail east takes you downhill in the direction of Fallen Leaf Lake. About halfway to the lake, you leave the wilderness area and begin to encounter private cabins. (There is now a building ban, limiting the proliferation of cabins.) As you approach civilization, your chances of catching a ride with a fellow backpacker increase. If you do not immediately catch a ride, you win the opportunity to see at least two impressive falls along the last mile to Fallen Leaf Lake.

By hitchhiking, I was able to get transportation in two segments to the airport in forty-five minutes. Alternatively, when you reach the phone at Fallen Leaf Lake, you can call a taxi.

## Winter Activities

Tahoe is a favorite stop for winter wonderland enthusiasts. Its ski area is America's largest, with twenty-two **downhill ski areas** within a fifty mile radius. Heavenly Ski Resort, 775-586-7000, the largest in town, has sixteen chairs and is located five miles north of the airport. Sierra-at-Tahoe, 530-659-7453, is somewhat south of town.

If you have never ridden a **horse-drawn sleigh**, bundle up for a forty-minute ride to a high plateau with panoramic view. Rides leave the downtown area from Borges Sleigh Rides, 530-541-2953. Camp Richardson's Corral also offers sleigh rides in winter, 530-541-3113.

Rent a **snowmobile** from the Zephyr Cove Snowmobile Center, 775-588-3833. Lake Tahoe Sport Center also rents machines and conducts tours, 530-577-2940.

The area offers a variety of **cross-country skiing** options for novice or expert. Four miles east of the airport are a number of safe and beautiful ski areas. You may be able to ski from the airport to these local areas without additional transportation. Nordic ski centers with groomed trails are plentiful in the area.

Words of caution: Skiing in the Desolation Wilderness Area southwest of the airport can be as dangerous as it is beautiful. In this area, the mountain sides are steep, and avalanches are a daily occurrence. Weather can change from a beautiful, clear-sky day to full snow whiteout in less than twenty minutes.

*- RW*

# Tuolumne Meadows

*Known for alpine flora and scenic views,
Tuolumne Meadows is a high-altitude hiking
area within the Yosemite National Park system.*

## Airport Information

Refer to Mammoth **C2-MAMM**, Mono Lake **C2-MONO**, and
Yosemite **C2-YOSE** chapters for information on nearby airports.

## Phone Numbers

Due to its popularity and accessibility from California population centers, Yosemite National Park has become highly regulated.  Obtaining proper information and permits can be as
frustrating as attempting to get support for Microsoft software.
(Just kidding; it's not that bad!)  I hope the following phone
numbers will make the process a breeze for you.

| | | |
|---|---|---|
| Yosemite Park Information | recording | 209-372-0200 |
| Tuolumne Permit Station | ranger | 209-372-0309 |
| Lee Vining Ranger Station, *east* | ranger | 760-647-3044 |
| Yosemite Permit Station, *west* | ranger | 209-372-0308 |
| Yosemite Public Information | ranger | 209-372-0265 |
| Yosemite Public Info., *alternate* | ranger | 209-372-0265 |
| Trail reservations , *always busy* | person | 209-372-0740 |
| Mistix Reservation, *campgrounds* | person | 800-436-7275 |
| High Sierra [Camp] Reservations | person | 209-253-5674 |
| Hotel/tent Reservations | menu, wait | 209-252-4848 |
| Concession Information | person | 209-372-1000 |
| Trail Ride Stables | person | 209-372-8348 |

## Permits

A $20 entry fee is required for each car that enters the national park. In addition, hiking permits are required. Permits cost $3 if ordered by phone, and are free at the station. The park permit system limits trail usage by quota.

To get the trail of your choice, obtain your permit in advance, or at least as soon as possible. Permits may be obtained from a booth in the parking lot near the west end of Tuolumne Meadows Lodge spur road. This is located off Highway 120, about one half mile east of the Tuolumne River. You can purchase maps and trail guides at the same booth.

Tip: When arriving from the east side, you have a better chance of obtaining a permit if you stop at the Lee Vining Ranger Station. However, Lee Vining rangers issue permits for the east side of Tuolumne Meadow, only.

During the months of February through May, permits may be obtained by writing to Backcountry Office, P.O. Box 577, Yosemite National Park, CA 95389. Either way, you must specify your intended route and itinerary.

Permits and reservations are required for nearly every activity except driving through the park. If you plan to camp, stay at lodging, or go horseback riding, be sure to make reservations through one of the phone numbers listed on the previous page.

## Overview

Along with the Yosemite Valley, the beautiful Tuolumne Meadows area was saved for the enjoyment of future generations, primarily due to the efforts of naturalist John Muir. In 1980, Congress created the Yosemite National Park, which includes Tuolumne Meadows. Today, the Tuolumne Meadows area offers nearly 100 miles of **high-elevation hiking** trails. Trail elevations typically range from 8500 to 11,000 feet. The high elevations limit backpacking to the summer months of early July through mid-September.

The hiking trails cover varied terrain. As one might guess from the area's name, a good percentage of the land is covered by alpine meadows. Some unwooded, rocky regions are painted with beautiful beds of wild flowers. Hillsides are predominately populated by lodgepole pine, with other trees occasionally offering competition. For example, Jeffrey pines can be found on some of the dryer slopes. In any case, tree population is generally sparse enough to allow good visibility in forested areas.

Since meadow trails can be muddy in places, bring appropriate footwear. Mosquito repellent is a must. Though not absolutely necessary, a compass is useful. As mentioned above, topo maps can be conveniently purchased from the permit booth. Bring a means for water purification. For all practical purposes, a camp stove is required.

The park's black bear population is perhaps the biggest threat to peaceful overnight camping. The park bears have never taken a human life, but pilfering campers' food is common. These bears appear to be more intelligent than the average dog, and have demonstrated that they have sufficient strength to smash and enter locked cars. Fortunately, over the years man has devised methods for protecting his food. These involve suspending the food at least twelve feet above the ground. Be sure to carry 30 feet of nylon cord. Follow the ranger's instructions to the letter.

The park offers an interesting option for hikers who wish to spend a number of days in the mountains without the burden of a heavy pack. The Yosemite Park and Curry Company has set up five **summer campsites**, complete with large tents and food services. The camps are placed in a circle at convenient intervals for an easy day's hike. Dormitory style living is provided in the tents, with beds, linens, and blankets provided. Breakfast and dinner are served. Perhaps best of all, each camp has hot showers. Prices are about $93 for lodging and meals.

Reservations are done by lottery. You can request applications by phone or mail from September 1 to November 30. You may return the applications between October 15 and November 30. The lottery is performed in mid December. Send your request to Yosemite Reservations, 5410 E. Home, Fresno, CA 93727, or call High Sierra Reservations. Thirty day notice is required for cancellations. Cancellations may enable you to get a slot at the last minute. If you find this process disturbing, think twice before doing anything that might increase the world's population.

**Overnight mule trips** are extremely popular, and reservations are therefore obtained by the same protracted lottery system. A four-day trip costs about $580, five-days costs $680, and six-days costs $915. If you specify alternative dates in request, your chances are improved.

**Daytime horseback trips** can be scheduled by simply calling the stables. Two hours cost $35, and half days cost $46.

Because of its beauty and location, Tuolumne Meadows is a popular vacation retreat. In order to maintain the environment's natural state, a number of regulations are enforced: Pets are not allowed on the trails. Wood fires are not permitted above 9600 feet. Camping is restricted to specified areas. For example, camping is not allowed within four miles of Tuolumne Meadows. Camping must be at least 100 feet from rivers, lakes, and trails. The ranger will provide you with a complete list of regulations.

## Mammoth Airport to Tuolumne Meadows

For information about Mammoth Airport, see the Mammoth chapter, **C2-MAMM**.

Leave the airport from the east side. Head north on Highway 395. After about 25 minutes, you enter the little town of Lee Vining. Turn west on Highway 120. After another 15 minutes, you pass through Tioga Pass. At 9945 feet, Tioga is the highest automobile pass in California. After the park's gate house, travel another six or seven miles to the ranger station near the Tuolumne Meadows High Sierra Camp. Total mileage to this point (very near the trailhead) is 47 miles.

Look for a booth in the parking lot. Here, you can obtain permit, maps, and information on coping with the bears. Meals and provisions may be purchased a half-mile further west on Highway 120. A utilitarian restaurant and small store are located just southwest of the Tuolumne River.

## Voglesang Loop

To get closer to the trailhead, drive a short distance east from the permit booth to the parking lot near the High Sierra Camp. A sign south of the parking lot marks the trailhead (distances in miles):

| | |
|---|---|
| **Tuolumne Pass** | **6.1** |
| **Voglesang Camp** | **6.7** |
| **Donahue Pass** | **11.9** |
| **Merced Lake** | **14.7** |
| **Yosemite Valley** | **27.5** |

All trails are well marked and easy to follow. Take the trail to John Muir Trail, which is just over the footbridge that crosses the Lyell Fork of the Tuolumne River. The walk from the parking lot to the John Muir Trail takes less than ten minutes. Follow the John Muir trail east another ten minutes until the Tuolumne Pass Trail intersection. Head south on the Tuolumne Pass Trail.

Along this stretch of trail, you can expect to see meadow, exposed rock, sparse trees, and people. The trail parallels the Rafferty Creek, and soon begins to climb at a comfortable grade. Expect to see more trees and less people. As the trail gets closer to Voglesang Camp, the trees give way to rock outcroppings and bits of meadow. Mount Dana, Mount Gibbs, and Mammoth Peak will become visible. After 3.5 to 4 miles from the trailhead, you will find yourself at Voglesang Camp.

Besides the High Sierra Camp tents, Voglesang offers a number of widely separated campsites for the do-it-yourself camper. As mentioned above, food and lodging may be available at the Curry Company's camps, but without reservations there are no guarantees.

The next leg is the six-mile Evelyn Lake Trail that leads from Voglesang Camp to the intersection of the John Muir Trail. It begins by passing Upper Fletcher Lake. The first half of the trail has several gradual ups and downs between elevations of 10,000 and 10,500 feet. Trees are few and rocks are many. You will pass several high-altitude lakes before the trail begins its descent. The second half is all downhill, and soon becomes wooded. At an elevation of 8880 feet, you intersect the John Muir trail. Time en route from Voglesang should be 2.5 to 3 hours. A nice campsite is located near Lyell Fork of the Tuolumne River intersection. At the time of my visit, the site was curiously mosquito-free.

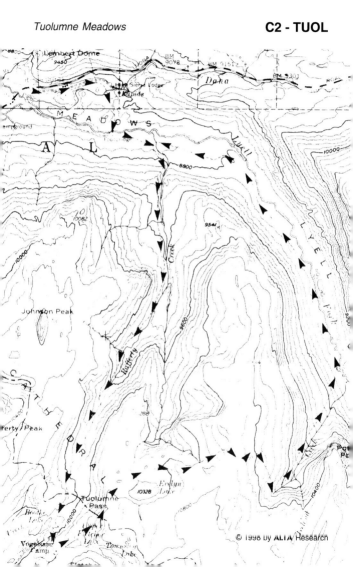

© 1998 by ALTA Research

The balance of the hike is a six-plus mile leg on the John Muir Trail, northwest back to the original trailhead. This section follows Lyell Fork along the valley floor, mostly at the edge of the meadows. Depending upon the time of year, you may have to practice mud avoidance. Although the pleasant scenery is a bit repetitious, this leg is a peaceful way to end an interesting hike. Time from joining the John Muir Trail to the parking lot is about three hours.

*- RW*

# Yosemite Park

## Mariposa-Yosemite Airport

| | |
|---|---|
| **Town** | Mariposa **ID** O68 (oh-68) |
| **Coord** | N-37-30.65, W-120-02.51 |
| **Elev** | 2250 feet, 1.1%, W high |
| **Runway** | 8rt - 26, 3310 x 50' asphalt |
| **Freq** | CTAF-122.7, Lights 122.7-5x |
| **Charts** | San Francisco sect., L2, Lo3 |

> ***CAUTION:*** *Airport information not for navigational use. Mountainous terrain nearby. Hang gliders. No line of sight between ends.*

*Yosemite Park is one of America's most beautiful scenic treasures. Views, hikes, backpacking, mule rides, and tours – a photographers paradise. $50-250. Chamber: 800-208-2434, 209-966-2456.*

## Airport Description

The runway is paved and in good condition. The east end is 31 feet lower than the west end. Even though Runway 26 runs uphill, consider departing on 26 when air is hot and wind is calm. In this direction, you can bear right and follow the road if climbing becomes difficult just after lift-off.

## Services, Lodging, and Transportation

Airport phone: 209-966-2143. Fuel: 80 and 100. Tiedown costs $3 per evening. A porta-potty is available for visitors who need to camp at the airport. The Airport Inn Cafe is within easy walking distance.

**Features**

B Full breakfast
C Continental
H Historic
P Pets OK
R Restaurant
T Transportation

The center for lodging is four miles east in Mariposa. Yosemite Motels Reservations books for seven area motels, 800-321-5261.

| | | | |
|---|---|---|---|
| Best Western Yosemite | CPT | $65-100 | 209-966-7545 |
| Comfort Inn | C | $70-385 | 209-966-4344 |
| E.C. Yosemite Motel | PT | $50-71 | 209-242-6800 |
| Ken and Flo's B&B | BT | $50-61 | 209-266-3515 |
| Mariposa Hotel | CHT | $92-107 | 209-966-4676 |
| Mariposa Lodge | PT | $72-77 | 209-966-3607 |
| Miner's Inn Motel | PRT | $70-165 | 209-742-7777 |
| Sierra House B&B | BT | $82-93 | 209-966-3515 |

Yosemite Park has a wide range of accommodations, from camping to cabins. Campsites cost $15, tent cabins are $44, rooms range from $95-270, and cabins cost $60-77. Ahwahnee Hotel is the most luxurious. Make reservations far in advance. Mix yourself a stiff martini before attempting to deal with the Reservation Office at 209-252-4848.

Enterprise delivers cars to the airport for rental, charging $50 and up. To be assured of transportation, reserve the car at least two days in advance, and by Thursday for weekend rentals. Call the FBO at 209-966-2143, or Enterprise at 673-6489.

VIA Yosemite Connection provides round-trip bus service from Mariposa to Yosemite, four times daily, 800-369-7275. VIA charges $20 per round trip, and less for children. Shuttle bus service is provided within Yosemite Valley at no cost. Yosemite Tours, 209-966-2816, is a retired couple who provide taxi and tour service out of Mariposa. Per group of up to 4 people, they charge $120 for a 6-hour tour through Yosemite.

Hitchhiking between Mariposa and Yosemite is difficult. Evidently, local folks have little use for tourists, and Winnebago drivers have little use for hitchhikers. I tested this mode of transportation with a sign that read *$5.00 to Yosemite*. It failed to produce a quick lift. The gracious couple who eventually gave the crusty pilot a ride refused to accept payment.

## Mariposa Area

Because Mariposa is primarily a food and lodging center for tourists destined for Yosemite Park, visitors often overlook opportunities in the Mariposa area. Close to town, you can visit the **Mariposa History Museum**; and just outside of town, the

**Gem and Mineral Museum**.  **Whitewater rafting** outfitters have offices in nearby towns; T provide transportation:

| | | |
|---|---|---|
| T | Ahwahnee Whitewater, *6 rivers* | 800-359-9790 |
| | All Outdoors Inc., *12 rivers, class 3-5* | 800-247-2387 |
| | Arta, *14 rivers, class 3-5* | 800-323-ARTA |
| T | Mariah Wilderness Experiences, *6 rivers* | 800-462-7424 |
| | Whitewater Excitement, *4 rivers* | 800-750-2386 |
| | Whitewater Voyages, *11 rivers* | 800-488-RAFT |
| T | Zephyr Whitewater, *5 rivers, class 3-5* | 800-431-3636 |

## Yosemite Park Overview

Yosemite National Park is a striking natural phenomenon that man has converted into a naturalist's Disneyland.  The number of people processed in an orderly fashion on the valley floor is amazing.  Fortunately for the serious backpacker, a relatively small percentage of the masses penetrate the back country.  Though you encounter numerous day hikers en route to common sites, once past the assorted popular falls, population density drops to acceptable levels, due in part to a quota system.

| | | |
|---|---|---|
| Yosemite Park Information | recording | 209-372-0200 |
| Tuolumne Permit Station | ranger | 209-372-0309 |
| Lee Vining Ranger Station, *east* | ranger | 760-647-3044 |
| Yosemite Permit Station, *west* | ranger | 209-372-0308 |
| Yosemite Public Information | ranger | 209-372-0265 |
| Yosemite Public Info., *alternate* | ranger | 209-372-0265 |
| Trail reservations, *always busy* | person | 209-372-0740 |
| Mistix Reservation, *campgrounds* | person | 800-436-7275 |
| High Sierra [Camp] Reservations | person | 209-253-5674 |
| Hotel/tent Reservations | menu, wait | 209-252-4848 |
| Concession Information | person | 209-372-1000 |
| Trail Ride Stables | person | 209-372-8348 |

These phone numbers will help you make the necessary arrangements. Reservations should be made in advance. For some activities, reservations need be made nine months in advance, and winners are selected by lottery.

A $20 entry fee is assessed from each car that enters the national park. Tourist trails are often paved and do not require a permit. A permit is required for serious backpacking trails, which are limited by quota. Permits cost $3 if ordered by phone, and are free if obtained on site.

During the months of February through May, backpacking permits may be obtained by writing to Backcountry Office, P.O. Box 577, Yosemite National Park, CA 95389. Either way, you must specify your intended route and itinerary.

**El Capitan**

Photo by Mary Dryden

The park offers an interesting option for hikers who wish to spend a number of days in the mountains without the burden of a heavy pack. The park has set up five **summer campsites**, complete with large tents and food services. The camps are placed in a circle at convenient intervals for an easy day's hike. Dormitory style living is provided in the tents, with beds, linens, and blankets provided. Breakfast and dinner are served. Perhaps best of all, each camp has hot showers. Prices are about $93 for lodging and meals.

Reservations are done by lottery. You can request applications by phone or mail from September 1 to November 30. You may return the applications between October 15 and November 30. The lottery is performed in mid December. Send your request to Yosemite Reservations, 5410 E. Home, Fresno, CA 93727, or call High Sierra Reservations. Thirty day notice is required for cancellations. Cancellations may enable you to get a slot at the last minute.

**Overnight mule trips** are extremely popular, and reservations are therefore obtained by the same protracted lottery system. A four-day trip costs about $580, five-days costs $680, and six-days costs $915. If you specify alternative dates in request, your chances are improved.

**Daytime horseback trips** can be scheduled by simply calling the stables. Two hours cost $35, and half days cost $46.

Backcountry campers should note the park's list of camping regulations and guidelines for dealing with bears. To protect your food from bears, bring at least 30 feet of nylon cord. Follow the rangers' instructions to the letter. Bears are generally benign if proper precautions are taken, but they can be a very annoying problem in certain areas of Yosemite.

## Four Mile Trail / Happy Isles Loop Hike

Information and maps are readily available from California bookstores and the Visitor's Center. When you get your permit, the ranger can give you directions to the Four-Mile Trailhead.

The trail is about 95% uphill, from 4000 to 7200 feet. Because I was in a rush to beat the sunset when I visited, I reached the top (Glacier Point) in two hours and 45 minutes. Typical ascent time quoted by the ranger was four hours.

The ever-present beautiful view offers a legitimate excuse for frequent rest stops. But, save your film for the top half! Interestingly, the trail is blasted out of granite and mostly paved with asphalt. The asphalt presents a problem on descent because it becomes slippery when covered with rock particles; this is not a problem when going up.

At the top, you again find yourself among hordes of tourists who have taken a car or bus to the developed vista. A snack bar, rest rooms, drinking water, and a vista point are among the attractions featured at Glacier Point. After catching your breath, you can escape the masses by taking the Panorama Trail.

Aptly named, the Panorama Trail provides the hiker with a series of righteous vistas. After 1.6 miles, branch left on Illilouette Trail to Illilouette Falls. Keep following this trail along the Panorama Cliff until you reach the popular Nevada Falls.

After enjoying the falls, take the trail down toward Happy Isles. Part way down, the Mist Trail branches off. It is damp and slippery and best hiked without a pack. I recommend continuing on the donkey trail. Both are very scenic.

Including rest stops and lunch, I clocked five hours between Glacier Point and Happy Isles. At Happy Isles, you can catch a free shuttle bus to key points in the park.

Photo by Mary Dryden

# California South

**California Aeronautics**

916-654-4959

# Big Bear

## Big Bear City Airport

**Town**    Big Bear   **ID**  L35
**Coord**   N-34-15.82,  W-116-51.27
**Elev**    6748  feet
**Runway**  8rt - 26,  5850 x 75' asphalt
**Freq**    CTAF-123.05,  Lights-123.05-3x5x7x
**Charts**  Los Angeles sectional,  L3, Lo4

*CAUTION:* *Airport information not for navigational use. High mountain airport. Watch density altitude. See nav guides for noise abatement procedures.*

> *Big Bear is an alpine valley oasis with recre-*
> *ational lake and lots to do, summer or winter.*
> *$100-$300.   Chamber: 909-866-4608*
>
> *Lake Arrowhead is an upscale planned recre-*
> *ational development, 30 miles west of Big Bear.*
> *$175-400.   Visitors Center: 909-337-3715*

## Airport

Big Bear City Airport is located high in the mountains, 60 miles northeast of Los Angeles. Look for the airport just east of Big Bear Lake. Mountain peaks and high terrain surround the town in all directions, except directly over the lake. Skys are clear 300 days per year.

The airport authorities request compliance with noise abatement procedures. Essentially, this means conduct approach activity to the south, and depart to west or east over low terrain. The default runway is 26. Consult navagation guides or call the airport for details.

## Services, Transportation, and Lodging

Airport phone: 909-585-3219. Fuel: 100, JetA. The airport has several FBOs and a terminal building with American and Chinese restaurants. Maintenance is available at the FBOs. Big Bear Airport has one campsite for fly-ins; reservations advised.

Cars can be rented at the airport from Big Bear Rent-a-Car, 909-584-2000. Rates are reasonable, but the agency requires that cars remain in the area. Enterprise, 909-866-1156 or 800-

325-8007, provides service to the airport, but is closed Sundays. Taxi services: Big Bear Shuttle and Taxi, 585-3219; Dial-A-Ride, 866-4444; and Big Bear Cab Co., 866-4544. Arrowhead Airport Shuttle runs between the airport and Lake Arrowhead, 337-3579.

Economy-minded visitors should consider staying at the recently refurbished Motel 6, 0.8 miles west of the airport. The others listed below are more costly, but most are closer to the marina and Big Bear Lake Village. For lodging referrals, call 909-866-7000.

**Features**

B Full breakfast
C Continental
H Historic
P Pets OK
R Restaurant
T Transportation

| | | | |
|---|---|---|---|
| Apples B&B | BT | $136-201 | 909-866-0903 |
| Bear Manor Cabins | B | $90-400 | 909-866-3502 |
| Big Bear Inn | R | $120-220 | 909-866-6666 |
| Cozy Hollow Lodge | CHP | $80-150 | 909-866-9694 |
| Fireside Lodge | C | $90-400 | 909-866-2253 |
| Forest Shores Inn | | $89-400 | 909-866-6551 |
| Frontier Lodge | CP | $71-300 | 909-866-5888 |
| Gold Mountain Manor B&B | BHT | $108-208 | 800-509-2604 |
| Inn at Fawnskin B&B | BT | $94-192 | 888-329-6754 |
| Moonridge Manor B&B | BPT | $75-175 | 909-585-0457 |
| Motel 6 | P | $42-68 | 909-585-6666 |
| Switzerland House B&B | BT | $70-249 | 800-335-3729 |
| Thundercloud Resort | CP | $70-170 | 800-732-5386 |
| Truffles B&B Inn | BT | $125-162 | 909-585-2772 |
| Northwoods | RT | $100-175 | 800-866-3121 |
| Windy Point Inn B&B | BT | $137-247 | 909-866-2746 |

Northwoods and Big Bear Inn list their facilities as "hotels." Gold Mountain Manor claims to be the only historic B&B, and Moonridge Manor has great views. Truffles is south of town, near the ski mountain and golf course. The Inn at Fawnskin B&B and Windy Point Inn are on the north side of the lake.

For nicer lodging in a well-planned, attractive environment, you need to drive a scenic mountain road 30 miles west to Lake Arrowhead. The B&Bs, in particular, will not disappoint you.

| | | | |
|---|---|---|---|
| Arrowhead Pine Rose | HP | $75-354 | 800-429- PINE |
| Arrowhead Tree Top Lodge | P | $77-150 | 800-358-TREE |
| Arrowsmith Inn B&B | B | $105-158 | 909-337-7581 |
| Carriage House B&B | B | $104-147 | 800-526-5070 |
| Chateau du Lac B&B | B | $137-245 | 800-601-8722 |
| Eagles Landing B&B | B | $104-200 | 800-835-5085 |
| Lake Arrowhead Vil. Lodge | CH | $141-206 | 909-337-2544 |
| Lake Arrowhead Resort | R | $300-350 | 800-800-6792 |
| Gray Squirrel Inn | P | $49-154 | 909-336-3602 |
| Greystone in Forest B&B | BT | $128-270 | 909-337-0278 |
| North Shore Inn | R | $50-115 | 909-338-5230 |
| Prophet's Paradise B&B | BPT | $99-168 | 800-987-2231 |
| Sleepy Hollow Cabins | | $71-93 | 800-909-2718 |

You can rent a house in Big Bear or Arrowhead. Rates are competitive. Call 800-550-LAKE for reservations.

## Big Bear Lake and Village

When I arrived in the heat of summer, Big Bear seemed like heaven. At over 6750 feet, the alpine valley is paradise to visitors who arrive from the desert floor: Cool air, light breeze, clear skys, trees, and water. **Big Bear Lake** is eight miles long, extending west from the airport.

In winter, deprived snow worshipers migrate from Los Angeles to this convenient destination. Snow fall is typically 120 inches, and temperatures range from around 40 during the day to mid-20's at night – a pleasant environment for winter sports.

The Serrano Indians are believed to have been the first to visit, some 3000 years ago. In 1845, the valley was re-discovered by white man and named Bear Valley because "the place was alive with bear." Trappers, hunters, gold miners, and lumber companies paved the way for tourists. The first hotel opened in 1888, and the lake was dammed in 1912. The first airplane, a Thomas Morse Scout, landed in 1917.

While resorts quickly sprung to life to meet the needs of visitors, Hollywood was equally quick to capture the environment on film. Known as "Hollywood's back lot," Big Bear and Holcomb Valleys provided scenery for well-known films like "Paint Your Wagon." If you would like to learn more about area history, visit the historical museum in Big Bear City Park.

Today, visitors enjoy two local ski areas, golf, zoo, swimming, boating, fishing, hiking, horseback riding, and other forms of entertainment.

Shortly after I arrived, I spotted a unique **hang glider ride** on the hill just west of Motel 6. This ride is advertised as hang glider training. For $10, you get a few words of instruction, you jump, and you ride a funky hang glider down a cable. The training is of dubious value, but what the heck, it's a fun experience! Kids and adults enjoyed the rides, and some purchased subsequent rides at half price. Call 909-585-8585 for information.

In summer, water sports are popular in the valley. Marinas **rent boats**, **jet-skis**, **sailboards**, and provide **lessons** for **waterskiing** and **sailboarding**. Two outfits give **boat tours**: Big Bear Queen Boat Tours, 909-866-3218; and Capt. John's Lake Cruises, 866-2455. Call 866-IFLY for **parasailing**. The

**Simulated hang glide ride**

Alpine Slide at Magic Mountain offers **water slides**, **go-karts**, and other forms of family fun, 866-4626.

The lake has trout, bass, and croppie. **Fishing** information can be obtained from the Fishing Association of Big Bear Lake at 909-585-4007. Kids and adults who are patience-challenged should try the private Alpine Trout Lakes, 866-4532. Alpine charges $5 to fish at their lake, plus a variable charge for the catch. No license is required, and gear is available.

Although the authentic (bear-infested) wilderness is now mostly history, the area still offers **scenic hiking** and **horseback riding** with great views. For backcountry information and maps, contact the U.S. Forest Service at 909-866-3437. A number of trails loop from the lake and back. Baldwin Lake Stables offers trail rides year round, 585-6482. **Big Bear Jeep Tours** provides a number of tours in the area, 878-5337.

**Artist captures a scenic view, west end of Big Bear Lake**

Bear Mountain **Golf** Course is a nine-hole, links-style regulation course at the base of Bear Mountain Ski Resort, 909-585-8002. The two **ski areas** at the south of town are Bear Mountain, 585-2519, and Snow Summit, 866-5766. In summer, you can ride the Snow Summit chair to the top and enjoy incredible views at the View Haus while chasing barbecued food with cold beer. Snow Valley Ski Resort is a third facility, on the way to Lake Arrowhead.

Other points of interest include the **Solar Observatory**, 909-866-5791, and the Moonridge Animal Park **zoo**, 866-0183. **Bikes** of various styles can be rented from five different outlets. Or, kick back and enjoy a **carriage ride** from Victoria Park Carriages, 584-0162. If you have a car, be sure to **drive** around the lake and drive to Lake Arrowhead.

The Chamber of Commerce lists dozens of events, too many to list here  – call the Chamber at 909-866-4607.

## Lake Arrowhead Village

Old-time Los Angeles residents have fond memories of Santa's Village, which began operation outside of Lake Arrowhead in 1953. In 1997 the park was turned over to Wildhaven for development of an **animal rehabilitation center**. Santa's cottages have been transformed into rustic buildings, reminiscent of early pioneer days. I wish them generous donations and much success.

Lake Arrowhead and village were originally owned by a lumber company, which created the lake as a water project. The original village was burned in the late seventy's to make way for a planned development. The replacement is a testament to the power of coordinated planning. They did such a beautiful job that visitors seldom mourn its loss of soul. Actually, strolling

San

Ash Meadows

Cedar Glen

Lake Arrowhead

PRIVATE PROPE (APPRO)

Lake Arrowhead Boy Scout Camps

Santana Community Hospital

North Shore Campground

Papoose Lake

North Shore Tavern

Lake Arrowhead Community Services Dist.

Cumberland Dr.

The World

Mt. Sorenson Elev. 6273 Ft.

Helipad

County Diamond Site

Heaps Peak

San Bernardino National

Grass Valley Creek

Willow Creek

Golden Rule Dr

PRIVATE PROPERTY BOUNDARY

UCLA Conf. Ctr.

North Bay

Papoose Bay

Childrens Marina

South Bay Marina

Fire Sta.

Hook's Meadow

Lodge

Lake Arrowhead Village

Syl Carlson Dr.

Santas Village

Rim Of The World

Sky Forest

P.O.

Ranger Sta.

Sweatzer Park

Deer Lodge Park

North Bay Rd.

Peninsula Dr.

Blue Jay

Grass Valley

Twin Peaks

Ridge

Tunnel

Canyon

Lake Arrowhead Country Club

Green Valley Lake Rd

Rim Forest

Crest Park

Ice Castle Int'l Training Ctr. and Ice Rink

Agua Fria

Library

Visitor Ctr.

Dogwood Campground

Rim of the World High School

County Road Dept.

Arrowhead Ranger Sta.

P.O.

U.S. Forest Service Lookout

Eagle Park

Mtn Rock Elev. 5280 Ft.

County Diamond Site

Mountain Community Senior High

San Bernardino County Admin.

Sheriff Court House

State Hwy. 18

Eagle Park

arrowhead highlands

through the aesthetically-created new environemnt is a pleasure – absent are blinking neon, used car lots, overt fast food joints, and misplaced gas stations.

I strongly recommend the 30-mile drive to Lake Arrowhead. The village has a beautiful setting on the lake, with over 50 shops offering quality goods. The place is designed to take your money in a most pleasurable way. The beauty is that you feel good about spending in this setting! It's fascinating.

Cruise the **shops**. You will find **factory outlets** like Van Heusen or Bass Shoe, and many small shops for **clothing**, **jewelry**, **art**, and **leather**. The Sunglass Hut claims to be the largest **sunglass shop** in the U.S. By the **marina**, you can enjoy a meal while water skiers do their dance.

Young kids will love the interactive, creative **Children's Museum**, 909-336-1332: face paints, scientific experiments, and fire house, complete with little fireman's outfits – a class act. On Saturday at the **Children's Forest** off Highway 18, U.S. Forest rangers walk kids through the forest, 337-2444.

Adults can play at the **Lake Arrowhead Country Club**, 909-337-2441. The club has 18-holes of **golf**, **driving range**, **tennis courts**, and **swimming pool**. Excellent **restaurants** are sprinkled around the lake. Casual Elegance is an expensive, high-quality restaurant in the Agua Fria area. Woodys is a popular restaurant on the waterfront. Royal Oak is a nice restaurant in Blue Jay. And, there are more.

The whole family will enjoy a $7-$10 **boat ride** on the Arrowhead Queen, 909-336-6992. You can learn to **water ski** from the McKenzie's Waterski School, 337-3814. The beautiful Ice Castle **skating rink** in Blue Jay offers skating by day and a wide diversity of shows in the evening, 336-2111.

Outdoor Learning Adventures, 909-337-3276, offers all kinds of outdoor adventures for adults and families: adventure **rope courses**, **hiking**, **rock climbing**, and **back packing**. You can **rent a horse** or **mountain bike** at the Snow Valley Ski Area, 800-680-7669, east of town on Highway 18. For **hang gliding** in the greater area, call Natural High, 909-867-7961; or High Adventure, 883-8488.

Like Big Bear, Lake Arrowhead has a long list of events. Call the Visitor's Center at 909-337-3715 for detailed event information. Web: *www.lakearrowhead.net.*

**Lake Arrowhead Village waterfront**

# Catalina Island

## Catalina Airport

| | | | |
|---|---|---|---|
| **Town** | Avalon | **ID** | AVX |
| **Coord** | N-33-24.30, W-118-24.95 | | |
| **Elev** | 1602 feet, middle high | | |
| **Runway** | 4 - 22rt, 3240 x 100' asphalt | | |
| **Freq** | CTAF-122.7 | | |
| **Charts** | Los Angeles sectional, L3, Lo4 | | |

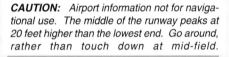

*CAUTION:* Airport information not for navigational use. The middle of the runway peaks at 20 feet higher than the lowest end. Go around, rather than touch down at mid-field.

---

*Catalina Island is a favorite weekend vacation
spot for southern California. Options range
from the hustle and bustle of Avalon
to the serenity of Two Harbors.
$30 - $300.  Chamber:  310-510-1520.*

---

## Airport Description

Catalina Airport is located on a ridge in the hills of Santa
Catalina Island.  At least 21 miles of ocean flight are necessary.
Unicom communication with the airport is mandatory.  An-
nounce intentions five to ten minutes before entering the pattern.

The airport (including runway usage) shuts down with punc-
tuality at the end of each day.  Closing times vary between 5:00
and 7:30, depending upon time of year.  Verify closing time
with Flight Service if you expect to arrive late in the afternoon.
When departing, plan on taxiing at least fifteen minutes before
closing time.

## Airport Services, Transportation, and Lodging

Airport phone:  310-510-0143, 800-255-8700 from CA.  No
fuel is available.  Though the field has an expansive tiedown
area, Catalina's popularity lures enough airplanes to cause problems at peak times of the year.  The landing fee for a single-
engine airplane is $5-15.  Try not to be discouraged by rigid
behavior from airport personnel;  spirits lighten up in town.

Located under the tower is a restaurant that specializes in
buffalo burgers.  The restaurant has a nice patio with a view of
surrounding countryside.  The restaurant is not open for dinner.

No other services are provided at the airport; food, lodging, and entertainment are available only in Avalon and Two Harbors.

Bus service runs between the airport and Avalon or Two Harbors six times daily during peak months. Fares to Avalon are $11 one way and $13 round trip. Call 310-510-0143 for schedule, and pay at the tower when you land. Reservations are required for the return trip. Avalon Taxi, 510-0705 or 510-0025, charges $60 for trips between Avalon and the airport.

**Boat tours** are provided by Discovery Tours, 310-510-2000; and Adventure Tours, 510-2888. Catalina Safari provides island-wide **bus service**, 510-2800. Golf carts can be rented from three agencies in Avalon for a tad less than a Cessna 152. Rent all shapes and sizes of small boats from Joe's Rent-a-Boat, 510-0455 at the central Avalon Pleasure Pier.

Most of the island's lodging is located in Avalon. The city offers several dozen options, including lodges, hotels, B&Bs, condos, and campgrounds. The following is a short list. Contact the Chamber of Commerce at 310-510-1520 for the full scoop.

**Features**

B Full breakfast
C Continental
H Historic
P Pets OK
R Restaurant
T Transportation

| | | | |
|---|---|---|---|
| Cloud Seven Hotel | CT | $44-164 | 310-510-0454 |
| El Torado | CHP | $82-300 | 310-510-0600 |
| Gull House B&B | C | $120-170 | 310-510-2547 |
| Hotel St. Lauren | CT | $44-313 | 310-510-2299 |
| Hotel Vista Del Mar | CH | $104-355 | 310-510-1452 |
| Inn on Mt. Ada | B | $280-690 | 310-510-2030 |
| Old Turner Inn B&B | BH | $131-202 | 310-510-2236 |
| Pavilion Lodge | CP | $65-206 | 310-510-2000 |

Camping is available within 15-minute walking distance of Avalon harbor. Head southwest from the main Catalina pier on

Catalina Street. At Tremont Street, make a quick right and left, and follow Avalon Canyon Road past the golf course and stables to Hermit Gulch Campground. For $8-10 per campsite, you receive showers, barbecue pit, and tables. Several trails radiate from the area, one of which leads to Wrigley Gardens. The camping facility is functional, but short on shade and privacy. Since space becomes limited on weekends, call 310-510-2000-x289 for reservations.

Feel the need for a quiet, laid-back vacation? **Two Harbors** may be a better match than the color and bustle of Avalon. Two Harbors is located northwest at the island's isthmus. The site has the look and feel of a tropical island hide-a-way. Facilities include one each of: restaurant, bar, snack bar, showers, scuba rentals, and laundramat. Experience a scenic hike in any direction.

Overlooking Two Harbors, Banning House features panoramic views and a homey environment for $108-191, 310-510-0688. Camping cabins and campgrounds are available for the budget minded. Call 310-510-0688 or 800-322-3434 for Two Harbors reservations, **diving** information, or just about anything else.

Other campsites are distributed about the island. They cost $8-10 per night and reservations are required, 310-510-2800-x0.

## Catalina Island

Catalina Island was discovered by Don Juan Rodriguez Cabrillo, a Portuguese navigator serving Spain in 1542. The sailors received a friendly welcome from sun-worshiping Indians who had arrived some 4000 years earlier. The island passed through many hands until 1975 when 86% of the land was purchased by the Santa Catalina Island Conservancy.

Santa Catalina is 20 miles tip-to-tip and is located 21 miles from the mainland (San Pedro). A network of hiking trails covers most of the island. Required hiking permits are available at the airport. **Hiking trails** wind through hills that are grazed by herds of buffalo and occasional goat and boar. The island coves and harbors are a favorite haunt for boaters. Beneath the surface, divers enjoy a treasure of marine beauty.

## Avalon

Avalon with its picture-postcard harbor has served as a Southern California playground for decades. Colorful, quaint buildings sit perched on the hills that protect the harbor. Restaurants spawn aromas that hitchhike on the ocean breeze. Snacks, from huge ice cream cones to buffalo burgers, beg to be enjoyed on every corner. This is no place for a serious dieter!

On your first day, I suggest that you poke your nose in every restaurant that looks interesting. Take inventory and plan your

**Avalon harbor**

restaurant stops for the balance of the stay. At the same time, visit the tour offices. Chances are, at least one of the nearly two dozen **tours** on land and sea will appeal to you. Consider the **Avalon Casino tour**, but be forewarned that overland tours may not be your best use of time.

The island supports a number of activities. **Ocean swimming** and **hiking** are still free, of course. The **Catalina Island Museum** is located in the Casino Building and the **Wrigley Gardens** are 1.2 miles southwest of town.

**Boats and bikes** can be rented at the harbor. Rent a boat from Joe's Rent-a-Boat, 310-510-0455. Brown's Bikes, 510-0986, rents bikes for $12-20 per day; and tandems for $30-40 per day.

Argo Diving Service, 310-510-2208, gives **scuba diving** tours and instruction. The following provide dive services and rent scuba

**Avalon: beach, bay, and casino**

and snorkeling gear, including underwater cameras: Catalina Diver's Supply, 510-0330; and, King Neptune, 510-2616.

Flip's Cheapo Charters provides **fishing excursions**, 310-510-2277 or 510-1416. Catalina Ocean Rafting gives thrilling rides on their inflatable powered rafts, 510-0211. Prices range from $50 for two hours to $260 for two days.

If you have never tried **parasailing**, Parasailing Catalina, 310-510-1777, will give you a thrill and even keep you dry for $45. A 9-hole **golf** course, 510-0530, and **tennis** courts are located at the southwest edge of town. Play **miniature golf** in a garden setting at Inland Plaza, one block from the beach. Several times daily, Catalina Stables, 510-0478, provides a 75-minute **horseback trail ride** into the local hills for $45. They are located past the golf course, southwest of town.

**Two Harbors**

A variety of events are staged in summer months. Nearly a dozen bars and restaurants offer entertainment on weekends. The **Sunset Buffet Cruise** provides food and entertainment on selected evenings. Enjoy an **afternoon cruise** along the coast and twilight dinner at Two Harbors. The Casino has **music** and **dancing** on most summer weekends, as well as **first-run movies**. Various dances, **races**, **art shows**, and **music (mostly jazz) festivals** are scheduled throughout summer. Call the Chamber at 310-510-1520 for dates.

## Blackjack Campground

Blackjack Campground is located within a one and one-half hour hike of the airport. The facility boasts just about every luxury one would expect to find in a camping area: toilet facilities, water, showers, electricity, telephone, picnic tables, Texas barbecue pit, and fire rings. Firewood is scarce, and the local ecology does not rapidly replenish this resource. This site can get very hot in midsummer.

To hike to Blackjack from the airport, follow the meandering paved road east from the airport toward Avalon. After about 45 minutes, you see a sign for Blackjack on the right. Turn right on the dirt road and follow it another 45 minutes to the campground. You will be heading toward a water tank visible at times en route to the campground. The campsites are located down and left of the tank.

Call 310-510-2800-x0 for information and reservations.

*- RW*

# Kernville

## Kern Valley Airport

| | |
|---|---|
| **Town** | Kernville **ID** L05 (L-zero-5) |
| **Coord** | N-35-43.70, W-118-25.19 |
| **Elev** | 2614 feet, middle high |
| **Runway** | 17rt - 35, 3500 x 50' asphalt |
| **Freq** | CTAF-122.8 |
| **Charts** | Los Angeles, L5, Lo3, Lo4 |

> ***CAUTION:*** *Airport information not for navigational use. Closed nights. Mountains N, W, E. No line of sight between runway ends.*

> *Kern Valley area is known for its whitewater
> runs. But there's more: lake boating, fishing,
> mountain biking, golf, hiking, archery, festivals,
> beautiful scenery, and the tallest trees on earth.
> $50 - $220.   Chamber: 760-376-2629
> www.kernvalley.com/KernCofC/index.htm*

## Airport

The Kern Valley airport is located in a valley between
Kernville and the north edge of Lake Isabella.  During daylight
hours, arrival and departure should be straightforward.  The
airport is closed at night.  The runway bows high at midfield,
restricting sight between ends.  Because the ramp isseriously
sloped, a functional emergency emergency brake is necessary.

## Services and Transportation

Airport phone: 760-376-2852.  Fuel: 100LL.  The airport has
a cozy café that doubles as fuel service and car rental agency.
Pilot's guides list a courtesy car at Kernville.  This is not
entirely in error. The one I rented looked like a typical airport
courtesy car, to the extreme.  Cars rent for $10 for two hours,
or $15 per day, plus $.20 per mile.  Tiedown is $3.50-5.00, and
airport camping costs $9.00.

## Lodging and Restaurants

Lodging and camping facilities are plentiful in the valley.
Outside of town, the riverside Whispering Pines Lodge is a
quality new facility with pool. The Kern River Inn B&B overlooks the town park, and serves the best breakfasts in town.

Also in town, the Kernville Inn has a pool and offers a good compromise between cost and quality. The River View Lodge has attractive older rustic cabins, but the units do not really view the river as the name suggests.

| | | | |
|---|---|---|---|
| Falling Waters | P | $39-98 | 760-376-2242 |
| Hi-Lo Resort Lodge | T | $50-110 | 760-376-2671 |
| Kern Lodge Motel | T | $55-110 | 760-376-2223 |
| Kern River Inn B&B | BT | $87-109 | 760-376-6750 |
| Kernville Inn | T | $54-109 | 760-376-2222 |
| McCambridge Lodge | PT | $52-73 | 760-376-2288 |
| River View Lodge | CHPT | $43-99 | 760-376-6019 |
| Western Motel | PT | $55-61 | 760-376-3222 |
| Whispering Pines Lodge | BT | $109-164 | 760-376-3733 |

**Campgrounds** are everywhere: at Lake Isabella, around town, and north of Kernville on Sierra Way. Campgrounds outside of town are typically run by the government.

**Features**

B Full breakfast
C Continental
H Historic
P Pets OK
R Restaurant
T Transportation

The best place for a romantic evening **meal** is Ewings on the Kern. Entrees of beef and seafood cost $14-25. You can dine to a river view, and on some evenings, music. I enjoyed a pleasant Italian meal at That's Italian in the heart of town. The Arcade Bar and Grill had the liveliest **nightlife** when I visited.

## Kern Valley

Kern Valley is known primarily for its **whitewater rafting**. The Kern River is one of North America's fastest dropping rivers, 30 feet per mile average, and 100 feet max. Because it has no serious waterfalls, the river is ideal for **whitewater sports**. For years Kernville has hosted Whitewater Wednesday, Kern River Festival, and Kern River Raft Races.

Seriously consider shooting the Kern in a rubber raft. Sierra South offers a one-hour trip for as little as $18. The guide takes you through several rapids and you are guaranteed to get wet. Expect to pay about $60-80/half-day, and $100-150/day for day- or multi-day raft trips. Various versions of kayaks are also available. Water levels are best in spring and early summer. Call the following to make the best match:

| | | |
|---|---|---|
| Chuck Richard's W.W. | *Lake Isabella* | 760-379-4444 |
| Kern River Tours | *Lake Isabella* | 760-379-4616 |
| Mountain River Adventures | *Kernville* | 760-376-6553 |
| Outdoor Adventures | *Woffordd.Hts.* | 800-323-4234 |
| Sierra South | *Kernville* | 760-376-3745 |

While in town, you can play a round of **golf**, or check out the **Fish and Game Hatchery** and **powerhouse**. The hatchery, open every day, is located a mile north of Kernville. Kids can feed young rainbow trout with handfuls of pellet grain. The nearby historic powerhouse is a rare treat. Schedule permitting, they will show you how they make electricity from water. Call them from the gate phone by entering 301.

**Fishing** is a big deal in Kern Valley. The Upper Kern river, from Lake Isabella upstream to Johnsondale Bridge, is open year round. Fishing is also available in the lake and south – couldn't ask for more variety. The valley is home to trout, crappie, bass, bluegill, squawfish, and carp.

The Kern River runs through Lake Isabella reservoir, a recent addition to the valley. Created in 1953 by

the U.S. Corps of Engineers, the lake provides 11,000 acres of water for recreation and commercial interests. The project included relocating Kernville to its present location. Before the dam, the lake area was known as Hot Springs Valley. Now, most of the springs are unavailable for public use. A dozen modern campgrounds and three marinas service the lake, offering serious **fishing**, **water skiing**, and various **watercraft for rent**.

The Forest Service has opened a **Visitor Center** off Highway 155, just south of the lake's main dam. Call the forest service at or 760-376-3781 for information about the lake and surrounding area. The following **marinas** offer fun ways to beat the heat: French Gulch Marina, 379-8774; Red's Kern Valley Marina, 379-1634; and North Fork Marina, 376-1812.

To the north and west of Kernville, you can drive by miles of **incredible scenery** to a grove of giant **old-growth Sequoia trees**.

**Rafters prepare for their first whitewater experience**

Follow the river north 22 miles. As the road veers west, about a mile above the bridge, the 150-foot South Creek Falls is visible from a pull-off. The road levels off at 7,000 feet at Johnsondale. Just beyond town, follow Parker Pass Road to the heart of Sequoia Forest and enjoy the view. After seven miles, turn right on Route 190 and stop at the **Trail of 100 Giants**. Plan some time to wander among the largest living things on earth.

Kern Valley offers a variety of other recreation. The Chamber, 760-376-2629, can provide additional details about the following: **art fairs**, **archery**, **target practice**, **hunting**, **fishing derbies**, **mountain biking**, **motocross races**, **boat and whitewater races**, **windsurfing**, **panning for gold**, and **skiing**. A sampling of **events** follows.

| | | |
|---|---|---|
| Feb, mid | Whiskey Flat Days, *rodeo, more* | 760-376-2629 |
| Feb, mid | Sierra Art Show, *arts and crafts* | 760-378-4109 |
| Mar, mid | Keyesville Classic Mountain Bike Race | |
| Mar, end | Lake Isabella Fishing Derby, *prizes* | 760-379-3867 |
| Apr,begin | Pow Wow International, *archery* | 805-631-9040 |
| Apr, mid | Kern River Races, *whitewater competition* | |
| Apr, mid | Celebration of the Bioregions, *ecology* | 378-2407 |
| May,begin | Whitewater Raft Race, *competition* | 376-2629 |
| May,begin | Discovery Drive Auto Show, *classics* | 376-2436 |
| May,begin | Spring Art Festival, *local artists* | |
| June,mid | Dirt Diggers Kernville Motocross, *dirt bike races* | |
| June,mid | Whitewater Wednesday, *whitewater* | 376-2629 |
| July,end | Personal Watercraft Race, *boat race,L.Isabella* | |
| Sep,begin | Sierra Art Fair, *local artists* | 760-378-4109 |
| Sep, end | Turkey Vulture Festival, *Kernville's favorite bird* | |
| Oct,begin | Kernville Rod Run, *classic cars* | 760-379-4926 |
| Oct, mid | Wild West Daze Rodeo, *rodeo* | 760-376-2629 |

*- RW*

# Oceano and Pismo Beach

## Oceano County Airport

| | |
|---|---|
| **Town** | Oceano    **ID**  L52 |
| **Coord** | N-35-06.08,  W-120-37.33 |
| **Elev** | 14 feet |
| **Runway** | 11rt - 29,  2335 x 50 asphalt |
| **Freq** | CTAF-122.7, Lights-122.7-3x5x7x |
| **Charts** | Los Angeles sectional |

*CAUTION:* Airport information not for navigational use.  Kites, birds, and power poles. Unpaved areas soft and unusable.

11rt

29

> *Oceano is a perfect afternoon fly-in on the Pacific coast. Walk from plane to beach and dunes. Places to eat near by. More in Pismo Beach. Rent ATVs, jet-skis, or horses.*
> *$20 - $250. Info: 800-443-7778.*

## Airport Description

Look for the airport less than a half mile from the ocean beach. There are no mountains or high obstructions in the area. In summer, low stratus sometimes covers the coast until noon.

## Services, Lodging, and Transportation

Airport phone: 805-473-2001. Fuel: 100 octane. Overnight tiedown is $5. Camping is permitted at the airport for an additional $3. Water and rest rooms are available. Just two minutes from the FBO is a park with picnic tables, barbecue pits, playground gear, and a duck pond. Campgrounds with showers are located within five minutes of the field.

| | | | |
|---|---|---|---|
| Cliffs at Shell Beach | RT | $160-413 | 805-773-5000 |
| Crystal Rose B&B | BHRT | $77-196 | 805-481-5566 |
| Edgewater Motel | C | $66-149 | 805-773-4811 |
| Pismo Landmark B&B | CHP | $87-127 | 805-773-5566 |
| Sandcastle Inn | CP | $121-197 | 800-822-6606 |
| Sea Crest Motel | T | $83-105 | 805-773-4608 |

The closest motels are located three miles north in Pismo Beach. Crystal Rose has an excellent restaurant.

The Oceano/Pismo area has over three dozen options for lodging. For help finding lodging that meets your needs, call 800-443-7778, Monday through Friday.

Oceano and local beach are a ten minute walk from the airport. A brisk pace will get you to Pismo Beach in one hour. If someone at the FBO can't give you a lift, Yellow Cab will take you there for $8, 805-489-1155. Enterprise rents cars Monday through Saturday noon, 800-RENT-A-CAR.

## Oceano

Oceano is perfect for a fly-in afternoon of play at the beach. Plan on arriving after noon and chances are, summer cloud cover will be gone when you arrive. Enjoy a **picnic** on the beach or eat at one of four **restaurants** within a ten minute walk. You have a choice of fish-and-chips, Mexican, Greek, or Italian.

**Parent supervises construction project at Oceano**

Oceano caters to lovers of sand, salt, and sun. Kites Galore sells a variety of **kites** and other fun **surf-side toys**. On the beach, you can rent 4-wheel **ATV sand vehicles**, which you can spin through the Pismo Dunes to the south. Rental packages include a one-person vehicle, helmet, and goggles. Prices start at $25 per hour and drop as time increases. If vehicles are unavailable at Oceana, call one of the ATV outfits at Grover Beach for pickup. Other options include **horse rental** and **jet-ski rental**.

If you decide to stay the night, why not enjoy the local culture at the **Great American Melodrama theater** in on Highway 1 in Oceano? Join the fun – cheer, laugh, boo, and hiss until you're red in the face. Tickets are $13 to $16.50 and reservations are recommended, 805-489-2499.

**Rent an ATV and tackle the dunes south of Oceano**

## Pismo Beach

If you choose to stay a day or two, don't miss the fun at Pismo Beach and area. With a focus on outdoor sports, festivals, and active night life, Pismo Beach typifies an old-fashioned California beach town.

Visit their new **million-dollar pier**, great for casting a line or just watching ocean and people. No license is required, and you may find a Red Snapper or Ling cod on your line. Throughout the year, **surfers** brave the waves in competition near the pier. **Triathlons** and **beach runs** give amateur athletes a chance to kick up the sand. You can **rent a horse** from Livery Stables for $20/hr and ride on the beach or elsewhere, 805-489-8100.

The Pismo Clam is usually the largest on the California coast. You can **dig for clams**, but you must have a license. Licenses

**Pismo Beach's Million Dollar Pier**

are available from sports shops and some liquor stores. Note the regulations regarding size, quantity, and times. To get results, you will need a bucket and a potato fork or similar tool with one-foot prongs.

Clam lovers will want to attend the **Pismo Beach Clam Festival** every October. In addition to a clam chowder cook-off, the clam festival offers a weekend of live entertainment and events. Competitions include fishing derby and the ever popular clam dig.

South of Pismo at Grover Beach, thrill-seekers can rent three- and four-wheel **ATVs** (All Terrain Vehicles) from: Arnie's ATV Rentals, 805-473-1610. Call for pickup from the airport. Speed through the dunes for two hours for $40-80.

Pismo Beach is home of some of California's more beautiful and exciting **golf courses**: Black Lake Golf Course (public) and San Luis Golf and country club (private). The oceanfront Pismo State Beach course, a 9-holer, is also popular. Several **tennis courts** are available in and around Pismo Beach.

A short distance to the southeast is Lake Lopez, 805-489-2095. Here you will find **camping**, **water skiing**, **windsurfing**, **canoeing**, **horseback riding**, **motor boating**, **sailing**, and **water slide**. On the way, you pass some beautiful scented **flower fields** which are usually in bloom in late summer.

San Luis Obispo County is fast becoming a popular place for wine tasters. Eight **wineries** are located within five to eight miles of Pismo Beach, and over twenty are located in the northern portion of the county.

Pismo Beach sponsors several **festivals** per month year-round: surfing contests, jazz festivals, Custom Car Show, World's Worst Poetry, Annual Clam Festival, and more. For dates and details, call the Convention and Visitors Bureau at 800-443-7778.

*- RW*

# Palm Springs
## San Jacinto Wilderness

### Palm Springs Airport

| | |
|---|---|
| **Town** | Palm Springs  **ID**  PSP |
| **Coord** | N-33-49.72, W-116-30.34 |
| **Elev** | 462 feet |
| **Runway** | 13R-31Lrt, 8500x150 paved |
| | 13L-31Rrt, 4952x75 paved |
| **Freq** | ATIS-118.25,  Twr-119.7, |
| | Gnd-121.9,  Lights-119.7-3x5x7x |
| **Charts** | Los Angeles sectional, L3, Lo4 |

*CAUTION:* Airport information not for navigational use.  High mountains surrounding desert valley.

Photo, courtesy of Nathan Levine, Sky-Flite Aerial Photography, Palm Springs

> *Palm Springs, an entertainment town in its*
> *own right, and doorway to the San Jacinto*
> *Wilderness. Ride a tram to mountain hiking*
> *trails and enjoy the view. $75 - $250.*
> *Info: 800-34-SPRINGS, www.palmsprings.org.*

## Airport Description

The airport has IFR approaches, parallel runway, and a full complement of services. When approaching the airport at night or in poor weather, be aware of the high mountains on either side of Banning Pass and for several miles west of the airport.

## Services, Lodging, and Transportation

Airport Office: 760-323-8161. All fuel and major repairs are available. AMR Combs Gates at 327-1201 is the more courteous of the two FBOs at the field. Tiedown is $7.50 for singles. A restaurant and coffee shop are located in the terminal.

Palm Springs has well over 100 inns. Accommodations have unique architecture and attractive landscaping; nearly all have a swimming pool. Competition forces them to be service oriented. Some specialize in attracting niche clientele. For example, there are resorts that specialize in families, health, Japanese visitors, and gays.

As a pilot, you can get <u>major discounts</u> on most of the following lodging, ranging from $38 to $100. However, you must make reservations through the AMR Combs FBO.

**Features**

B Full breakfast
C Continental
H Historic
P Pets OK
R Restaurant
T Transportation

| Holiday Inn | RT | $66-160 | 800-622-9451 |
| Hyatt Regency Suites | RT | $88-245 | 800-233-1234 |
| Las Brisas | B | $55-112 | 800-346-5714 |
| Marquis Resort | RT | $113-225 | 800-223-1050 |
| Palm Springs Hilton | PRT | $77-775 | 800-522-6900 |
| Shilo Inn | CT | $77-145 | 800-222-2244 |
| Spa Hotel | RT | $66-200 | 800-854-1279 |
| Wyndham Hotel | RT | $77-145 | 800-972-0264 |

Call 760-322-8380 in the air terminal for the Ground Transportation Information Desk. Taxis: VIP, 322-2264; and Rainbow Cab, 325-2868. A list of rental car agencies follows:

| Avis | 760-327-1353 | 800-331-1212 |
| Budget | 760-327-1404 | 800-527-0700 |
| Dollar | 760-325-7333 | 800-421-6868 |
| Hertz | 760-778-5100 | 800-654-3131 |
| National | 760-327-1438 | 800-CARRENT |

An Aerial Tramway located six miles from the airport provides vertical transportation up into the San Jacinto Wilderness. The tramway has a connecting bus that charges $10 per person from the airport. Taxis charge about $15-18 per group for the same run. The AMR Combs Gates FBO has been known to drive groups to the tramway when not too busy.

The Aerial Tramway, 760-325-1391, is a Swiss gondola suspended by cables that climbs from 2643 to 8516 feet at 700 feet per minute. The tramway was installed in 1963 at a cost of about eight million dollars. Your cost is $18 per round trip. Ask about tram and Alpine Restaurant discount packages. Hours of operation are approximately 9:00 AM to 9:00 PM.

## Overview

The Palm Springs area has golf courses, country clubs, desert and mountain hiking, hot springs, hot air balloon rides, and an active night life. The principal season for valley-floor activities is October through May. For Palm Springs resort information, call the Desert Resort Area Visitor's Bureau at 800-34-SPRINGS.

The new **Palm Springs Air Museum** is a must-see stop for pilots at the airport, 760-778-6262. The museum has over 30 prime WW II aircraft, all of which are flown regularly.

**Balloon rides** are popular in the valley. Flights last approximately one hour and are available from: Dream Flights, 800-933-5628; and Fantasy Balloon Flight, 800-GO-ABOVE. Or, try a five-minute tandem **parachute jump** from 5000 AGL with Parachutes over Palm Springs, 800-535-JUMP.

Windy Point, north of town, is a center for **dune buggy** activity. Rent dune buggies and ATVs from Off-road Rental,

**Palm Springs Air Museum**

760-325-0376. Or, **rent a Harley** from Route 66 Harley Rentals, 800-567-HAWG. Smoke Desert Adventures, 324-5337, offers **jeep tours**. South of town near the Indian reservation, Tree Stables is a center for **horseback riding**, 327-1372.

Palm Springs has two dozen **museums** that cover history, culture, and desert wildlife. The **Living Desert Museum**, 760-346-5694, is a 360 acre **zoo** and **desert garden** that is dedicated to deserts of the world. The facility is in Palm Desert, 1.5 miles south of Highway 111.

Palm Springs has a number of diverse warm-water activities. Oasis Waterpark, 760-327-0499, four miles southeast has an unusual collection of aquatic amusements: **wave-pool,** free-fall and **speed slides**, **hydro-tubes**, and **hot spas**. Palm Springs Swim Center, 323-8278, has an Olympic-size **pool** and high diving boards. The Spa Hotel in downtown Palm Springs, 325-1461, has natural **hot mineral water pools** for $20 per person.

The greater valley is home to 92 **golf courses**, nine of which are in Palm Springs. The town hosts the famous Bob Hope/ Chrysler Classic Golf Tournament and others. Golfers may want to drop by the Poynter Golf Museum, 760-341-2491.

Five **performing arts** centers provide a variety of choices for evening entertainment: Annenberg Theater, 760-325-4490; Plaza Theater, 327-0225; McCallum Theater, 340-ARTS; Palm Canyon Theater, 323-5123; and Top Hat Playhouse, 416-4339.

Palm Springs has an incredible number of **events** throughout the year. For example, the town hosts one of the few winter rodeos, The **Palm Springs Mounted Police Rodeo**, which occurs in late January. The **National Date Festival** occurs 22 miles southeast at Indio in mid-February. This ten-day celebration includes parades, cultural exhibits, music, and **camel races**.

Located high above the desert, **San Jacinto Wilderness** is a place of alpine beauty with convenient access. The tramway lets you hike to San Jacinto Peak, starting from 8516 feet – a mere 2300-foot gain in elevation to 10,804 feet.

You follow trails that meander past pine trees and granite boulders, punctuated by mountain streams and stunning views of the valley. Because snow is a possibility any time of year, hikers should carry a compass in case trails become unreadable.

Depending upon season and day of week, hordes of people may be in the area near the upper tram station, **donkey ride**, and restaurant. You can, however, hike far enough to be free of the masses. Ask a ranger to recommend options.

## Tramway / Round Valley / San Jacinto Peak Hike

The 12-mile hike to the peak and back can be done in one or two days. Thanks to the tramway, elevation gain on this hike is only 2300 feet. The trail to the peak is worthy, and the reward is one of the best views in Southern California. Use the *Palm Springs* topo map for this hike.

Call the Long Valley Ranger Station at 760-327-0222 to reserve a permit. Ride the tramway to Mountain Station. Walk ten minutes to the ranger station and pick up the permit. From the ranger station, walk two miles to Round Valley. The trail to San Jacinto Peak gradually climbs next to a small mountain stream. Round Valley is a dependable source of water.

From Round Valley, follow the trail north as indicated by signs *Tamarack Valley* and *San Jacinto Peak*. The trail meanders for a half mile to the grassy clearing of Tamarack Valley. Visible here is the prominent Cornell Peak, a formation that may tempt experienced climbers. Follow the trail through two miles of switchbacks to the trails from Saddle Junction and Wellman Divide. Turn right and follow the trail one mile to the south ridge of San Jacinto Peak. As you reach the Summit Trail, turn right and follow it 1000 feet to the top. Before reaching the top, you pass a stone shelter built by the CCC in 1936.

Some claim that the view from San Jacinto is Southern California's best. John Muir, a naturalist whose credentials are beyond doubt, exclaimed as he watched a sunrise from the peak in 1936: "The view from San Jacinto is the most sublime spectacle to be found anywhere on this earth!"

You will be unable to witness this spectacle unless you camp overnight, which should be done in designated areas. Campers will have time to return to the tramway by a different route. This increases the round-trip distance by half again as much, but provides additional scenic variety. Follow the trail to Saddle Junction via Wellman Divide. Between the Divide and the Junction, you pass running water at Wellman Cienga. Along this stretch, hikers are rewarded with scenic views into the valley and across Lily Rock and Tahquitz Peak.

At Saddle Junction, a vista in its own right, follow the trail back to the tramway at Mountain Station. The sign says *Willow Creek* and *Long Valley*. Follow the trail through a forest of ferns and Jeffrey pines for one and one-half miles to Willow Creek Trail Camp. Continuing on the trail, you see splendid views of the desert and Santa Rosa Mountains. After Hidden Lake and Desert View, you encounter an intersection. Bear right and follow the trail approximately one mile to Mountain Station.

**Living Desert Museum**

# Solvang

## Santa Ynez Airport

**Town**     Santa Ynez   **ID**  IZA
**Coord**    N-34-36.41,  W-120-04.53
**Elev**     671 feet, W end high
**Runway**   8rt - 26,  2804 x 75 asphalt
**Freq**     CTAF-122.8,  Lights-122.8-5x7x
**Charts**   Los Angeles sectional,  L3, Lo4

> **CAUTION:**  Airport information not for naviga-
> tional use.  Glider, ultralight, and helicopter
> operations.  Depart 26 for noise abatement.

> *Solvang is a working replica of a turn-of-*
> *the-century Danish town:  colorful, tidy,*
> *tempting eats, and a theater for evening*
> *entertainment.  $100-250.*
> *Info:  805-688-6144, www.solvangusa.com.*

## Airport Description

With IFR approach navagation aids, Santa Ynez airport is
easy to locate.  Pay attention to nearby restricted areas and
mountains to the south.  Note noise abatement procedures.

## Airport Services, Transportation, and Lodging

Airport phone:  805-688-8390.  Fuel 80 and 100LL.  Maintenance is available from Sunwest Aircraft, 688-2574.  **Glider
rides** are offered on the weekends by Windhaven Glider, 688-
2517.

Solvang is several miles west of the airport – too far to walk.
Sunwest Aircraft rents cars for $38-77 per day. Yellow Cab,
688-0069, charges $10 per trip between airport and town.   San
Ynez Valley Transit provides bus service, 688-5452.  They run
approximately every 1.5 hours and charge $1.25 per person.

After arriving in Solvang, you can rent a variety of **pedal-
powered carriages** for $12-34 per hour from Surrey's Cycles,
688-0091.  Or, purchase a **horse-drawn tour** through the streets
of Solvang.  The ride takes 20 minutes and costs $5.

| | | | |
|---|---|---|---|
| Alisal Guest Ranch | BRT | $408-505 | 800-425-4725 |
| Best Western King Frederick | C | $70-90 | 800-549-9955 |
| Chimney Sweep Inn | C | $83-300 | 800-824-6444 |
| Danish Country Inn | BP | $76-98 | 800-447-3529 |
| Peterson's Village Inn | C | $148-205 | 800-321-8985 |
| Quality Inn | C | $94-215 | 800-457-5373 |
| Solvang Royal Scandinavian | CRT | $77-160 | 800-624-5572 |
| Svendsgaard's Danish Lodge | C | $53-138 | 800-733-8757 |
| Three Crowns Inn | C | $41-165 | 800-848-8484 |

The nearby Alisal Guest Ranch is an upscale, full-featured **ranch** and **country club resort**. Besides western **horseback riding** on its 10,000 acres, the Alisal offers **tennis**, **golf**, and a number of other activities. The base price of $408-505 for two includes a tasty breakfast and dinner, but does not cover activities. Minimum stay is two nights.

**Features**

B Full breakfast
C Continental
H Historic
P Pets OK
R Restaurant
T Transportation

## Solvang

History of local settlement dates back to 1804 when the Mission Sante Ynez was founded. Though the Mission suffered a turbulent history, most of it still stands at the edge of town.

Today, Solvang is known for its pervasive Danish architecture, food, and atmosphere. This chapter of local history began prior to World War One when a group of Danes emigrated to the Santa Ynez Valley. They named their new home Solvang, which means sunny field. In 1956, a prominent citizen built a windmill home and other Danish buildings around Copenhagen Square. In the thirty years that followed, towns folk have transformed central architecture to "authentic" Danish. You simply have to see it to believe it.

   Solvang is a great site for an overnight visit. You may begin by taking a leisurely **stroll around town**. Professional **shoppers** will need the better part of a day. Other options include **local tours** or **wine tastings**.

   Later, enjoy a dinner at one of the town's many good restaurants. I thoroughly enjoyed the evening play at the **Theater Fest**. Tickets run $11-20; call 805-922-8313 for reservations.

   When you wake next morning, enjoy a **sinful breakfast** at one of Solvang's dozen Danish bakeries. If you have not yet taken the self-guided tour of the **Santa Ynez Mission**, the mission tour is a good way to walk off calories before returning to the airport.

**Danish architecture is literally the rule in Solving**

## Festivals

The **Fairy Tale Festival** in mid July features a wide range of events, including street-corner story tellers. **Danish Days** in mid to late September bring out the local color – dancing in the streets, costumes, parades, etc. **October Harvest Festival** in late October is geared toward wine and beer tasting. Other yearly events include **bicycle rides** and **horse treks**.

Christmas holidays are special in Solvang;  a great time to visit for color and boundless shopping opportunities. Call the Solvang Visitor's Bureau at 800-468-6765 for details on any of the above festive events.

*- RW*

**Shop keepers in costume play a hand of cards after lunch**

Photo by Ed Krieger

# Colorado

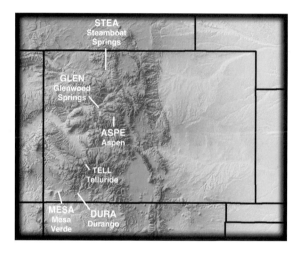

**Colorado Aeronautics**

**303-792-2160**

# Aspen

## Aspen - Pitkin County Airport

| | |
|---|---|
| **Town** | Aspen **ID** ASE |
| **Coord** | N-39-13.39, W-106-52.13 |
| **Elev** | 7815 feet, 2%, S end high |
| **Runway** | 15 - 33rt, 7004 x 100' |
| **Freq** | Twr-118.85, ATIS-120.4, |
| | Gnd-121.9, Apc-134.9, 128.5 |
| **Charts** | Denver sect., L5, L6, Lo9 |

> **CAUTION:** Airport information not for navigational use.
> High mountains, birds, balloons, hang gliders, and ultralights.
> Special procedures. Night operations not permitted for GA.
> Watch mountain weather and density altitude!

Photo by Nancy Rose

> *Aspen and Snowmass, world class ski centers in a*
> *beautiful alpine valley.  Fun to visit any time of*
> *year; wide range of outdoor activities. $120-300.*
> *Chamber:   970-925-5656, www.aspen.com*

## Airport Description

Except for a valley to the southwest, high mountains guard the airport in all directions.  In spite of these picturesque alpine obstructions, Aspen's high elevation, and mountain weather, Alpine airport hosts daily scheduled airline traffic.

Although Aspen has good radar coverage and an IFR approach, I cannot imagine why anyone but a seasoned mountain pilot would opt to make the approach in IMC conditions.  Either way, you arrive and depart under approach and tower control. To avoid mountain turbulence or thunder storms,  plan to arrive and depart before 11:00 AM.

## Services and Transportation

Airport phone:  970-920-2016--0, 920-5384.  Fuel:  100 and JetA; expensive.  Overnight tiedown for a single is $15, and $20 for a twin.  Further, a landing fee of $1.33 per 1000 pounds is charged, and you are charged an additional 10% of your car rental fee if you rent a car at the airport.

My first impression at the airport was, "Hey, this is a service-oriented kind of place!"  Baggage handling, information desk, etc.  The side effects are expense and procedures that you would expect at an airport many times Aspen's size.  Perhaps such attention to detail is prudent at commercial, mountain airports. For less hassles, expense, and elevation, see the Glenwood Springs chapter, **CO-GLEN**.

The following taxi services charge $13-20 per group for rides to town: High Mountain Taxi, 800-528-TAXI; Lightning Limo, 970-925-7505; and Airport Valet, 970-920-9099. Roaring Fork Transport service, RAFTA, gives <u>free</u> rides between airport and town every 15 or 30 minutes. For $6, RAFTA provides service between Glenwood Springs and Aspen, 925-8484.

Reserve your rental car in advance during tourist seasons. All provide service to the airport.

| | | |
|---|---|---|
| Alamo | 800-327-9633 | 970-920-2603 |
| Avis | 800-331-1212 | 970-925-2355 |
| Budget | 800-527-0700 | 970-925-2151 |
| Eagle Rent-A-Car | 800-282-2128 | 970-925-2128 |
| Hertz | 800-654-3131 | 970-925-7368 |
| Rocky Mtn. Rent-A-Car | *no airport fee* | 970-925-2880 |
| National | 800-CAR-RENT | 970-925-1144 |
| Thrifty | 800-FOR-CARS | 970-920-2305 |

Most of the above rent 4x4s for an extra $10 to $20. Blazing Adventures, 800-282-RAFT, and High Mountain Taxi, 800-528-TAXI, offer 4x4 tours through ghost towns and the mountains. Expect to pay about $60 per person for a jeep or bike tour.

Timberline Cycle Center, 970-920-1170, rents bikes for $20 per day and up. Aspen Sports, 925-6331, rents bikes at higher rates. Bicycle tours are popular in the area, and a number of tour services are listed later in this chapter.

## Lodging

Prices for lodging in Aspen range from $60 to $4000, summer prices are lower. Choices include B&Bs, lodges, motels, hotels, condos, mountain-side cabins, and ranches. Aspen's lodging and reservation system is well organized:

| Aspen Central Reservations | 800-262-7736 | 970-925-9000 |
| Aspen Reservations Inc. | 800-421-SKIS | 970-925-4000 |
| Snowmass Central Res. | 800-598-2004 | 970-923-2010 |
| Snowmass Resort Assoc. | 800-598-2004 | 970-923-2000 |

In addition to seemingly unlimited modern accommodations, Aspen has a handful of B&Bs, some of which are rather large:

| Aspen B&B | C | $85-310 | 800-837-5728 |
| Hearthstone House | C | $95-400 | 888-925-7632 |
| Independence Sq. B&B | CHT | $95-400 | 970-920-2313 |
| Sardy House | BHPR | $108-500 | 800-321-3457 |
| Molly Gibson Lodge | CT | $80-400 | 888-271-2304 |

Baby sitting services are available from Baby Sitters Incorporated, 970-923-6080, and a half-dozen others.

## Aspen

What was once a silver mining boom town is now a world class resort. Although Aspen hints of her heritage with Victorian architecture, her focus is on you and your vacation. Aspen and Snowmass are expertly designed for visitors.

Winter sports, zesty luxury, and service are words that describe my impressions of the town. Even in summer, you can't ignore the impact of winter sports on this berg. Ski slopes tower above the village and ski lifts can be boarded several blocks from the center of town.

Though winter is Aspen's biggest season, summer offers advantages of easier flying conditions, lower prices, and diverse activities. Raft trips, hiking, horseback rides, golf, parasailing, music, and theater are samples from Aspen's summer menu.

The Aspen Chamber Resort Association has put together a number of **affordable summer packages**. Attend five days at the Aspen Music Festival with prices starting as low as $60 per person for room and entertainment. Their four-day Outdoor Adventure package includes lodging and four half-days of **rafting**, **downhill biking**, **back-country 4x4 riding**, and **horseback riding**. Some of these are surprisingly affordable. For information, call 800-262-7736 or 970-925-9000.

In town, you can spend a day or two simply **browsing the shops**. Shop keepers seem hospitable, receptive, and delighted to have people come in and just visit. Stores are well stocked. You'll find **jewelry stores** with discounted prices on Indian-made jewelry and western-style goods, over two dozen **art galleries**, and wonderful **sporting goods stores**. The Ute Mountaineer is a great place to get maps and advice on **where to hike**.

When your feet get tired, find an ice cream shop or outdoor restaurant.  Or, ride the **Silver Queen Gondola** to Aspen Mountain peak for lunch at the Sundeck Restaurant.

With two of the most spectacular **golf clubs** in the Rockies, Aspen and Snowmass have become popular with duffers.  The Snowmass Lodge and Golf Club Links, 970-923-3148, was designed by Arnold Palmer and Ed Seay.  The City of Aspen Municipal Golf Course, 925-2145, is located one half mile west of town.  **Tennis courts** are abundant in the area.

You can start the day with a **balloon ride** from one of several companies: Above It All Balloon Company, 888-927-9696; Blazing Adventures, 800-282-RAFT: or Unicorn Balloon Company, 800-468-2478.  Expect to pay about $175 per person.  Paragliding Incorporated, 970-925-7625, offers tandem mountain **paraglider rides** and private training.  Contact Gliders of Aspen, 925-3694, for conventional **glider rides**.

**Downhill bicycle tours** are openly advertised, and torturous uphill bicycle tours are available by special request.  Blazing Adventures, 800-282-RAFT, and Timberline Cycle Center, 970-920-1170, offer a variety of downhill and mountain bike tours.

**Whitewater adventures** are a speciality of the area.  The Aspen **Kayak** School teaches classes for $400 per week, or $300 per weekend.  Aspen Kayak and other whitewater experts offer half-day to one-week excursions:

| A Aspen Adventure | *canoe, raft* | 800-920-4386 |
| Aspen Kayak School | *kayak* | 970-925-4433 |
| Blazing Paddles | *balloon, horse, raft* | 800-282-RAFT |
| Colorado Riff Raft | *paragliding, raft* | 800-759-3939 |
| River Runners | *raft trips* | 719-539-2144 |

The Rocky Mountains are perfect for summertime **horseback adventures**. The following **outfitters** offer experiences from **lunch-rides** to week-long **pack trips**:

| | | |
|---|---|---|
| Bush Creek | *hourly, dinner* | 970-923-4252 |
| Capitol Peak Outfitters | *hourly, pack* | 970-923-4402 |
| Moon Run Outfitters | *day, pack* | 970-923-4945 |
| Rocky Mtn. Cattle Moovers | *cattle drives* | 800-826-9666 |
| T-Lazy-Seven Ranch | *lunch, hay, pack* | 970-925-4614 |

Looking for something different? Aspen Alpine Guides, 800-643-8621, and Aspen Expeditions, 970-925-7625, will teach you **rock climbing** in their half- to multi-day classes. Or, for $40-60 per person, you can enjoy a gourmet **llama lunch trip** from Llama Treks, 925-1971. The T-Lazy-7 Ranch, 925-4614, offers a range of **western experiences**, including **stage-coach** and **hay rides**.

While A. Aspen Adventures offers a unique **tour** of Aspen's rich and famous homes, most visitors opt to tour the mountains. The following offer **4x4 rides** that take you through spectacular scenery to old mining sites .

| | | |
|---|---|---|
| A. Aspen Adventure | *jeep tours* | 800-920-4386 |
| Alpine Safaris | *jeep tours* | 970-925-6643 |
| Aspen Readhead Tours | *jeep tours* | 800-560-3451 |
| Blazing Trails | *jeep tours* | 800-282-RAFT |

Before the day ends, consider making reservations for evening entertainment. The historic Wheeler Opera House, 920-5770, continues to present **ballet**, **concerts**, and other entertainment. June through August, you can enjoy **Theater in the Park**, 925-6813. Check with the Chamber for festivals, 800-26-ASPEN.

The following **outfitters** meet the needs of **hikers**, **fisher-men**, and **hunters**, from novice to serious sportsman:

| | | |
|---|---|---|
| Aspen Alpine Guides | *hiking* | 800-643-8621 |
| Aspen Outfitters | *fishing, hunting* | 970-925-3406 |
| Aspen Sports, Inc. | *fishing* | 970-925-6332 |
| Aspen Trout | *fishing guides, supplies* | 970-920-1050 |
| Capital Peak Outfitters | *pack trips...* | 970-923-4402 |
| Bush Creek Stables | *fall hunting* | 970-923-4252 |
| Elk Mountain Guides | *hiking* | 970-920-2659 |
| Oxbow Outfitting | *fly fishing, hunting* | 800-421-1505 |
| T-Lazy-Seven Ranch | *pack trips, fishing* | 970-925-4614 |

Aspen, of course, is acclaimed as a world-class **ski center**. Aspen Mountain is the closest ski hill, being located literally at the edge of town. Walk several blocks from the center of town, hop a ski lift or the Silver Queen Gondola. Within minutes you

are in skiers heaven.  The **gondola** takes you up 3267 vertical feet to the 11,212-foot peak.  Snowmass Ski Area is eleven miles from Aspen and is accessible by shuttle bus.  Snowmass has an awesome array of runs, with maximum vertical rise of 3555 feet.  Buttermilk Mountain and Highlands are the other local hills.  Call 800-525-6200 for information about ski areas.

**Dinner sleigh rides** are provided by Snowmass Stables, 970-923-3075, and T-Lazy-7 Ranch, 925-4614.  The T-Lazy-7 also rents **snowmobiles**.  Krabloonik Kennels gives **dogsled rides**, 923-4342.  Their gourmet lunch package costs $195 per person.  Contact Ashcroft Ski Touring at 925-1971 for **cross-country ski tours**.

## Events and Festivals

Aspen has a continuous flow of events throughout the year.  The Aspen **Theater** Company, Snowmass/Aspen Repertory Theater, and Annual Aspen **Music Festival** give performances through the summer months.  A sampling of other **major summer events** follows:

| | |
|---|---|
| June, mid | Aspen/Snowmass Food and Wine Classic |
| June, mid | Dance Aspen Summer Festival |
| June,late | Jazz Aspen Festival |
| June,end | Snowmass Hot Air Balloon Festival |
| June, end | Aspen Air Show |
| July 4th | Parade, Fireworks, Race... |
| July, mid | Buttermilk Mtn. Festival of Arts & Crafts |
| Aug, end | Tour of Aspen Mountain & Road Bike Races |
| Sept, end | Aspen FilmFest |

For the latest updates and more information, call the Aspen Visitor's Center at 800-26-ASPEN.

*- RW*

# Durango and Silverton

## Animas Air Park Airport

| | |
|---|---|
| **Town** | Durango **ID** 5CO0 (5c-o-zero) |
| **Coord** | N-37-12.19, W-107-52.15 |
| **Elev** | 6684 feet, 0.8%, N end high |
| **Runway** | 1rt -19, 5000x50' asph/grav. |
| **Freq** | CTAF-122.8, AWOS-135.17 |
| **Charts** | Denver sectional, L5, Lo9 |

**CAUTION:** *Airport information not for navigational use. Mountains nearby. Airport on 200' mesa. Check density altitude. Depart 19 unless tail wind is greater than 10-15 knots.*

> *Durango is a lively town with western entertain-*
> *ment, interesting shops, and good restaurants.*
> *Silverton is an enchanting mining town with*
> *charm and history to spare.  The two are con-*
> *nected by a coal-fired steam train.  $110 - $250.*
> *Durango:  800-525-8855, www.durango.org*
> *Silverton:  800-752-4494, www.silverton.org*

## Airport Description

Durango has two airports, Animas Airpark and La Plata County. Durango Animas is closest, located about four miles south of town. The runway sits on a 200-foot mesa, with hills and high mountains (over 13,000 feet MSL) located to the north.

The strip is paved and is in good condition. The south end is 50 feet lower than the north end. Runway 1 is the default for arrivals. Due to the runway grade, consider departing on Runway 19 unless winds favor an up-hill departure.

Runway lights may be requested in advance by phone.

## Airport Services

Animas Airpark phone: 970-247-4632. Fuel: 100 amd JetA. Airframe and powerplant repair are available for small aircraft. There is a $5 landing fee and a $5 tiedown fee. Free camping is permitted within a grove of trees northwest of the service area. If you plan to rent a car, consider landing at La Plata County Airport.

Returning to Animas Airpark by car can be tricky, especially since local tourist maps are misleading. From Durango, follow 550 and 160 east. At the stop light after Motel 8, make a right and quick left at the Animas Air Park sign. Continue following signs to the airport.

## Transportation

Bus and Limo services run between Durango and La Plata County Airport. Limo cost is $15 per person; call Durango Transportation at 970-259-4818 for taxi or limo service. Asterisks denote rental agencies at La Plata County Airport:

| | | |
|---|---|---|
| Avis * | 800-331-1212 | 970-247-9761 |
| Budget * | 800-527-0700 | 970-259-1841 |
| Dollar * | 800-421-6868 | 970-259-3012 |
| Enterprise | 800-325-8007 | 970-385-6860 |
| Hertz * | 800-654-3131 | 970-247-5288 |
| National * | 800-CAR-RENT | 970-259-0064 |
| New Country Ford | | 970-385-4822 |
| Rent-A-Wreck | 800-421-7253 | 970-259-5858 |

New Country Ford, Enterprise, and National will pickup from Animus Airpark. Rent-A-Wreck has 4x4s in Durango. In Silverton, you can rent 4x4s from Silver Summit, 800-574-8679; or Triangle Service Station, 387-9990.

The hottest recreational transportation opportunity in town is the historic **Durango and Silverton Narrow Gauge Railroad**, which runs between Durango and the mountain mining town of Silverton. Round trip fare is $49. Make arrangements <u>in advance</u> by calling 970-247-2733. **Stage coach rides** are available near the train station at 6th and Main.

# Lodging

Durango supports over four dozen inns, motels, and hotels. Prices for double occupancy range from $35 to over $100 per unit. Call Purgatory/Durango Central Reservations at 800-525-0892 to arrange accommodations. The local Chamber is another good source of information, 800-525-8855 or 970-247-0312.

| | | | |
|---|---|---|---|
| Best West. Mtn. Shadow | CR | $63-103 | 800-521-5218 |
| Iron Horse Inn | PRT | $75-108 | 800-748-2990 |
| Jarvis Suite Hotel | H | $65-120 | 800-824-1024 |
| Double Tree | PRT | $80-325 | 800-222-TREE |
| Strater Hotel | BHRT | $108-210 | 800-247-4431 |
| Vagabond Inn | P | $37-96 | 800-259-5977 |

The Iron Horse Inn gives a $5 discount to AAA members and provides excellent pilot transportation. Every evening they run a van to the Bar D Chuckwagon Dinner and Western Show. The Strater Hotel has a fun location in the heart of town.

**Features**
B Full breakfast
C Continental
H Historic
P Pets OK
R Restaurant
T Transportation

Silverton has a dozen diverse places to stay – 800-752-4494 or *www.silverton.org* for information. Ask for AAA and AARP discounts:

| | | | |
|---|---|---|---|
| Alma House B&B | BHP | $60-109 | 800-259-5977 |
| Grand Imperial Hotel | HPR | $59-163 | 800-341-3340 |
| Teller House Hotel | CHR | $42-74 | 800-342-4338 |
| Wyman Hotel & Inn | BHP | $83-180 | 800-609-7845 |
| Wingate House B&B | C | $90-160 | 970-387-5520 |

You can camp at Silverton Lake Campground, 970-387-5721, just north of Silverton. For $13, they pick you up from the train station and provide a tent-site.

# Durango

Durango, a colorful town of 13,000, is located in the Animas River valley surrounded by the San Juan Mountains. My first impressions were imprinted at dusk: A lively Main Avenue, western-flavored shops and restaurants aglow, and lots of people promenading from train station to river and back.

If you're like me, your first thought at supper time is **food**. No problem in Durango, you will find plenty of enticing alternatives on Main or 6th Street, all within walking distance.

**Shoppers** will enjoy the diversity and quality of shops in the area: jewelry, clothing, leather, outdoor wear, camping gear, and more. Durango supports over a dozen **art galleries**. A **microbrewery** is conveniently located right on Main. By day, you can tour the **train yard**, visit the **museum**, play a round of **golf**, or ride the **steam train** to Silverton – a must! (See the section on Silverton for details.).

At night, enjoy lively **western saloons** or attend a **theatrical production**. For just pure fun, try the Diamond Circle Theater, which presents **old west melodramas** in the Strater Hotel, 800-247-4331. **Old-time music** is played in the Strater's Diamond Bell Saloon. The Sundance Saloon at 601 E. 2nd Street is known for **country and western music**.

Nine miles north of town, the Bar D Ranch serves a **chuckwagon supper** at 7:30 sharp, followed by an entertaining **stage show**. The evening costs $14 for adults and $7 for children. Arrive early to browse the Bar D shops and gallery, or ride the **Bar D train**. The ranch is open nightly from Memorial Day through Labor Day, and reservations are required; call 970-247-5753. Save Tuesday or Wednesday night for the Durango Pro **Rodeo** in town.

Looking for something different?  Visit the **Ute Reservation**, 970-565-3751.  Or, how about a soak in the Trimble Hot Springs. Trimble, 247-0111, is a full-service **hot springs** facility, six miles north of Durango.  Watch **hand-crafted glassware** made at the Harmon Art Glass Company, 259-3976, two miles north of town. **White water rafting** companies provide thrills on the Animas for $12 for an hour to $200 for a day or more:

| | | |
|---|---|---|
| Flexible Flyers | *lowest $, raft* | 970-247-4628 |
| Mild to Wild | *train and raft* | 800-567-6745 |
| Mountain Waters Rafting | *raft* | 800-748-2507 |

Local outfitters can set you up for a half-day **horseback ride**, or for a week-long adventure in the mountains:

| | | |
|---|---|---|
| Duranglers | *fishing* | 970-385-4081 |
| Rapp Guides and Packers | *pack* | 970-247-8923 |
| Silverado Outfitters | *hunting, pack* | 970-387-5747 |

Mountain Bike Specialists rents **bikes**, 970-259-6661.  Durango Singletrack Tours organizes **bike tours**, 888-336-TOUR.

In **winter**, the following offer excellent **skiing** conditions and beautiful views:  Purgatory Ski Area, 970-247-9000, 25 miles north of Durango; and Wolf Creek Ski Area, 731-5605, 60 miles east at Pagosa Springs.  Two smaller hills, Hesperus, 259-3711, and Chapman Hill, 385-2967, are located close to town.  **Cross-country skiing**, **snow shoeing**, **ice climbing**, **ice fishing**, **skating**, and **snowmobiling** can be pursued anywhere in the region. **Sleigh rides** are offered by the following outfits.  Remember to bundle up!

| | | |
|---|---|---|
| Astraddle-A-Saddle | *short rides* | 970-731-5076 |
| Buck's Livery | *rides, x110* | 970-247-9000 |
| Mayday Livery | *sleigh, wagon* | 970-385-6772 |
| Red Mountain Ranch | *sleigh, pack* | 970-247-9796 |

# Silverton

Silverton is located in the San Juan Mountains at an altitude of 9300 feet. It sprang to life as a gold mining town in 1874 after the U.S. Government relieved the Ute Indians of their land. Without the Indians to worry about, prospectors rushed the area. The Denver and Rio Grande Railroad (D&RG) lost no time in building a narrow gauge line to Silverton. After completion in 1882, the town began to boom. Mining reached its peak between 1900 and 1912. Most of the beautiful old buildings you see today were built during this colorful period.

After decades of hard times, the mining industry was given a boost by the American Tunnel, which was driven over to the lower portion of the Sunnyside mine. In 1978, miners were working in an area close to the base of Lake Emma. On Sunday during a major rainstorm, the lake broke through and emptied its contents into the mine. The water flooded the workings and came out through the American Tunnel. Many consider it a miracle that the disaster occurred when no one was in the mine, and nobody was hurt.

After years of hard times, a Florida citrus grower rescued the failing D&RG line in 1981. He financed major improvements and changed the name to Durango and Silverton Narrow Gauge (D&SNG).

Today, the D&SNG is the only regulated, 100% **coal-fired narrow-gauge railroad** in the U.S. Trains make several trips per day between Durango and Silverton, offering hours of sights through the San Juan National Forest. Hikers use the train to **access trailheads** at the western boundary of the beautiful Weminuche Wilderness.

Round-trip tickets cost $49 for adults and somewhat less for children. Reservations are essential. Payment and ticket pickup is awkward and inefficient, so plan well in advance – it's worth the effort. Call 970-247-2733 for reservations. Board the train at 5th and Main in Durango.

You can enjoy Silverton in one day by riding the train up in the morning, enjoying lunch and a walk around town at noon, and returning to Durango by train or bus in the afternoon. Or, do Mild and Wild's **train and raft trip combo**, 800-567-6745. Silverton is very picturesque and you will leave with lasting memories, even if you eat and run.

Should you decide to stay for the evening, consider staying at the Alma House or Wyman Hotel. The historic Teller house offers rooms and breakfast starting at $42. These old inns maintain their 1900-era Victorian charm, while providing modern-day amenities. If you stay the evening, you have time for a

**walking tour**, which takes you by the **County Jail** and **Museum** at the north edge of town.  Evening entertainment for $5.00 is provided by A **Theater** Group, 970-387-5522.

Unlimited **hiking** opportunities to high lakes, breathtaking vistas, or abandoned mine-workings abound. Sportsmen will enjoy lake and stream **fishing**, miles of **4x4 trails** to historic **ghost towns**, and a wide choice of **camping** opportunities. Or, simply take a **relaxing drive** to scenic Ouray.

## Events and Festivals

Durango is a center for **bicycle competition**, with nearly a half-dozen events scheduled each year.  The season begins on Memorial Day weekend with the Iron Horse Bicycle Classic. Over 1500 bike riders challenge the D&SNG steam train over a grueling 50-mile course to Silverton.  A listing of **major area events** follows:

| | | |
|---|---|---|
| May, late | Iron Horse Bicycle Classic | *Durango/Silverton* |
| June,early | Arts and Crafts Fair | *Durango* |
| June,early | Champion White Water Races | *Durango* |
| July 4th | Parade, Music, Fair, and Fireworks | *Silverton* |
| July, mid | Four Corners Gem and Mineral Show | *Durango* |
| July, end | Silverton Jubilee Folk Music Festival | *Silverton* |
| Aug, early | Hardrockers Holidays (mining festival) | *Silverton* |
| Aug, mid | Brass Band Festival | *Silverton* |
| Sept, mid | Christmas in September | *Silverton* |
| Sept, late | Mountain Man Rendezvous | *Silverton* |
| Oct, early | Durango Cowboy Gathering | *Durango* |

Call Durango Chamber of Commerce for details, 800-525-8855 or 970-247-0312.  For Silverton, call 800-752-4494 or 970-387-5654.

*- RW*

# Glenwood Springs

## Glenwood Springs Airport

| | |
|---|---|
| **Town** | Glenwood Springs **ID** GWS |
| **Coord** | N-39-30.50, W-107-18.69 |
| **Elev** | 5916 feet |
| **Runway** | 14 - 32, 3305 x 50' asphalt |
| **Freq** | CTAF-122.8 |
| **Charts** | Denver sect., L5, L6, Lo9 |

*CAUTION:* Airport information not for navigational use. Mountains in vicinity; trees at ends. Deer and other animals. Land 32 and depart 14. No night operations. Watch density altitude.

> *Glenwood Springs, an affordable mountain*
> *resort town, world's largest hot springs pool,*
> *scenic side trips – lots to do:  rafting, horseback*
> *riding, hiking, hunting, fishing, more. $50-200.*
> *Info:  970-945-6589, www.glenscape.com.*
> *Carbondale  Chamber:  970-963-1890.*

## Airport Description

Glenwood Springs airport is three miles south of town in a
river valley that rests between two tall mountain ridges.  Though
winds may be gusty due to nearby mountains, airplanes have
adequate maneuvering space above the airport.

For noise abatement, land on Runway 32 and depart on 14
unless winds require otherwise.  Note that the runway is short
for its elevation, and no night operations are allowed.

## Services and Transportation

Glenwood Aviation phone: 970-945-2385.  Fuel:  100 octane.  Outside tiedown is $5.  Informal camping with rest room
access is available.  At mid-field, Glenwood Aviation rents cars
for $20 overnight, $10 for the day, and charges even less if you
buy fuel.

Alpine Taxi charges about $13 per ride into Glenwood Springs,
970-947-1818.  At specific times of day, you can hop the Roaring Fork Transit and ride between Aspen and Glenwood Springs
for $6, exact fare.  Call 925-8484 for the current schedule.
Western Slope RV Rental rents recreational vehicles, 945-5155.

If the airport cars are unavailable, no problem. Rental cars are plentiful and inexpensive in Glenwood Springs. The following will pickup from the airport, most have 4x4s.

| | | |
|---|---|---|
| Enterprise | 970-945-8360 | 800-325-8007 |
| Glenwood Aviation | *least expensive* | 970-945-2385 |
| Glenwood Springs Ford | | 970-945-2317 |

Glenwood Springs attracts bicycle enthusiasts. Among the sources of rental bikes are Sunlight Ski & Bike Shop, 970-945-9425; and Rock Gardens, 945-6737.

## Lodging

Glenwood hosts over 60 options for lodging, ranging from camping and $25-motels to charming historic hotels and B&Bs. Glenwood Springs Chamber Resort Association can help get you connected, 888-4-GLENWOOD. Or, try Colorado Accommodations, 800-221-0098. Hotel Colorado is a national historic landmark, located east, a block from the big hot springs pool. The low-priced motels are in West Glenwood. A partial list follows:

**Features**

B Full breakfast
C Continental
H Historic
P Pets OK
R Restaurant
T Transportation

| | | | |
|---|---|---|---|
| Adducci's Inn, *G.Spr.* | BHT | $52-81 | 970-945-9341 |
| Back In Time B&B, *G.Spr* | BHT | $92 | 888-854-7733 |
| Hot Springs Lodge, *G.Spr.* | RT | $92-115 | 800-537-7946 |
| Hotel Colorado, *G.Spr.* | HPR | $97-340 | 800-537-7946 |
| Kaiser House, *G.Spr.* | BH | $65-100 | 970-945-8827 |
| Lavender Swing, *G.Spr.* | BHT | $76-87 | 970-945-8289 |
| Riverside Cottages, *rustic* | H | $55-250 | 800-544-3998 |

Also consider staying at a lodge in the beautiful Crystal Valley. Worthy alternatives include the following:

| Avalanche Ranch, *R.* | **BHT** | $80-175 | 970-963-2846 |
| Redstone Castle, *R.* | **BHR** | $112-315 | 800-643-4837 |
| Inn at Raspberry Ridge, *M.* | **BP** | $65-90 | 970-963-3025 |
| Prospect Mtn. Ranch, *R.* | | $42 | 970-963-2323 |
| Redstone Inn, *R.* | **HP** | $32-130 | 970-963-2526 |
| Ute Meadows Inn, *M.* | **BPR** | $75-140 | 888-UTEMEAD |

Inns marked with *R* are in Redstone, and *M* in Marble. Prospect Mountain Ranch is funky, but has a beautiful alpine setting. Redstone Castle has day **spa** facilities, with massage and chiropractor services available.

Rock Gardens, 800-958-6737, is a satisfactory place to camp. Follow I-70 or the bike trail 1.5 miles east of the hot springs pool to "No Name" Exit 119. The facility is at river edge, and the owners run a whitewater rafting operation. Camping costs $19 per tent. Airport transportation is sometimes provided.

## Glenwood Springs

Glenwood Springs is a four-season family resort community. Surrounded by mountain wilderness and located at the confluence of the Colorado and Roaring Fork Rivers, this little town is a base for all types of outdoor seasonal activities, and boasts the largest **hot springs pool** in the world.

Located at the eastern edge of town, Glenwood's Hot Springs Pool, 970-945-7131, is two blocks long and open year-round. The source is Yampa Springs, which produces 4,000,000 gallons of 124.4 degree water per day – said to be the hottest large-scale springs in the world. The large pool is cooled to 90 degrees, and the therapy pool is 104. The water has a slight sulphur smell. Facilities include water slide, kiddie pool, miniature golf, and pool-side dining. Admission is $7.50 plus $1.50 for a towel and $2.50 for a bathing suit.

Hot springs enthusiasts should visit Glenwood's buried treasure: Yampah Hot Springs **Vapor Caves**. Located one block east of the big pool, the facility has **natural steam baths** in underground caves. The name "Yampah" means "big medicine" in Ute Indian language. The Utes originally lowered themselves into the caves with ropes to savor the healthy effects of the vapors.

Today, lighting and stairs have been added, but the process remains the same. Sit in the humid vapors until you can stand the heat no more. Then dose yourself with cold water. Boy, does that feel good!

Admission is $8.75. Their serene on-site spa provides **massage**, **facials**, herbal body **mud treatments**, and private hot baths. Body work costs $32 to $74 per treatment. Call 970-945-0667 for information.

**Largest warm-water hot springs pool in the world**

Golfers can make the rounds on three local **golf courses**: Battlement Mesa, 970-285-9480; Glenwood Springs, 945-7086; Rifle Creek, 970-625-1093; and, Westbank Ranch, 945-7032.

**Shopping** is less sophisticated and less expensive than in Aspen: mostly crafts and sporting goods stores, and a modern covered mall. Two miles south of town on Highway 82 is the Factory Surplus store, with low prices on most surplus gear, sporting goods, and tools. At 10th Street and Grand Avenue, you find a great camping goods store, along with natural foods store and book store. The town's information center is across the street, and well worth a visit.

While in town, consider visiting the following **museums**: Frontier Historical Society, 970-945-3249; or, the Glenwood Springs Center for the Arts, 945-2414.

After dark, you can attend a **movie** at one of two theaters. Or, put on your **dancing** shoes and visit a local pub. Mother O'Leary's is a jumping smoke-filled bar on Grand Street, which caters to the under-thirty crowd (and to thirsty pilots who enjoy dancing, like me). Even younger folks hang out at the Bayou on the west end of town. Both are almost guaranteed to have music on weekends.

Several **hiking** and **biking trails** head for the hills, right from the edge of town. The Red Mountain Trail is short and steep. The views are rewarding, and the 1600-foot elevation gain will burn off excess calories from the night before. The trailhead is at the southwest edge of town, and a nice hiking/biking map is available from the Chamber at 1102 Grand Avenue.

Hanging Lake Trail in Glenwood Canyon is one of Glenwood's most photographed attractions. The trailhead is located nine miles east on I-70, and is open year-round. The somewhat rugged 1.2 mile hike takes you up 900 feet to Deadhorse Canyon. At the top, waterfalls rain into beautiful Hanging Lake.

A number of trails lead hikers up to the Flat Tops, a plateau in the White River National Forest. Also known as the Ute Trail, the Flat Tops were used by Ute Indians for summer migrations and as a path to the hot springs. Ask the Forest Service about the numerous trails in the area, 970-945-2521.

Inexpensive, 1.5- to 6-hour **whitewater raft** trips are offered by the following providers:

| | | |
|---|---|---|
| Blue Sky Adventures | *rafting: $24-35* | 970-945-6605 |
| Rock Gardens | *rafting: $23-59* | 800-958-6737 |
| Whitewater Rafting | *rafting: $23-59* | 970-945-8477 |

Glenwood Springs is a center for **hunting**, **fishing**, **trail rides**, and **pack trips**. Local outfitters:

| | | |
|---|---|---|
| AJ Brink Outfitters | *fishing, riding* | 970-524-9510 |
| Canyon Creek Outfitters | *riding, fishing* | 970-984-2000 |
| Funland, Inc. | *horseback riding* | 970-945-5278 |
| Roaring Fork Anglers | *wade, float trips* | 970-945-0180 |
| Rocky Mtn. Cattle Moovers | *cattle drives* | 800-826-9666 |
| Sunlight Stables | *trail rides* | 970-945-5500 |
| Twin Pines Stables | *Marble: riding, packs* | 970-963-1220 |

In winter, Glenwood's Ski Sunlight **ski** facility springs to life. The hill is ten miles southwest of town and features four lifts, 2010 feet maximum vertical drop, and over 20 km of groomed cross-country ski trails. Sunlight lays claim to one end of Colorado's longest groomed **snowmobile** trail, which can be traveled all the way to Powderhorn. Contact the Sopris Snowriders Snowmobile Club for information, 970-963-3671. Rocky Mountain Sports rents machines and conducts tours, 945-8885.

For more information about lodging or recreation, contact the Chamber Resort Association, 888-445-3696; or the Chamber of Commerce at 970-945-6589. Contact the White River National Forest office at 945-2521 for information on wilderness recreation.

## Crystal Valley

Crystal Valley, south of Glenwood Springs, offers some of the most **beautiful scenery** to be found anywhere. You will find **outdoor activities** and traces of **history** at every turn. Pack your camera, snack, walking shoes, and rain gear – you're about to treat yourself to an afternoon you'll remember.

Follow Highway 82 ten miles to Carbondale. Turn right and follow Highway 133 into the mountains. You pass the Ava-

**Avalanche Inn**

lanche Inn and other places of lodging listed above. In some places, you can see what is left of the old railroad bed. Soon you will see white hunks of marble lying aside the bank. Years ago, the railway went to Marble, our final destination, where some of the world's best white marble was mined. The Tomb of the Unknown Soldier is marked by a six-ton slab from this mine.

Don't miss the turnoff to Redstone. Turn left, cross the river and drive about one mile into town. Once a coal mining town, Redstone is now a tourist and arts community with **antique** and **art gift shops**. The Redstone Inn was built for housing miners, but is now the home of Redstone's visitors. Just beyond Redstone on your left is the mine-owner's former residence, Redstone Castle. At 1:30, you can tour the castle, which is now a B&B and contains a restaurant. The folks at the castle can connect you to local tours and activities, 970-963-2551. (See Lodging, above.)

**View of Crystal River from art/antique shop in Redstone**

Chair Mountain Stables, 970-963-1232, offers **trail rides** for beginners at $18/hr.  **Fishing** is available in the Crystal River and other spots.  For riverside lodging with on-site **hot springs**, **outdoor tubs**, and **pool**, you can stay at Filoha Meadows, a Christian retreat site several miles north of town, 963-1806.

After enjoying Redstone, continue south and turn left toward Marble.  The road twists and narrows as it climbs;  mountain peaks seem to grow higher.  You pass through a marble dump where eerie white monoliths proudly mock the passage of time.  As you drive into Marble, you see streets that have earned the right to be lazy, weathered buildings that have endured the rise and fall of a mining empire – if only they could tell their tales.

And, was I in for a surprise!  My first clue was an inordinate number of people in town;  it simply did not make sense.  As luck

would have it, I had stumbled on the **annual Marble Symposium**. As an artist pointed me toward the forest two blocks from town, we were jolted by a flash and sudden clap of thunder. The mountain skies had begun their afternoon ritual.

Try to visualize a forest with huge chunks of snow-white marble poking through the green. Bright blue tarps are suspended from tall trees. Red air hoses and yellow extension cords radiate through the woods like tentacles of a giant alien creature. Power tools whine as artists toil to release their dreams in stone. A white eagle is frozen in escape from a block of marble to my left, a pensive face peers out of another. Marble works in progress wherever I look. More lightning, thunder, and now rain. It was surreal.

You can attend the Marble Symposium and create a work of your own. The event runs twice in July each year. Contact the Art Students League of Denver Sculptures at 303-297-1429 for information.

The Colorado Yule Marble Mine closed in 1942, but re-opened in 1990. Crystal River Jeep Tours, 970-963-1991, provides **tours to the mine** and to the historic Crystal City Mine. Tours cost $20 per person for a 2-2.5 hour ride. You can hike or ride six miles on horseback to Crystal City as well. Either way, it's a **photographer's paradise**.

A **private turf airstrip** is located one mile west of Marble. Experienced mountain pilots may land at the strip if they write a "hold-harmless letter" to Robert L. Conger, 4505 S. Yosemite #116, Denver, CO 80237, 303-690-3722. The 4000 foot strip is at elevation 7800; most pilots land east and depart west.

The Avalanche Ranch B&B, 970-963-2846, is a good source of local information about the valley. They have created an easy-

to-read guide that covers the Crystal River Valley. The local
history books at their inn are absolutely fascinating.

## Events and Festivals

Glenwood Springs and nearby communities host from four to
a half dozen events per month. Starting in June, the town
sponsors their Summer of **Jazz** Series on Wednesday nights at
6:30 in Two Rivers Park.

Glenwood Springs is home to several **theater** companies.
The Defiance Theater, 970-945-8418, does shows with a cast of
over 100. The CMC Theater, 945-8619, performs several diverse
pays every year. Thunder River Theater Company, 963-0399,
specializes in Pulitzer prize-winning plays.

The following is a list of major regular events:

| | | |
|---|---|---|
| June, mid | Annual Strawberry Days Festival | *week of events* |
| June, mid | Crystal Valley Balloon Festival | *Carbondale* |
| July, early | Meeker Range Call | *parade, rodeo, concert* |
| July | Marble Carving Symposium | *do it yourself* |
| Feb-July | Dance Festival | *shows, workshops* |
| July, mid | Aircraft Fly In | *antique, unique aircraft* |
| July, end | Carbondale Mountain Fair | *arts, food, music* |
| August | Doc Hollidays | *shoot-out, drama* |
| Sept, mid | Oktoberfest | *entertainment, arts, food, beer* |
| Sept, late | Fall Arts Festival | *at Hotel Colorado* |

Call the Glenwood Springs Chamber at 970-945-6589, or
Carbondale Chamber, 963-1890, for Crystal Valley information.

*- RW*

# Mesa Verde

## Cortez-Montezuma County Airport

| | |
|---|---|
| **Town** | Cortez **ID** CEZ |
| **Coord** | N-37-18.18, W-108-37.68 |
| **Elev** | 5914 feet, middle high |
| **Runway** | 3 - 21, 7205 x 100' asphalt |
| **Freq** | CTAF-122.8 |
| | Lights-122.8-3x5x7x |
| **Charts** | Denver sectional, L5, Lo9 |

> ***CAUTION:*** *Airport information not for navigational use.*
> *Intensive flight training, heliocopters, and crop dusters.*
> *Trees Runway 3. No line of sight between runway ends.*

> *Mesa Verde contains the most extensive and*
> *completely preserved Native American ruins in*
> *the U.S. Park Service development is top-notch;*
> *the ruins and scenery are visual treats. $75-200.*
> *Park Service: 970-529-4461, www.mesaverde.org*

## Airport Description

The Cortez airport is located ten miles northwest of the Mesa Verde National Park. The airport's large runway is easy to spot, 2000 feet below the green-top mesa. Cortez UNICOM is active.

## Services , Lodging, and Transportation

Airport phone: 970-565-3721. 100 and JetA. Tiedown is $3. There are no food services at the airport, but numerous restaurants are located three miles northeast in Cortez.

In Cortez, the Super 8 Motel has rooms for $50-85. Call 800-843-1991 or 970-565-8888 for reservations. Numerous other motels are located in nearby Cortez. Two provide free pickup and allow pets: Turquoise Motor Inn, $65-110, 970-565-3778; and Sands Motor Hotel, $43-83, 970-565-3761.

The Far View Lodge in Mesa Verde Park costs $80-100, depending upon time of year and number of guests, 800-449-2288. Guests get a great view, but no TV in the rooms. The park's campground, Morefield Village, does not accept reservations. Over 400 campsites are available at the Village, which is located four miles after the park's entrance. The $12 tent sites have access to general store, restaurant, showers, and laundry. The lodge and campground are not open in winter.

Call Save-A-Buck Taxi for a taxi, 970-749-5009. U-Save Auto Rental, 565-9168, is at the airport and the only source of cars in Cortez. Their older vehicles rent for $42-up.

## Mesa Verde National Park

To get to the park from Cortez, drive ten miles east on Highway 160. Turn right on the road to the park and pay the $10 entry fee. Drive 19 miles to the mesa.

Because there are so many options, plan your day either at the Far View Visitor Center (open only in the summer) or the Chapin Mesa Museum. The park rangers provide literature, maps, and advice. Food, gasoline, and lodging are available in the park from mid-May through mid-October.

Mesa Verde contains the most extensive and completely preserved **Native American ruins** in the United States. The multi-level villages were preserved because of their sheltered locations in the recesses of canyon walls. They were first inhabited by the Anasazi Indians in A.D. 550. By 1100 to 1300 the Anasazi population peaked at several thousand. Some recessed cliff villages had as many as two hundred rooms.

You can explore several exceptional villages and view other interesting artifacts at Mesa Verde. This is truly a national treasure. Plan on spending two full days in the park.

The park has many interesting sites to visit. Be forewarned that long waits are in store for those in the wrong place at the wrong time. Plan ahead! Here are some tips for making the most of your time:

As you view a fee map of Mesa Verde at the far Visitor's Center, note that you can branch left for Chapin Mesa, or right toward Weatherill Mesa. Either alternative requires the better part of a day.

Of the two, Chapin Mesa is more oriented toward the tour-bus crowd. It has sites you will not want to miss. Balcony House is a must. To avoid a 45-minute to hour wait, arrive at Balcony House 15 minutes before it is scheduled to open. Between visits to the other ruins, you can enjoy a visit to the museum and gift shop.

The right branch, Weatherill Mesa, is less traveled and the more serene of the two.  The long, windy access road apparently keeps buses and RVs at bay.  After arrival at the central parking lot, you move from site to site by tram.  The system is well coordinated.  After making a tram reservation, you can grab a snack while waiting your turn to visit the sites.

If your schedule permits, consider attending a Native American **craft demonstration** at Far View Terrace.  Adults will enjoy browsing the authentic jewelry, which is available at the craft stores located near the four restaurants in the park.  **Horseback riding** trips leave from  Point Lookout.  **Evening entertainment** is provided at the Morefield Campground.  Ask at the park or at your motel for information about Native American-related activities in the evening.  For park information, call  970-529-4461, or 529-4475 for nature tours.

# Steamboat Springs

## Steamboat Springs Airport

| | |
|---|---|
| **Town** | Steamboat Springs **ID** SBS |
| **Coord** | N-40-30.98, W-106-51.98 |
| **Elev** | 6878 feet |
| **Runway** | 14 - 32, 4452 x 100' asphalt |
| **Freq** | CTAF-122.8 |
| | Lights-122.8-3x5x7x |
| **Charts** | Cheyenne sect., L8, Lo7, Lo9 |

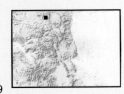

> *CAUTION:* Airport information not for navigational use. Hills and mountains surround. Balloons, gliders, hang gliders, and deer. Watch density altitude, mountain weather.

32

14

> *Steamboat Springs, a downhill ski center and*
> *home of international ski jumping trials.  In*
> *summer, Steamboat reveals its western heritage,*
> *offering: whitewater, hot springs, riding, hunting,*
> *fishing, and backpacking.  $80-200.*
> *Info:  970-879-0880, www.steamboat-chamber.com.*
> *Res:  800-922-2722, www.steamboat-ski.com.*

## Airport Description

The Steamboat Springs airport sits in Colorado's northern
Rockies, two miles west of town.  Airport authorities make a
point of cautioning unfamiliar pilots against visiting, especially
in marginal weather.  In favorable weather, I feel Steamboat
Springs is a safe destination for pilots with mountain experience.

## Services, Transportation, and Lodging

Airport phone:  970-879-1204 for Steamboat Aviation.  Fuel:
100LL JetA.  Tiedown is $6 for singles.  They may have a
courtesy car by the time you read this.

Alpine Taxi Limo, 970-879-TAXI, carries couples to town for
about $10.  Due to the lack of rental cars at Steamboat, consider
landing at Hayden Airport.

| Avis, *Hayden* | 800-331-1212 | 970-879-3785 |
| Hertz, *Hayden* | 800-654-3131 | 970-276-3304 |

Several shops in town rent bicycles: Awsome Cyclery, 970-
879-8989;  Ski Haus Conoco, 879-0385; and Sore Saddle Cyclery,
879-1675.

Steamboat has over a hundred places to stay. Special Places, 800-848-1960, is a lodging reservation service for private duplexes, homes, and condos . Steamboat Reservation Services handles all kinds of lodging and offers interesting package deals. For prices that range from $125 to $250 per person, you can purchase a multi-day package that includes **balloon rides**, **gondola rides**, **rodeos**, **hot springs**, **vintage car races**, etc. Call 800-922-2722 or 970-879-0740 for details.

**Features**

B Full breakfast
C Continental
H Historic
P Pets OK
R Restaurant
T Transportation

| | | | |
|---|---|---|---|
| Bristol Hotel | BHPR | $65-200 | 800-851-0872 |
| Caroline's B&B | B | $94-121 | 800-856-4029 |
| Crawford House | BH | $45-65 | 970-879-1859 |
| Elk River Guest Ranch | | $130-185 | 800-750-6220 |
| Old Town Inn | H | $55-137 | 800-355-0484 |
| Sheraton Steamboat Resort | PR | $115-400 | 800-848-8877 |
| Steamboat B&B | BH | $99-170 | 970-879-5724 |
| Strawberry Park Hot Spr. | | $20-45 | 970-879-0342 |

## Steamboat Springs

Long before Steamboat Springs was discovered and developed by the white man, Ute Indians claimed the area as their summer playground. Abundant game and the inviting waters of numerous hot springs made the area a true paradise.

White trappers appeared in the mid 1800s and gave Steamboat Springs its modern-day name. Of the area's some 100 hot springs, one steamer made a unique chugging sound. At a distance of 200 yards, the spring reportedly sounded like a steamboat laboring upstream. Though it still flows just east of the depot, it lost its voice when the railroad bed was cut through at the turn of the century.

By 1913, Steamboat Springs was a thriving ranching and coal mining community. A Norwegian visitor spotted the hill across from the Yampa river and decided to make it a ski jump. Though locals were amused by the foreigner's crazy plan, it became a quick success. In 1914, the worlds best ski jumpers descended on the hill for a meet. The famous Steamboat Winter Carnival was born. Today the hill is a site of major national and international Nordic skiing competitions.

Steamboat's visitors experience a curious mix of western charm and tourist-town hospitality. While the Norwegian's ski hill looms virtually at the edge of town, the large downhill ski area is a totally separate complex. With this activity focused several miles east, "Old Town" Steamboat has retained a measure of its traditional western flavor.

There's lots to do in Steamboat and the town's social calendar is rich with events. For tips about **events** like **outdoor concerts**, check with the Chamber of Commerce at 970-879-0880 or Parks and Recreation at 879-4300.

Lincoln Avenue is the main street through town. If you have time to spare, take a relaxing stroll down Lincoln and browse the shops. You will find a cute **shopping** complex at 7th and Lincoln, and the Information Center is at the west edge of town. Steamboat has over a dozen galleries and art-related stores.

The Silver Bullet **Gondola Ride** is another way to have a couple of hours of fun. Located at the ski hill, the gondola takes you up thousands of feet to **hikes**, **horseback rides**, and food at the top. Enjoy a BBQ lunch at Thunder Deck, or Saturday dinner or Sunday brunch at Hazie's. The Routt National Forest offers horse or **hayride** combos from the gondola, as well. A wide variety of **free music** is staged at Gondola Square, evenings 5:00-7:00 in summer. Call 970-879-7300 for info, and note that the ride is closed on some days.

Steamboat Springs has two **hot springs** facilities. The Steamboat Health and Recreation Pool, 970-879-1828, is located on Lincoln at the east edge of town. Its pools are 82 and 100 degrees Fahrenheit, and it has a wonderful **hydro slide** which works year-round. Other features include weight room, sauna, massage, and child care. Entry is $6 and the slide costs $4 per ten rides. Hint: I don't care how old you are, try the slide!

Strawberry Hot Springs, 970-879-0342, is a natural facility located in the hills outside of town. It is rustic and pretty, surrounded by forest and tall trees – an inverse image of the in-town facility. Bring your own drinking water and food. Clothing is optional, or change into your bathing suit in a tepee. Relax in cascaded pools and watch the deer visit the springs. The cost for the springs is $5-10 per day. Campsites, tepees, and cabins cost $20-45. Strawberry is eight miles north of town; the last 3.6 miles is dirt road.

Fish Creek **Falls**, just three miles east of town, is a great spot for a **picnic**. The kids will enjoy hand-feeding the chipmunks, and the 283-foot falls provide a perfect backdrop for family photos. The Falls serve as a trailhead for hiking into the mountains. You can follow Fish Creek Trail 6.7 miles past the Continental Divide to Long Lake at 9850 feet. Trails take you along the Divide and to lakeside campsites.

**Golf** enthusiasts can get their fix at the Sheraton Golf Club, 970-879-1391, or Steamboat Golf Club, 879-4295.

On hot summer afternoons, **tubing** the Yampa is a preferred low-cost activity. Rent your inner tubes from Backdoor Sports at 9th and Yampa or from Boinkers at 11th and Yampa. **Boats** can be rented at Steamboat Lake Marina, 970-879-7019. Steamboat Lake Outfitters rents **horses** and 4-wheel **ATVs**, 879-4404.

Friday and Saturday evenings at 7:30, you can see the **Pro Rodeo** for $7, 970-879-4300. Several of the outfitters listed later offer afternoon rides followed by dinner. I had a satisfying meal and good laughs at the Ore House **dinner theater**, 879-1190. The 7th Street Playhouse Theater, 879-3254, and Community Players, 879-9596, produce dance and theater all summer long. Check the papers for local events. The **ice skating rink** is covered, and is another spot to check for events.

The Yampa Valley is one of the most serene, forgiving, beautiful places to **fly a balloon** in the U.S. Within the bowl of the valley, balloonists find incredibly maneuverable winds that often allow them to circle back to their takeoff site. Prices range from $85 to $250 for flights from 15 minutes to the ultimate, a 1.5 hour flight over the Continental Divide. Try one of the following: Balloons over Steamboat, 970-879-3298; Pegasus Balloon Rides, 800-748-2487; Wild West Balloon, 970-879-7219.

**Steamboat Springs Health and Recreation Pool hot springs**

The Yampa River, right through town, is a classic run for both experienced and beginning kayakers.  The Yampa River Park, across from the downtown hot springs pool, is a mile-long **whitewater park** – one of only a few in the world.  It consists of long poles, cables, and gates.  For **kayak training** or **treks**, contact Mountain Sports Kayak School, 970-879-8794, or Steamboat Kayak School, 879-6249.  **Whitewater outfitters**:

| | |
|---|---|
| Bucking Rainbow Outfitters | 970-879-8747 |
| Buggywhip's Fish & Floats | 800-759-0343 |
| Canyon Canoeing Adventures | 970-870-8127 |
| Colorado River Runs | 800-826-1081 |
| Streamboat Rafting Co. | 888-888-RAFT |
| Western Water sports Inc. | 970-879-7019 |

**Strawberry Hot Springs, eight miles north of town**

**Rock climbing** experiences and instruction are provided by Rocky Mountain Adventures, 970-879-4857. Owing to Steamboat's rich western heritage, **horse-related services**. are abundant:

| | | |
|---|---|---|
| Black Mountain Ranch | *cattle drives* | 970-653-4226 |
| Broken Skull Cattle | *cattle drives* | 970-879-0090 |
| Bucking Rainbow Outfitters | *rides* | 970-879-8747 |
| Del's Triangle 3 Ranch | *meal rides, packs* | 970-879-3495 |
| Dutch Creek Ranch | *meal, rides* | 800-778-8519 |
| Elk River Guest Ranch | *meal, rides* | 800-750-6220 |
| Saddleback Ranch | *cattle drives* | 970-879-3711 |
| Sombrero Ranch | *rides, hunts* | 970-879-2306 |
| Stampede Adventures | *cattle drives* | 970-871-9102 |
| Steamboat Lake Guides | *rides, pack* | 800-342-1889 |
| Sunset Ranch | *meal, rides* | 970-879-0945 |
| Windwalker Tours | | 970-879-8065 |

Colorado hunting and fishing information is available from Colorado Division of Wildlife, 970-879-1870 (at U.S.F.S.). Straightline Sports specializes in fly fishing and conducts fly-fishing schools. There are over two dozen licensed **fishing** and **hunting outfitters** in the area; an abridged list follows:

| | | |
|---|---|---|
| Buggywhip's | *fly & float fishing* | 800-759-0343 |
| Del's Triangle 3 Ranch | *hunting, fishing* | 970-879-3495 |
| Elk River Guest Ranch | *fishing* | 800-750-6220 |
| High Meadows Ranch | *ride, fish, hunt* | 800-457-4453 |
| Steamboat Lake Fishing | *fishing* | 970-879-6552 |
| Steamboat Lake Guide | *hunt, fish* | 800-342-1889 |

## Winter Activities

Steamboat residents claim that their mountains have created more Olympians than any other town in the U.S. Besides their

**ski-jump hill** mentioned earlier, Steamboat is the home of an impressive downhill ski facility.

The **downhill ski** complex is located southeast of town, complete with lodging, dining, and shops. Known for champagne powder and tree skiing, Steamboat has over 2500 acres of skiable terrain with a maximum vertical drop of 3600 feet. Nordic skiers will enjoy the 30 km of groomed track and endless trails through the National forest.

The regular season lasts from early December to early March. Call 970-879-7300 for ski reports, and 800-922-2722 for reservation services.

Local stables offer **sleigh rides** of all flavors, including lunch and dinner. See the list of "horse-related activities" on a previ-

ous page, or call Windwalker Tours for dinner sleigh rides, 800-748-1642.

Like everywhere else in the mountains, snowmobiles have become a major pastime for residents and visitors. A list of **snowmobile outfits** follows:

| | |
|---|---|
| Bucking Rainbow Outfitters | 970-879-8747 |
| High Mountain Snowmobiles | 970-879-9073 |
| Steamboat Lake Outfitters | 800-342-1889 |
| Steamboat Snowmobile Tours | 970-879-6500 |

## Events and Festivals

Steamboat Springs hosts a continuous flow of events through summer months, as well as international-class sporting events in winter. Music and rodeo events fill the summer, summing to a whopping total of 200 events per year!

Call the Steamboat Chamber of Commerce at 970-879-0880 for details. A list of major summer events follows:

Photo: Larry Pierce

| | | | |
|---|---|---|---|
| June,early | Yampa River Festival | *kayak events* | 879-6249 |
| June, late | Western Weekend | *rodeos, poetry...* | 879-0880 |
| June, late | Chili Cookoff & Pepper Root | *eats...* | 879-0880 |
| July,begin | Cowboy Roundup Days | *parade,music* | 879-0880 |
| July, mid | Rainbow Weekend | *balloons, art, food* | 879-0880 |
| Aug, end | Vintage Auto & Art Race | *elegant cars* | 879-0880 |

# Telluride

## Telluride Airport

| | | | |
|---|---|---|---|
| **Town** | Telluride | **ID** | TEX |
| **Coord** | N-37-57.23, W-107-54.51 | | |
| **Elev** | 9086 feet, both ends high | | |
| **Runway** | 9rt - 27, 6870x100' asphalt | | |
| **Freq** | CTAF-123.0, Lights-3x5x7x | | |
| **Charts** | Denver sectional, L5, Lo9 | | |

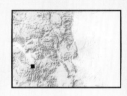

> ***CAUTION:*** *Airport information not for navigational use. Extemely high altitude airport; watch density altitude. Mountainous terrain. Drafts and gusty winds. Hang gliding, helicopter operations, and soaring.*

> *Telluride caters to skiers when it's white, and to*
> *lovers of music and outdoor recreation when it's*
> *green. Pretty as a post card any time of year.*
> *$100-350.  Info: 88-TELLURIDE,*
> *www.telski.com, www.tvs.com.*

## Airport Description

Telluride's airport sits at an extremely high elevation; ponder your aircraft's capabilities and piloting skill before opting to land at this mesa in the sky. Early mornings are safest for arrival and departure. The airport is closed to night operations. Noise abatement is requested. When arriving, fly the highway corridor to Placerville. Turn left and land on Runway 9.

Because temperature changes quickly in the mountains, departure is safest at or before sunrise. In summer months, the sun rises before the FBO opens. Consider settling airport financial obligations prior to day of departure. Depart on Runway 27 and fly to Placerville before turning right.

## Services, Transportation, and Lodging

Airport phone: 970-728-5051. Fuel: 100 and JetA. Telluride Executive Service provides tiedown at $8 for singles, fuel, oxygen, and refreshments. Budget Rental is on site.

Once in town, transportation is not essential. Lodging, restaurants, and shops are all within walking distance. Free shuttle buses run throughout town. Telluride Shuttle and Taxi, 970-728-6667, and Telluride Transit, 728-6000, provide rides to and from the airport for $7 per person.

Telluride rental agencies will service the airport. Telluride Outside specializes in 4x4 vehicles. If vehicles are unavailable, consider landing at Montrose, an 80-minute drive to Telluride.

| | | |
|---|---|---|
| Budget, *airport* | 800-527-0700 | 970-728-4642 |
| Dollar, *Montrose* | 800-421-6868 | 970-249-3770 |
| Enterprise, *Montrose* | 800-325-8007 | 970-240-3835 |
| Hertz, *Montrose* | 800-654-3131 | 970-249-9447 |
| Telluride Outside | 800-831-6230 | 970-728-3895 |
| Thrifty, *Montrose* | 800-367-2277 | 970-249-3770 |

Bikes can be rented from the following for $20-up per day: Olympic Sports, 970-728-4477 and Paragon Sports, 728-4525.

Telluride has lodging for over 3500, but demand can exceed supply during ski season and summer festivals. Prices fluctuate radically, depending upon season and festival. Telluride Central Reservations coordinates bookings for all properties, 888-827-8050. Ask about their vacation packages. Camping is available at the east end of town.

**Features**

B Full breakfast
C Continental
H Historic
P Pets OK
R Restaurant
T Transportation

| | | | |
|---|---|---|---|
| Alpine Inn B&B | BH | $75-250 | 800-707-3344 |
| Bear Creek B&B | B | $75-250 | 970-728-6681 |
| Johnstone Inn B&B | BH | $75-185 | 800-752-1901 |
| Manitou Lodge B&B | CH | $65-330 | 800-538-7754 |
| Mountainside | | $77-200 | 888-728-1950 |
| New Sheridan Hotel | BH | $75-400 | 800-200-1891 |
| Oak Street Inn | | $63-80 | 970-728-3383 |
| Skyline Guest Ranch | | $140-225 | 888-754-1126 |
| The San Sophia B&B | BR | $125-325 | 800-537-4781 |

The Skyline Guest Ranch offers **riding**, **hunting**, and **fishing** in summer, and horse-drawn **sleigh rides** in winter.

## History

Some say Telluride was named for tellurium, a gold-bearing ore in the area. Others claim the name is a corruption of "to hell you ride," after its 1880s reputation for mining, gambling, and infamous brothels.

Until 1900, gold financed the town's growth and bustling activity. Hundreds of miles of mines honeycomb the area. Telluride mining engineers pioneered the use of AC power in mines using Nicola Tesla's power generation and distribution system (the basis of our modern system). As mining profits diminished, the population dwindled to five hundred in the Thirties.

**Telluride Balloon and Wine Festival**

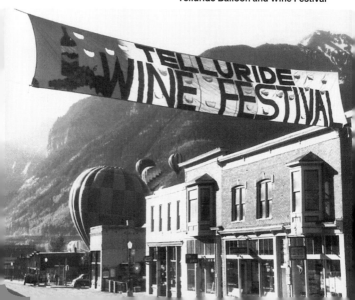

In 1968 a new resource was discovered in the mountains —
skiing. By 1971 the Telluride Ski Area became a reality, and
Telluride boomed once again. Through care and zoning restrictions, it maintains its historic charm.

## Recreation

Telluride lies in an alpine valley between mountains that
tower above its 8745 foot floor. It is clearly one of the prettiest
towns in Colorado. In winter, Telluride caters to advanced and
expert **ski** enthusiasts. In summer it hosts a series of **festivals**,
nearly one per week. Events include film festivals, music, wine
and beer, and sporting events. The Airmen's Rendezvous in
mid-August is a world class hang glider and paraglider meet.

The Telluride Ski and Golf Club has a 6739-yard, par 71 **golf
course** with great views, 970-728-6157. For a more serious dose
of scenery, ride the free **Gondola** from Telluride to Mountain
Village and Coonskin Ridge.

The San Juan Mountains are a limitless resource for outdoor
recreation. Numerous **hiking** trails begin their ascent in town or
at the airport. Destinations include mine ruins, canyons, waterfalls, peaks, and streams — an overwhelming variety. Maps and
info are available from the Chamber of Commerce, Olympic
Sports, and Telluride Whitewater. **Warning:** Drink purified
water only, and entering mine structures is a high-risk venture.

**Fishing** is available at Alta, Woods, Silver, and Trout lakes.
Stream fishing is excellent on the San Miguel, South Fork, and
Dolores. Licenses are available from sport shops like Olympic
Sports, 970-728-4477.

Telluride Outside, 800-831-6230, specializes in outdoor recreation, offering the following diverse list of activities: **jeep
tours**, **ATV tours** and rentals**, whitewater rafting**, **fly fishing**,

horseback rides, and **bicycle tours**. In winter, they provide **sleigh rides, snowmobile tours, helicopter skiing**, and **dog sledding**.

Hot air **balloon rides** can be chartered from San Juan Balloon Adventures, 970-626-5495. Scott MacLowry provides **tandem paraglider rides**, 728-4098.

Paragon Sports, 970-728-4525, rents **wind surfing** gear for use on nearby lakes. **Mountain climbing** services and instruction are offered by Antoine Savelli Guides, 728-3705; and Fantasy Ridge Mountain Guides, 728-3546. Mountain Adventures, 728-6052, does hiking, biking, and **rock climbing for kids**. Learn **whitewater kayaking** from San Juan Paddling School, 729-2579.

Time between dinner and the dance floors can be enjoyed at the Nugget **Theater**, or the Mountain Splendor **multi-image slide show** at the Masonic Hall. After 9:30 PM, dance to live music at the Fly Me To the Moon Saloon or Roma Bar and Cafe. These two hot spots are located across from one another on Colorado Avenue at the east end of town.

Orvis Hot Springs at 970-626-5324 is the closest **hot springs** to Telluride, twenty miles north and 1.3 miles south of Ridgeway on Highway 550. It includes a natural hot mineral pond, private tubs, and lodging. Continue driving to Ouray and you will discover another. Ouray Hot Springs at 325-4638 has a million gallon, continuous-flow pool.

Almost without trying, you can experience a Telluride **festival**. The town sponsors over two dozen festivals per year. Examples are the Jazz Festival, Bluegrass Festival, Wine and Balloon Festival, and a number of film and photo festivals.

*- RW*

Photo by Grafton M. Smith

# New Mexico

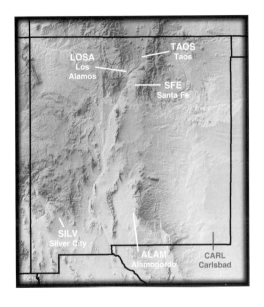

**New Mexico Aeronautics**

**505-827-1531**

# Alamogordo

## Alamogordo White Sands

| | |
|---|---|
| **Town** | Alamogordo   **ID** ALM |
| **Coord** | N-32-50.40, W-105-59.44 |
| **Elev** | 4197 feet |
| **Runway** | 13rt-21, 7005 x 150' asphalt |
| | 16 - 34rt, 3512 x 200' dirt |
| **Freq** | CTAF-122.8, Lights-122.8 |
| | AWOS-127.825 |
| **Charts** | Albuquerque, L4, Lo10 |

**CAUTION:** Airport information not for navigational use. Military traffic. Restricted areas. Mountains NE.

13rt

34rt

16

21

> *Alamogordo, gateway to White Sands National*
> *Park, has an exceptional space museum.*
> *Nearby mountain sites add spice to this*
> *inexpensive destination.  $50-200.*
> *Chamber: 800-826-0294, www.alamogordo.com*

## Aiport

When planning a trip to Alamogordo, note that easy access is
available only from the northeast quadrant, which is guarded by
the Sacramento Mountains.  Except for a narrow access corridor
from the south, restricted areas block travel from other directions.

From a distance, Holloman Airforce Base is easy to spot, east
of the White Sands national monument.  Keep an eye out for
Holloman's stealth fighters, and land at Alamogordo's White
Sands Regional.  The airport has an on-field NDB, ALM at 341
KHz, and Boles VOR a couple miles south, BWS at 109.6.

## Services, Transportation, and Lodging

Airport phone: 505-439-4110; Ed's Flying Service, 437-4330.
Fuel: 100 and JetA.  Tiedown is $3.  Ed's has the feel of an old-
time FBO, a good place to chat while waiting for transportation.
A taxi to the motel district in town costs about $7.  Call Dollar
Cab, 434-8294; or Radio Cab, 437-2292.

There are no rental cars at the airport.  Hertz and National
have pulled out, leaving Enterprise (which does not service the
airport) and two others that will pick you up: Avis is at the
Holiday Inn, 505-437-3140 or 800-331-1212.  And, Rental Cars

of Alamogordo, 439-9723, has inexpensive junkers for $14.95, up. They rented me a Geo without air conditioning. It was a typical sweltering afternoon, so I wise-cracked, "Gee, this must be the only car in Alamogordo without air conditioning." The gal behind the counter answered, "Oh no, I think we have another one."

Motel prices in Alamogordo range from less than $25 for a semi-clean, low-class room, to $60 for the best. Prices and class rise accordingly at mountain resort areas like Cloudcroft and Ruidoso. The Lodge in Cloudcroft is a beautiful high-mountain inn and country club. The Inn of the Mountain Gods in Mescalero has gambling and good food.

**Features**

| | |
|---|---|
| **B** | Full breakfast |
| **C** | Continental |
| **H** | Historic |
| **P** | Pets OK |
| **R** | Restaurant |
| **T** | Transportation |

| | | | |
|---|---|---|---|
| Alamo Inn | | $25 | 505-437-1000 |
| Desert Aire Best Western | CP | $41-55 | 505-437-2110 |
| Hotel Alamogordo | CP | $56 | 505-437-7100 |
| Inn of Mtn.Gods, *Mescalerio* | RT | $106-110 | 505-257-5141 |
| Insbruck Lodge, *Ruidoso* | | $31-52 | 800-680-4447 |
| The Lodge, *Cloudcroft* | HR | $100-237 | 800-395-6343 |
| Motel 6 | P | $38 | 505-434-5970 |
| Super 8 Motel | CP | $43-60 | 505-434-4205 |
| Townsman Motel | | $27-33 | 505-437-0210 |

## Alamogordo

Alamogordo began as a railroad town, a "planned community" even before anyone used the term. The El Paso and Northern Railroad arrived in 1898. Owner Charles Eddy created wide thoroughfares with irrigation ditches lined with cottonwoods. "Alamogordo" is derived from the Spanish name for "fat cottonwood."

Eddy wanted no liquor in his model community. However, he followed the advice of a trusted employee, and limited consumption of alcohol to one city block located across from Eddy's office. The deed of every other lot included a clause prohibiting liquor. Failure to comply meant that ownership would revert back to the company. Amazingly, this provision stayed in effect until 1984.

Today, Alamogordo is known primarily for the White Sands National Monument and the missile proving grounds to the west. After visitors arrive, they discover additional fun sites to visit. Stop by the Chamber of Commerce for maps and brochures. Drive north from the airport through town on Highway 70. The Chamber is located between the zoo and Toy Train Depot.

The **International Space Hall of Fame** is a must-see site. To get to the museum, drive north from the Chamber to Indian Wells Road. Turn right and follow Indian Wells up to the museum. The

**International Space Hall of Fame**

museum and grounds are artfully executed, a real tribute to man's exploration of space. The property includes everything from personal objects to satellites and a massive rocket. Many of the displays are fascinating. For example, instead of displaying a mock-up rocket, they show an authentic cut-away, so you can see how it works. The presentation is educational, but you will enjoy the visit even if you come only to look.

The film at the adjacent **Omnimax** 140-degree wrap-around theater is another must-see. When I visited, they showed a fascinating film that was shot in the MIR space station. The fee for museum and film is $6. In summer, they offer a Shuttle Camp for kids, 800-545-4021. At the air base, you can have a close look at a **stealth F117** on the 3rd Thursday of the month, 505-475-5406.

Another popular spot in town is the **Toy Train Depot**, 505-437-2855. Located near the park and Chamber of Commerce on

White Sands Boulevard, the Depot has over 1200 feet of model train track in the five-room facility. In the past, they operated a miniature train along a 2.5 mile track around Alameda Park. The Depot is closed on Tuesdays and holidays.

The **Alameda Park Zoo** is south of the Toy Train Depot. Established in 1889, it is the oldest zoo in the Southwest. Other nearby places to visit include **Alameda Park** and **Tularosa Basin Historical Society**, adjacent to the Chamber. **Art** enthusiasts should stop by the Eagle Ranch Pistachio Groves, 505-434-0035.

Alamogordo has dozens of **restaurants**, most of which are non-gourmet. The Holiday Inn is a safe bet for breakfast or lunch. More down home, Memories of Millie serves breakfast and lunch in an old house. Kegs serves a wide spectrum of food. Compass Rose is a brew pub on First Street. Angelina's is the place for Italian. For Mexican, try My Place, Ramona's, or Si Senor. The Chinese Dragon serves Chinese American and Mexican food, a curious mix. Yee's Oriental Express serves exclusively Chinese.

While enjoying a satisfying Italian meal at Angelina's, I learned why a number of the signs in town are written in German. Angelina explained that the signs are a courtesy for 3000 German pilots who came to town for military flight training. Existing housing quality fell short of the Germans' expectations. This triggered a housing boom of high-quality housing. Meanwhile, the extra flight training created noise levels that caused farmers to complain about decreased milk production. A battle ensued. Angelina believes the farmers will win, leaving a glut of new houses in the area.

After dinner on some evenings, you can enjoy **cultural entertainment** at the Alamogordo Music Theater, 505-475-5541, and Community Theater, 434-2719. The Flickinger Center has family theater and music performances, 437-2202. Also check the New Mexico State Rohovec Center, 439-3676.

## Outside Alamogordo

Virtually all Alamogordo tourists visit **White Sands National Monument**, 505-479-6124. They come for the sands, really gypsum, white as snow. This is a rare phenomenon because calcium sulfate is soluble in water. The best time for photos is a narrow window of time at sunset and sundown.

The dunes are located 15 miles southwest of Alamogordo off Highway 70. There is no public transportation. Occasionally, Highway 70 is closed due to missile testing. Entrance fee is $3. The Park Service offers various tours, 505-679-2599.

Need a break from the heat? In less than 45 minutes from Alamogordo, you can enjoy the cool mountain air of **Cloudcroft** at 9000 feet. Head north from town and turn right on Highway 82. The 16-mile road climbs 4600 feet to Cloudcroft. In town, turn right and follow signs to the **Lodge at Cloudcroft**, 800-395-6343. The Lodge is an upscale resort with scenic **golf**

**Lodge at Cloudcroft**

**course** and access to a variety of recreation.  They offer **golf** packages in summer and **ski** packages in winter.  The Lodge is a good place to enjoy that special meal.  Cloudcroft has a half dozen diverse restaurants, including a serious BBQ house.

You can **rent horses** from the Chippeway Riding Stables, 800-471-2384.  Cloudcroft Trolley Company, 800-349-4535, offers the same, plus **hay rides** and **sleigh rides**.  Horse lovers should drive north to Ruidoso Downs to visit the race track and **Museum of the Horse**.

In winter, there are various places to **ski** near Cloudcroft. You can rent **snowmobiles** from Tripple M's Snow Play Area, 800-766-7529.  For more recreation information call the Cloudcroft Chamber at 505-682-2733.

The **Sunspot National Solar Observatory** is 17 miles east of Cloudcroft off Highway 82.  You can actually walk into one of the huge telescope chambers and watch scientists do experiments.

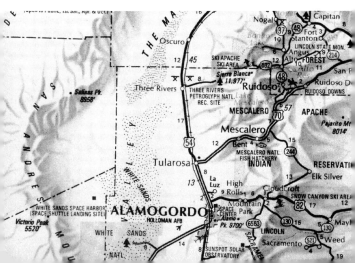

The site is also an excellent vantage point for viewing the valley. The best way to soak up local alpine scenery is to **hike** a mountain trail in the Lincoln National Forest, 505-682-2551.

Those who prefer to do their walking on a **golf course** can pick from the following: Cloudcroft Lodge Golf Course, 800-395-6343; Ponderosa Pines in Cloudcroft, 505-682-2995; Desert Lakes in Alamogordo, 437-0290; Links at Sierra Blanca, 800-854-6571; and public golf course in Carrizozo.

With several days to play, you can explore the territory to the north. The **Three Rivers Petroglyphs Area** , for example, is due north of Tularosa off Highway 54  Continue the drive, and **scenic roads** take you past **historic sites**, **museums**, and through **Native American culture**.  Consider exploring Tularosa, Carrizozo, White Oaks, Ancho, Capitan, Lincoln, Ruidoso Downs, Ruidoso, Mescalero, and, of course, Cloudcroft.

**White Sands National Monument – Yes, it really does look like snow!**

# Carlsbad

## Cavern City Airport

| | |
|---|---|
| **Town** | Carlsbad  **ID** CNM |
| **Coord** | N-32-20.25, W-104-15.80 |
| **Elev** | 3293 feet |
| **Runway** | 14L-32Rrt, 4705x150, asph. |
| | 14Rrt-32L, 5830x150, asph. |
| | 3 - 21, 7854 x 150, asphalt |
| | 8 - 26, 5477 x 150, asphalt |
| **Freq** | CTAF-122.95, Lights-122.65 |
| | ILS-111.9, RCO-122.65 |
| **Charts** | Albuquerque, L4, L15, Lo10 |

*CAUTION:* Airport information not for navigational use. Powerlines runways 32L, 32R, and 26. Arroyo 26. Gliders.

> *Carlsbad is known for the world-class Carlsbad*
> *Caverns. The area also offers hiking, back-*
> *packing and other outdoor activities.*
> *$100 - $225. Chamber: 505-887-6516,*
> *www.caverns.com/~chamber*

## Airport

Carlsbad sits at the southeastern corner of New Mexico. The town's Cavern City Airport is 5 miles southwest of the city. The airport is a complex of four paved runways, the longest measuring 7854 feet. The airport is not obstructed by mountains, nor imprisoned by restricted air space, as are New Mexico airports to the west. Cavern City has ILS approaches that use VOR CNM at 116.3 MHz, 5.5 miles southeast of the airport. AM broadcast station KMAQ at 1240 can be used as an unofficial ADF guide to the area.

## Services, Transportation, and Lodging

Airport phone: 505-887-3060. McCausland Aviation, 887-1500, has 100LL and JetA and offers various repair services. Hertz rental cars may be obtained from McCausland, 887-1500. Enterprise, 887-3039, picks up from the airport. Enterprise has the best prices, but inconvenient hours for weekend travelers. Either way, cars are frequently in short supply; reserve in advance. A taxi costs about $10 from airport to town, 885-5115.

Lodging can be inexpensive in Carlsbad. Prices begin at $20, and you can easily find a tolerable room on Highway 62 for $30. Because it is prudent to inspect before renting a low-cost motel,

$20-30 motels are not listedbelow. White City's Best Westerns have a number of tourist attractions within walking distance of the motels. Low-end prices include tax and AAA or AARP discounts. Motels marked with an asterisk are within walking distance of Carlsbad.

### Features

- **B** Full breakfast
- **C** Continental
- **H** Historic
- **P** Pets OK
- **R** Restaurant
- **T** Transportation

| | | | |
|---|---|---|---|
| * Best Western Stevens | **PRT** | $57-63 | 800-730-2851 |
| Best Westerns, *White's City* | **PR** | $65-77 | 800- CAVERNS |
| Continental | **PT** | $32-50 | 505-887-7800 |
| Days Inn | **CP** | 68-80 | 800-325-2525 |
| | | | 505-887-7800 |
| * Economy Inn | **PT** | $30-45 | 505-885-4914 |
| * Holiday Inn | **PRT** | $78-95 | 800-742-9586 |
| Lorlodge Motel | **PT** | $35-51 | 505-887-1171 |
| Motel 6 | **P** | $34-40 | 505-885-0011 |
| Quality Inn | **PRT** | $51-74 | 800-321-2861 |
| * Stage Coach Inn | **CPRT** | $31-105 | 505-887-1148 |
| Super 8 | **C** | $44-55 | 800-843-1991 |
| | | | 505-887-8888 |

## Carlsbad Caverns

Carlsbad Caverns is the premier developed cave network of the world. To get there, drive 20 miles south on Highway 62 through White's City, and another seven to the caverns. The entry fee is $6, and less for children and seniors.

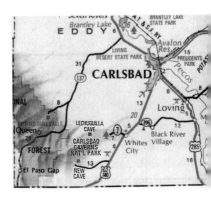

Inside the Visitor's Center, you can ponder your options by inspecting a 3D model of the caverns. I recommend taking the longest walk down and through the caves. You enter at an amphitheater that surrounds a large hole in the ground. The amphitheater is for observing the thousands of Mexican free-tail bats that exit at dusk. The caves are cool, but I was comfortable with a long-sleeves shirt.

I remembered when I visited the Carlsbad Caverns at the age of seven. My parents wanted my sister and I to see the wonders of the west, and this was one of our stops. At the time, I happened to be ill with a high fever. My father carried me through the caves on a sometimes-slippery path of dirt and gravel. The trail into and through the caves is now paved with a high-tech blacktop of emery chips and epoxy glue. Although most of my memories of that childhood trip have faded, I clearly remember experiencing the underground wonderland from the comfort of my dad's arms.

The one-mile trail from the Natural Entrance takes you to a depth of 755 feet. This point has lunchroom, restrooms, and an elevator to the surface. From there, you walk another one-mile loop that tours the Big Room. The two mile circuit requires an hour to an hour and a half. An optional ranger-guided tour leads you another mile through the scenic rooms of the King's Palace.

The cave's geologic history began 250 million years ago with the formation of a 400-mile reef in an inland sea. The sea evaporated, leaving vast limestone deposits. A few million years ago, slightly acidic rain water began dissolving the limestone to produce the caverns. The erosion process was accelerated by hydrogen sulfide gas from below that combined with water to become sulfuric acid.

Well over 1000 years ago, prehistoric Native Americans left mysterious drawings on the cave walls near the entrance. In the

1800s, white settlers were drawn to the cave by spectacular swarms of bats. Some settlers stayed to mine the huge deposits of bat guano for fertilizer. A cowboy named Jim White is credited with publicizing the wonder. In the 1920s, the Department of Interior finally believed the fantastic stories they heard about the cave, and it became a national monument.

For information about the caverns, call the Best Western complex in White's City at 800-CAVERNS, the park's Visitor's Center at 505-785-2232, or visit the park's web site at *www.nps.gov/caca*.

White's City is the gateway to the park. To me, the place looked like a classic tourist trap. Being a tourist, I stopped. In fairness, the Best Western facilities are nice, and the **Million Dollar Museum** was interesting. It contains an antique doll house collection, carriages, clocks, and lots of interesting implements of early settlers. There's an **arcade** for the little ones, and **ice cream** for big

**Photo from a photo machine in White's City**

kids, like me. Granny's Opera house shows an old fashioned **melodrama** on most summer evenings, reservations required.

Just outside of town, I visited the Apache Canyon Trading post to see their collection of **rattle snakes**. This is the kind of place where, as kids, my sister and I would have said, "Mommy daddy, please can't we see the snakes!" The parents would reply, "That's a waste of money," but would occasionally give in. Perhaps that is why I appreciate the art of a good roadside attraction – I paid a buck to see and smell a couple dozen sleepy snakes. Even in captivity, the sound of a rattle gives me the chills! Compared to the cost of my last flight, it was worth the dollar.

Hikers who enjoy **rugged mountain trails** should plan a visit to the **Guadalupe Mountains National Park**, a mountain wilderness area 35 miles south of White's City. The park can be fully appreciated only by foot from 80 miles of trails that criss-cross the

**Apachie Canyon Trading Post, a stop for curios and rattle snakes**

mountains. The easiest access is the scenic McKittrick Canyon trail, a popular site for fall colors. Call Guadalupe Mountains National Park at 915-828-3251 for details.

## Town of Carlsbad and Area

Chances are, you will have time to do additional sightseeing. I recommend visiting the **Living Desert Zoo and Gardens** at the north end of town, 505-887-5516. A 1.3 mile self-guided tour takes you past plants and animals in their natural habitat.

If you stroll around town, you find that Carlsbad has a touch of history and culture. The **Carlsbad Museum** is both historic and artsy. Various **galleries** show a variety of local art: Old Pecos Gallery downtown, Indian Point Art Gallery to the north, and The Artists Gallery at Pecos River Village.

Although I was unable to locate a truly outstanding restaurant, Carlsbad has a number of satisfying **places to eat**. The Red Chimney specializes in BBQ. For Italian, try Manicotti's or the Holiday Inn. Beaver's Restaurant serves fish. Night life and Mexican food can be had at Lucy's Comedy Club. The Elk's Club serves the best steaks in town, members only.

Wild Wade's Fun City, 505-887-0564, offers **family recreation**, including go-carts, miniature golf, and batting cages. Carlsbad's city-owned 680-acre Shooting Complex has a half dozen **gun ranges** and an area for radio-controlled model airplanes. More recreation can be found at the Riverwalk Recreation Center.

**Golfers** can enjoy a round at the Lake Carlsbad Municipal course, or at the Riverside Country Club. The Lake Carlsbad Tennis Complex has nine **tennis** courts and three handball courts.

Carlsbad has 28 parks in town. At the Lake Carlsbad park, you can rent a paddleboat or ride the George Washington **paddlewheeler** along the Pecos River, 505-885-1600. Kids will enjoy the motor-

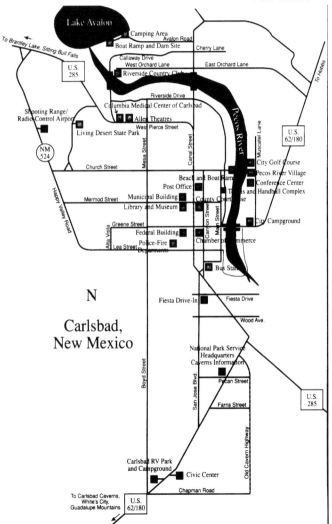

Carlsbad,
New Mexico

ized bumper boats.  Another spot for **water sports** and **fishing** is Brantley Lake State Park, 12 miles north of Carlsbad.

The Lincoln National Forest borders Carlsbad to the southwest. Its Chihuahuan desert terrain ranges in elevation from 3500 to 7600 feet.  Sitting Bull Falls is a short walk from the parking lot.  Many visitors **hike** 4.5-mile Trail 226 through Last Chance Canyon. Others explore undeveloped caves.  There are no developed camp-grounds, but **camping** is allowed in the forest.  Call the Forest Service at 505-885-4181 for details.  Small and big game **hunting** is lucrative in the forest; contact Game and Fish at 827-7911.

Carlsbad's main event occurs in the third week of May.  The **Mescal Roast** is a four-day celebration of the traditions of the Mescalero Apache people.  The event includes food, art, prayer, and Native Mountain Spirit Dances.  The **Western Week Rodeo and Celebration** occurs in early July.

**Collored Peccarys at the Living Desert Zoo and Gardens**

# Los Alamos

## Los Alamos Airport

**Town**    Los Alamos    **ID**    LAM
**Coord**    N-35-52.47, W-106-16.09
**Elev**    7171 feet, 1%, W end high
**Runway**    9 - 27, 5550 x 113' asphalt
**Freq**    CTAF-123.0, Lights-3x5x7x
**Charts**    Albuquerque sect., L4, L6

> **CAUTION:** *Airport information not for naviga-*
> *tional use. Phone ahead for flight briefing. Radio*
> *contact required. Expect land 27, depart 9. Avoid*
> *R-5101. Flashing beacon means field is closed.*

> *Los Alamos, paradox of the Southwest: birth place*
> *of atom bomb, rich in Native American history and*
> *scenic beauty.  Fascinating historic and technical*
> *museums, ancient ruins, outdoor recreation.*
> *$90 - $180.  Chamber:  800-444-0707*

## Airport Description

The airport occupies a finger a of plateau, bordered by canyons on either side.  Expect crosswinds up to 15 knots at any time. The town center is within walking distance, one mile west.

Los Alamos is being transitioned from federal to county control.  Gone are the days of unconventional protocol.  Still, the airport manager asks that you call for a briefing before landing, 505-662-8420.  You need permission to land.  Prior to approach on 27, establish airport contact on 123.0.

## Services, Transportation, and Lodging

Airport phone:  505-662-8420.  Fuel: 100LL, credit card.  The FBO is Stafford Aviation, 662-5002.  Taxi: 660-3426.  Budget Rental agency has an office at the airport, 505-662-4226.  Avis will deliver to the airport, 662-5046.  Note the combination on the automatic airport gate before leaving the airport.

The interesting points in town are within walking distance, less than two miles from the airport.  The Bradbury Museum is one mile due west.  Most local motels pick up from the airport with prior arrangement.

The following is a reasonably complete list of lodging in the Los Alamos area.  Location key:  *L.A.* for Los Alamos, *W.R.* for

**Features**

B Full breakfast
C Continental
H Historic
P Pets OK
R Restaurant
T Transportation

White Rock, *J.S.* for Jemez Springs, and *L.C.* for La Cueva. La Cueva Lodge is less than two miles from Spence Hot Springs.

| | | | |
|---|---|---|---|
| Adobe Pines B&B, *L.A.* | **CT** | $71-87 | 505-662-6761 |
| Bandelier Inn, *W.R.* | **CP** | $56-100 | 800-321-3923 |
| Bud's B&B, *L.A.* | **BHT** | $56-78 | 800-581-BUDS |
| Canyon Inn B&B, *L.A.* | **C** | $56 | 800-662-2565 |
| Castella del Alba B&B, *L.A.* | **BT** | $71-115 | 505-672-9494 |
| Dancing Bear B&B, *J.S.* | **B** | $78-133 | 800-422-3271 |
| Hilltop House, *L.A.* | **BHRT** | $40-85 | 800-462-0936 |
| Jemez Mtn. Inn, *J.S.* | **HB** | $100-140 | 888-819-1075 |
| La Cueva Lodge, *L.C.* | **P** | $58 | 505-829-3814 |
| Los Alamos Inn, *L.A.* | **HPR** | $55-90 | 800-279-9279 |

## Los Alamos Center

Although Los Alamos is known as the town that built the bomb, it has history and beauty that rival its neighbors. Early inhabitants of the area were the **Anasazi**, "The Ancient Ones." These Pueblo ancestors were a classic hunting-and-gathering society. Make time to visit the nearby remains of their Frijoles Canyon village, now known as **Bandelier National Monument**. The Anasazi community flourished until the 1500's.

Swedish anthropologist Adolf Bandelier "discovered" the ruins in 1880. He did an extensive anthropological study of the Frijoles Canyon settlement using methods based on keen observation and speculation – avant garde in his day.

Four years after Bandelier died, Ashley Pond purchased the Los Alamos Ranch with the dream of creating an environment in which "sickly east-coast boys could become robust, learned men." The ranch became a reality, and for 25 years its young men completed their commencement on horseback.

In 1943, the feds took over Ranch School land and buildings to make way for the Manhattan Project – the top-secret project to build an atom bomb. In no time, a makeshift town was constructed to house the country's greatest scientific minds. J. Robert Oppenheimer steered these brilliant, eccentric men on a common course to build the ultimate weapon. Even today, only a handful of countries have solved the puzzles that Los Alamos scientists solved in two short years with mechanical calculators.

In 1957, the community of Los Alamos was opened to the public, though portions of the plateau still remain off limits. Today, Los Alamos looks like a normal, prosperous American town, except that half the people on the streets wear picture IDs around their necks.

The University of California manages the Los Alamos National Laboratory under contract with the Department of Energy, which owns 28,000 acres of Los Alamos land. With an annual operating budget of one billion dollars, the laboratory is responsible for 13,000 jobs, including contractors. Although the labs remain Los Alamos' largest employer, the community of 18,000 is attracting new businesses, as well as a steady stream of tourists.

Historically, much of the lab's hardware has been focused on nuclear and particle physics. Today, research at the labs is shifting toward practical, peacetime pursuits. Materials, weather, environmental issues, and human biology are now being studied. The Human Genome Project, for example, is part of a nationwide effort to map the 100,000 human genes.

The new **Bradbury Science Museum**, 505-667-4444, and **Los Alamos Historical Museum**, 662-6272, are must-see stops in Los Alamos. If you are interested in science, plan two or more hours at the Bradbury Museum. Even if you're not, the museum's coverage of the Manhattan Project and its impact on the course of world history are fascinating. Take time to see the historical film and read about the historical artifacts. Scientific exhibits include a variety of models and interactive displays. As a courtesy to the "other side," museum curators have included an exhibit that shows the incredible destruction and clean-up costs associated with nuclear development.

You get to the museum from the airport by walking due west on Trinity Drive, and continuing west on Central Avenue to the heart of town, a 20-minute walk.

Five minutes after crossing 20th Street and passing the old Fuller Lodge, you turn right for the Chamber of Commerce and Historical Museum. The **Historical Museum** does a fine job of presenting a humanistic view of area history, interesting information that is often overshadowed by the Manhattan project. **Visitor information** is available at the adjacent Fuller Lodge building. While there, enjoy the New Mexico art at **Fuller Lodge Art Center**.

If you stay several days, you have time to enjoy the community's amenities. The **Los Alamos Golf Course**, 505-662-8139, is home of the Atomic City Invitational Golf Tournament. The county has 22 **tennis courts**. Their **aquatic center** at 7245 feet elevation is the highest indoor Olympic training pool in the world. **Bicycle** enthusiasts may contact Land of Ox Bicycles at 662-9790 for information on trails and events.

## Beyond Los Alamos

Outside of White Rock, you can visit the **Balagna Winery**, phone 505-672-3678. Owner John Balagna, a retired chemist from the bomb era, serves samples of his white and red. His tasting room and residence have a spectacular view of the Rio Grande valley. I especially enjoyed his La Bomba red.

Most visitors spend a day or more visiting nearby **Native American ruins** and **pueblos**. Both **Bandelier** and **Puye Cliff Dwellings** are worth a visit. Also consider the **Tsankawi** ruins between Los Alamos and White Rock, and **Santa Clara Pueblo** near Espanola.

**Bandelier** is located ten miles southwest of White Rock. The scenic monument includes 32,737 acres of wilderness with striking land formations, some of which were home to Anasazi Indians between 1100 and 1550 AD.

After entering **Frijoles Canyon**, you find the Visitor's Center and remains from cliff houses and a pueblo. The cliffs, which may remind you of Swiss cheese, are the first clue of early human habitation. Nature conveniently provided volcanic cliffs full of holes; the Anasazi enlarged the holes and integrated multistory housing.

**Bandelier Cliff Dwellings**

Take time to view the ten-minute slide show at the center. Allow at least two hours to enjoy the cliff dwellings, pueblo, and Ceremonial Cave. **Backpacking** and daily **hikes** are popular on trails to Lower Waterfall and Painted Cave.

Another site, my favorite for the area, is the **Puye Cliff Dwellings**. It is northeast of Los Alamos, Highway 601 off State Road 30. After paying a fee to the local tribe, you arrive at the base of the cliffs, elevation 6870 feet. You can drive to the top, but I suggest climbing the 170 feet of trails and ladders that take you to the top. There's not much left except caves carved into the walls, holes for rafters, and building remains at the top.

The view from the top is both serene and beautiful, 360 degrees of mountains and valleys. As I took time to be still and let the wind blow through my hair, I felt a wonderful sense of peace. Could it be that the souls of this 1500-person community had in some way touched me?

**Santa Clara Pueblo**

Drive west from Los Alamos, and you enter the beautiful **Jemez Mountains**. Looking for a nice drive? Take State Road 4 through Jemez Springs, and eventually toward Albuquerque. Better yet, slow down and enjoy the mountains' treasures.

If you are a hot springs addict like me, your first stop will be **Spence Hot Springs**. These beautiful natural hot springs are located on a mountain side at 7300 feet, 10 minutes from an unmarked parking area. With four mountain-side pools formed of boulders and view of timbered canyon, Spence rates among the top. Clothing is optional, the norm for unimproved springs. The USFS warns that water quality is not monitored: "Visitors should avoid getting water in their nose" to minimize the possibility of ingesting an extremely rare amoeba found in warm water.

To get to Spence Hot Springs, leave Los Alamos on 501 and turn right on State Road 4 (not marked). Travel west twenty or so miles to La Cueva, and turn left on 4. In less than two miles, you

**Spence Hot Springs**

pull over at the second gravel parking area on the left. The parking turnoff is not marked, but you will probably see several parked cars. Walk straight down to the river, bear left, cross the river on a log, and climb straight up any of several trails that parallel warm water running down the mountain.

**McCauley Springs** are the other natural springs of interest, not far from Spence. Ask the U.S. Forest Service in Los Alamos (Central and 20th) for maps. **Commercial hot springs** are located eight miles south of La Cueva in Jemez Springs, 505-829-3303.

About 15 miles west of Los Alamos is Valle Grande, the collapsed summit (caldera) of an **ancient volcano** that erupted 1.4 million years ago. Fifteen miles in diameter, it is one of the largest caldera in the world. The **Pajarito Mountain Ski Area** uses an outer slope of the rim, offering a vertical drop of 1200 feet. The ski facility has 30 trails, four lifts, lodge, cafeteria, and rental shop. Call 505-662-SNOW for conditions or 662-5725 for other information. Call the USFS ranger station at 829-3535 for cross-country ski information.

The mountains are rich in **hiking trails**, and the USFS can show you dozens of options. **Fishing** is found in all directions from Los Alamos. The Jemez River is a fly fisherman's favorite. **Hunters** bag elk in the high country, deer, bear, turkey, and other small game. For information, contact the Sports Bag at 505-662-2454, Smiths at 672-3811, or Fish and Game at 827-7911.

## Events

Los Alamos Chamber of Commerce brochures show a long list of minor events that change from year to year. Call 505-662-8105 for information. Gordon's Music, 662-7279, sponsors interesting music events, like their traditional Michael Martin Murphey concert in April. **Major yearly events**:

| May, mid    | Chamber Trade Fair     | 505-662-8105 |
| June, early | Bridge the Gap Festival | 505-665-5000 |
| Dec, mid    | Lighting of the Lights  | 505-662-8105 |

**Bradbury Museum**

# Santa Fe

## Santa Fe Airport

| | |
|---|---|
| **Town** | Santa Fe  **ID** SAF |
| **Coord** | N-35-37.01, W-106-05.29 |
| **Elev** | 6345 feet, N side high |
| **Runway** | 2 - 20, 8323 x 150' asphalt |
| | 15 - 33, 6304 x 150' asphalt |
| | 10 - 28, 2900 x 100' asphalt |
| **Freq** | ATIS-128.55, Apc/Dep-132.8 |
| | Twr-119.5, Gnd-121.7, |
| | Lights-119.5-3x5x7x |
| **Charts** | Albuquerque, L4, L6, Lo10 |

> **CAUTION:** Airport information not for navigational use. Hills nearby. Downdrafts over arroyos. Helicopter operations. No line of sight between 15-33 ends.

> *Santa Fe, home of 250 art galleries and world-class opera. Adobe architecture, pervasive art, handmade jewelry, colorful clothing shops, and spicy food. Nearby Native American ruins, pueblos, and other historic sites. $150-400.*
> *Info: 800-777-CITY,   www.santafe.org*

## Airport Description

Santa Fe Airport is a multi-runway, tower-controlled facility with multiple instrument approaches.  At night, be aware of local mountains.

## Services, Transportation, and Lodging

Airport phone: 505-473-7243.  Fuel: 100 octane and JetA. Tiedown is $4.  Santa Fe Jet Center, 471-2525, and Zia Aviation, 471-2700, will loan their courtesy cars for short runs.

Santa Fe's better motels and hotels offer free airport transportation from the airport.  Select lodging near the town square where there is lots to see within walking distance, and you can avoid the expense of a rental car for several days.

Capital City Cab, 438-0000, provides taxi service to town center for $20 plus one dollar for each additional person.  Roadrunner Shuttle, 434-3367, charges $16 per couple.

| | | |
|---|---|---|
| Avis, *terminal* | 800-331-1212 | 505-471-5892 |
| Budget, *pickup* | 800-527-0700 | 505-984-1596 |
| Enterprise, *pickup* | 800-325-8007 | 505-473-3600 |
| Hertz, *terminal* | 800-654-3131 | 505-471-7189 |
| Thrifty, *Jet Center* | 800-367-2277 | 505-471-2525 |

Note that car rental agencies stationed at the airport levy an additional 9% airport tax.

To get to town from the Santa Fe Airport, drive east on Airport Road, turn left on Cerrillos Road (Highway 14), and drive seven miles into town. The inexpensive motels lie between the airport and the Santa Fe River. When you cross the river, you are only three blocks from the town Plaza.

Santa Fe has over 100 motels, hotels, condos, and B&Bs. Christmas and summer are the most difficult times to secure reservations. Other times, you can locate lodging after arrival. A representative list of lodging:

**Features**

| | |
|---|---|
| **B** | Full breakfast |
| **C** | Continental |
| **H** | Historic |
| **P** | Pets OK |
| **R** | Restaurant |
| **T** | Transportation |

| | | | |
|---|---|---|---|
| El Rey Inn | C | $66-140 | 800-521-1349 |
| Garrett's Desert Inn | | $90-130 | 800-888-2145 |
| Inn at Loretto | R | $200-400 | 800-727-5531 |
| Hotel Santa Fe | PRT | $130-230 | 800-825-9876 |
| La Fonda Hotel | HR | $130-560 | 800-523-5002 |
| Super 8 Motel | C | $55-65 | 800-800-8000 |

Two upscale hotels, Loretto and historic La Fonda, are close to the town Plaza; both are quite special. Garrett's Desert Inn is also near the Plaza, but has less charm. The Hotel Santa Fe is seven blocks from the Plaza. The others listed above are on Cerrillos Road, not within walking distance of the Plaza. To find a perfect match in lodging, call the following reservation services:

| | | |
|---|---|---|
| Alternative Reservations | 800-995-2272 | 505-820-2468 |
| Bed & Breakfast of NM | | 505-982-3332 |
| Santa Fe Detours | 800-338-6877 | 505-986-0038 |
| NM Central Reservations | 800-466-7829 | 505-766-9770 |
| Santa Fe Central Res. | 800-776-7669 | 505-983-8200 |

## Santa Fe Center

Archeologists believe that first residents of Santa Fe were ancestors of the Pueblo People. In 1540, rumors of gold spurred conquistadors to enter the land. By 1598, they had establish a settlement near San Juan Pueblo. In 1610 the Spanish government built their capital city for Nuevo Mejico where the palace of the Governors in Santa Fe now stands.

In 1690, the Pueblo People managed to evict the Spanish invaders until 1692 when the town was recaptured by Don Diego de Vargas. Santa Fe became a crossroads, first on the highway to Mexico City, and later in 1821 as the final stop on the Santa Fe Trail. The U.S. Government took New Mexico from Mexico in 1850, but it did not become a state until 1912.

Due to the strict building code of 1957, Santa Fe consistently maintains the adobe look of its heritage. Even fences in feed lots and the federal tower at the airport have the Pueblo look. Today, a community of 50,000 people inhabit the adobe structures on wandering, Spanish-named streets. Santa Fe now has 200 restaurants, 250 art galleries, and 70 jewelry shops.

The logical place to begin exploration is the **Plaza**. It was, and is, the center for commerce, gatherings, parades, and **people watching**. Today, it is flanked by some of Santa Fe's best **shops** and most interesting **museums**. The north side is bounded by the **Palace of the Governors**, the oldest government building in the U.S. **Saint Frances Cathedral** stands to the east. To the southeast, across the Santa Fe River, is the famous Canyon Road with eight dozen fine **galleries** and shops.

Other points of historical interest can be found all around town in areas like the **Railroad District** and sites along the Old Santa Fe Trail. The **Loretto Chapel** with its "Miraculous Staircase" is a popular stop for visitors. The staircase was built by a mysterious carpenter who built the structure without nails or visible means of support, and who then vanished without accepting payment. Amongst the historic sites, you can enjoy interesting diversions like **Santa Fe Pottery** on South Guadalupe, where artists throw pots before your very eyes.

The **Museum of New Mexico** is comprised of five Museums in Santa Fe and five monuments throughout New Mexico. You can purchase a three-day pass for all five museums for $10. **The Palace of the Governors,** 505-827-6483, on the Plaza now houses settlers' and governors' artifacts. Native Americans sell **handmade art** and **jewelry** along the building's long, covered porch. Just down the street, the **Museum of Fine Arts,** 982-1311, houses more than 8000 works from the likes of Georgia O'Keefe and other New Mexican masters. Photographic multimedia exhibits that play on the Los Alamos atom bomb project seem strangely juxtaposed.

Further from the Plaza, on Camino Lejo, you can visit the **Museum of International Folk Art**, 505-827-6350. This museum is one of the largest of its kind, including a collection from more than one hundred countries.  Also on Camino Lejo, you'll find the **Museum of Indian Arts and Culture**.  This museum focuses on the historical and contemporary lives of the Pueblo, Navajo, and Apache cultures.  Other interesting Native American museums include the **Institute of American Indian Arts Museum**, 827-6344,  and the **Wheelwright Museum of the American Indian**, 982-4636.

The **Santa Fe Children's Museum** is one mile south of the Plaza at 1050 Old Pecos Trail, 505-989-8359.  This museum offers international exhibits and programs for entry fees of $1.50 to $2.50.  Kids will also enjoy the **El Rancho de las Golondrinas** located 15 miles south of Santa Fe near La Cienegena. This 200-acre Spanish ranch is a **living historic museum** that recreates the life-style of early Spanish settlers.  The ranch is closed throughout winter.  Call 471-2261 for times, costs, and special events.

Santa Fe has close to two hundred **restaurants**, many of which rival cosmopolitan standards in decor as well as cuisine  Don't be afraid to poke your head in a restaurant door, if only to appreciate local interior architecture.  I enjoyed a variety of great restaurants in Santa Fe.  For a taste of New Mexican cuisine, try Tomasita's Cafe at 5005 South Guadalupe.  Remember, when New Mexicans say  a meal is "hot," they mean  HOT!

## Greater Santa Fe

Past the adobe structures of Santa Fe, rolling hills and valleys hold treasures in **art** and **history**, including a wealth of ancient finds.  Curious art aficionados can experience artwork in the making in many studios throughout the area.  Local arts and crafts include **painting**, **weaving**, **pottery**, **tinware**, **glass blowing**, **sculpture**, **woodcarving**, **jewelry-making**, **basketry**, **wrought ironwork**, and **beadwork**.

**Shidoni Gardens**, a must-see treat for those with even a mild interest in art, is located five miles north of Santa Fe, just south of Tesuque.  An international resource for sculptors and collectors, Shidoni includes an **art foundry** with 40 employees, an **outdoor gallery** for very large sculpture, **indoor galleries**, and adjacent **glassblowing** studio.  I have never seen so many huge unique pieces of sculpture in one place.  Suggestion:  Wander the eight-acre gallery grounds and break for a picnic lunch under the trees by the Rio Tesuque.

On Saturday, don't miss the open **bronze pourings** at noon.  Call 505-988-8001 for information and appointment.  Most any time of day, you can see **glass blowing** at the Tesuque Glass Works, 988-2165, located to the right of the entrance to Shidoni.  Charles Miner, the "dancing glass blower," founded the works in 1975.  You get a front-row view as Charlie and his students work magic with molten balls of glass.

The Shidoni Gardens are located five to six miles north of Santa Fe. Follow Washington north from the Plaza area. The name changes to Bishop's Lodge Road, but keep heading north until you see the gardens on the left. If you run into the small town of Tesuque, you went one-half mile too far.

The **Santa Fe Opera**, a must-do for music lovers, is located a little further north on the road to Taos. The spectacular outdoor theater is active in summer months, only. Call 505-986-5900 or 986-5955.

Several day-or-longer scenic drives are worth considering. The **Los Alamos Loop** to the west and south takes you past Los Alamos, **Bandelier National Monument**, south past Bernalillo, and back to Santa Fe. (See chapter **NM-LOSA** for details on the Los Alamos area.) As you turn south on State Road 4, you can explore a 12th century **pueblo** and enjoy **hot springs** at Jemez

**Shidoni Gardens**

Springs. Turn onto NM 44 to visit **Coronado State Monument**, a large pueblo that conquistadors visited in 1540.

The **Taos Loop** swings north to Taos along the "high road" and back to Santa Fe via State Road 68. Exit Santa Fe on US 84-285 to Pojoaque. Turn right on State Road 503 and drive through a lovely valley. You can picnic at **Nambe Falls**. Back on State Road 503, drive until the sign to Chimayo'. Turn onto 520 to get to this sleepy village, famous for its **church** and **weavers**.

**Santuario de Chimayo'**, completed in 1816, is believed to contain a source of **holy dirt** with miraculous healing powers. After sitting quietly in the church, you can scoop up a small amount of holy dirt from a room to the left of the altar. Near the church are several shops and vendors that specialize in hot peppers and other local culinary additives. Perhaps because I took extra time to enjoy this quiet stop, it left a lasting impression.

At Route 76, head for **Truchas**, the location of Robert Redford's Milagro Beanfield War movie. Next, you enter Las Trampas with its beautiful **San Jose Church**. The other towns are worth a drive-through, if you have the time and inclination to amble. The next stop is Taos, worth a week all by itself. (See chapter **NM-TAOS**.) Highway 68 takes you quickly back from Taos to Santa Fe.

The Southern Loop is sometimes known as the "**Turquoise Trail**" or "the back road to Albuquerque." From Santa Fe center, follow Cerrillos, State Road 14 southwest. You leave town, passing the turnoff to **living history museum** El Rancho de las Golondrinas (mentioned earlier).

**Cerrillos**, the first town you encounter, was once a **mining town** and major railroad stop. Now a sleepy little community, it's the home of several dusty shops and the Casa Grand **Trading Post** and **Petting Zoo**. A sign marks the Wordley Hotel, which is not really a hotel – just a sign left in place after the filming of <u>Young</u> <u>Guns</u>. The town has a personality all its own, worth as much as an hour of exploration. Kids will enjoy the petting zoo, and adults may appreciate the funky What Not Shop.

The next stop is **Madrid**. Once a **coal-mining town**, Madrid is now a **colorful tourist stop** with shops to browse and places to snack. If you have been in New Mexico for several days or so, Madrid will look different – no adobe! The wood-frame miners' cabins that line the main street arrived on flat-bed rail cars when the town was booming.

I enjoyed visiting the **mine museum** at the Mine Shaft Tavern. The museum includes a tin-roofed **melodrama theater**, the only theater in the world with an authentic coal-fired steam engine as a backdrop. The train's engineer is "Casey Bones," a skeleton. You can join Casey in the cab for a photo opportunity. As an added

**Santuario de Chimayo'**

educational bonus, the controls are labeled so you might guess how the old contraption was actually made to go.

The **tavern** is a treat. Yummy aromas of greasy burgers tempt the appetite, old dollar bills paper the wall behind the rows of bottles, and local-looking folks seem to be at home on both sides of the bar. There are lots of smiles and jokes – a great place to take a break and sip a beer. When nature calls, patrons can enjoy the town's only public flush toilets.

Other stops on the Turquoise Trail include 10,678-foot **Sandia Peak**, the ranching community of **Moriarty**, and the scenic **Galisteo area**. On the way back, consider taking a side-trip to **Lamy**, home of Santa Fe's original **train station**. Lamy's historic **Legal Tender Saloon** and restaurant includes many period pieces from the Victorian Era.

A number of interesting **pueblos** and **Indian ruins** are sprinkled within a couple hours of Santa Fe. Local tourist information includes descriptions, maps, and etiquette. I particularly enjoyed the **Puye Cliff Dwellings** and **Bandelier National Monument cliff dwellings** near Los Alamos.

**Backpacking**, **hiking**, **mountain-biking**, **fishing**, and **hunting** are available in appropriate seasons. Discover **high desert fly fishing** with High Desert Angler, 505-98-TROUT. **Whitewater rafting** is a popular three-season sport in the Rio Grande and other rivers. Ride the class-five rapids of the Taos Box, or take a more serene float through the White Rock or Rio Chama Canyons. The following outfitters can take you there:

| | | |
|---|---|---|
| Far Flung Adventures | 505-758-2628 | 800-231-7238 |
| Los Rios River Runners | 505-776-8854 | 800-544-1181 |
| New Wave Rafting Co. | 505-984-1444 | 800-984-1444 |
| Santa Fe Detours | 505-983-6565 | 800-338-6877 |
| Southwest Wilderness | 505-983-7262 | 800-869-7238 |

Santa Fe Detours can set you up with a **balloon ride**, **whitewater rafting**, **pack trip,** or **trail ride**. Trail rides are offered by Rancho Encantado, 800-722-9339; and by Gan Eden Ranch, 505-474-7400. Bishop's Lodge, 800-732-2240, provides both overnight and day rides.

In winter, you can **ski** just 30 minutes from Santa Fe. The Santa Fe Ski Area, 800-776-SNOW, peaks at 12,000, with 40 runs that drop 1650 feet. **Cross-country skiing** is popular on Aspen Vista, a Forest Service road two-thirds of the way up to the downhill area.

## Festivals and Events

Santa Fe is rich in **music**, **art**, and **cultural events**. Contact the Santa Fe Convention and Visitors Bureau for the rundown on current events, 800-777-CITY. A list of major annual events follows:

| Jun, begin | Spring Festival | 505-471-2261 |
|---|---|---|
| July, early | Santa Fe Opera begins | 505-986-5900 |
| July, early | Rodeo de Santa Fe | |
| July, early | Santa Fe Chamber Music Fest | 505-983-2075 |
| July, mid | Northern Pueblos Artists Show | 505-852-4265 |
| July, end | Spanish Market - Plaza | |
| Aug, early | Stampede Pro - Woman's Rodeo | 505-982-6694 |
| Aug, mid | Mountain Man Rendezvous Fair | 505-476-5094 |
| Aug, mid | Indian Market | 505-983-5220 |
| Sept, early | Banjo and Fiddle Contest | 505-471-3462 |
| Sept, early | Fiestas de Santa Fe | |
| Oct, begin | Harvest Festival | 505-471-2261 |

# Silver City

## Grant County Airport

| | |
|---|---|
| **Town** | Silver City   **ID**   SVC |
| **Coord** | N-32-38.19, W-108-09.39 |
| **Elev** | 5443 feet |
| **Runway** | 8 - 26,  6800 x 100' asphalt (Also, multiple dirt runways.) |
| **Freq** | CTAF-122.8, AWOS-126.725 VOR:SVC-110.8, Lights-122.8 |
| **Charts** | Albuquerque,  L4, Lo10 |

**CAUTION:** Airport information not for navigational use.  Military traffic.  Dirt runways soft when wet.

> *Silver City, rich in wild-west history, is a center*
> *for mining operations and scenic mountain*
> *country to the north.  Gila Cliff Dwellings, hot*
> *springs, mine tours, fishing, and more.  $75-200.*
> *Chamber:  800-548-9378, www.silvercity.org.*

## Airport

Whiskey Creek Airport (94E), the closest airport to town, has
no rental or courtesy cars. Grant County Airport (SVC) has
rental cars and on-field VOR – the airport of choice for most
visitors.

Grant County Airport is a flat-land airport, clear of the mountains to the north.  Prominent landmarks include stacks four
miles north, a large pit mine ten miles north, and Silver City ten
miles southwest.  The main asphalt runway is wide and free of
obstructions.  A number of ancillary dirt runways branch out to
the north.

## Services, Transportation, and Lodging

Grant County Airport Phone: 505-388-4554.  Grimes Aviation: 538-2142.  Fuel: 100LL and JetA.  Grimes provides a
variety of rental vehicles with an informal touch.  They charge
$30 per day and $.30 per mile, which can work out to a sizeable
tab if you tour the beautiful country to the north and east.

Less convenient transportation alternatives include two rental agencies in Silver City.  Ridgwood Mortors, 505-538-5311, has cars for $40 and $.15/mile after 50 miles.  They pickup from either airport.  Taylor Car Rental, 388-1800, charges $25/day and $.25/mile.  They service Grant County Airport for a surcharge of $25, and Whiskey Creek for $12.  Silver City Grant County Taxi Service provides rides from Grant County Airport for $25, up.  Call 538-1852 or 538-0925.

Of the following, Larson's Gateway Plaza in Hurley is closest to the airport.  Bear Mountain Guest Ranch is three miles from town on 160 acres against the Gila National Forest.  The others are in Silver City.  Remember to ask for the usual discounts.

**Features**

**B** Full breakfast
**C** Continental
**H** Historic
**P** Pets OK
**R** Restaurant
**T** Transportation

| | | | |
|---|---|---|---|
| Bear Mtn. Guest Ranch | BHPRT | $68-85 | 800-880-2538 |
| Carter House B&B | BH | $72-84 | 505-388-5485 |
| Copper Manor | R | $50-54 | 800-853-2916 |
| The Cottages | BH | $145-99 | 800-938-3001 |
| Drifter Motel | PRT | $45-50 | 800-853-2916 |
| Econo Lodge | CP | $56-61 | 505-534-1111 |
| Holiday Motor Motel | PRT | $45-50 | 800-828-8291 |
| Larson's Gateway Plaza | PRT | $39-42 | 505-537-5001 |
| Palace Hotel | CHP | $33-54 | 505-388-1811 |
| Super 8 Motel | P | $48-54 | 505-388-1983 |
| | | | 800-800-8000 |

The next group includes interesting choices east or north of Silver City.  Lodging marked with S have access to hot springs.  Faywood Hot Springs and City of Rocks have camping only.  Wildwood Hot Springs has primitive facilities, like yerts and tepees.

| Bear Creek Cabins, *Pinos A.* | P | $143-176 | 505-388-4501 |
|---|---|---|---|
| City of Rocks State Park | | $5 | 505-536-2800 |
| Faywood Hot Springs | S | $18 | 505-536-9663 |
| Hot Spr. Vacation Cent., *Gila* | PS | $52 | 505-536-9551 |
| Lake Roberts Gen. Store, *L.R.* | P | $33-88 | 800-224-1080 |
| Lake Roberts Motel, *L.R.* | P | $40-50 | 505-536-9393 |
| Sapillo Crossing Lodge | PR | $45 | 505-536-3206 |
| Wilderness Lodge, *Gila* | BHPS | $50-61 | 505-536-9749 |
| Wildwood Hot. Spr., *Gila* | S | $33 | 505-536-9777 |

When driving north, you can camp at any number of scenic public and private campgrounds. There are pleasant places to camp near Gila Hot Springs and the Gila Cliff Dwellings.

## Silver City

Mining has always been a mainstay of Silver City and the mountains to the north. Early Native Americans mined turquoise, and in 1804 the Spanish began digging for copper. In 1859, a group of '49ers from California discovered gold seven miles north in the foothills, now Pinos Altos. In 1870, exciting silver deposits were discovered just above the Silver City marsh.

The rush was on! In ten short months, the city grew from one cabin to over eighty sturdy brick buildings. On the leading edge by period western standards, Silver City was one of the first in the territory to have a public school. Railroad and telephone connections soon followed. They completed an electric light plant just two years after New York City installed its first electric system.

Because the mineral deposits were diverse and extensive, Silver City managed to avoid the usual death that follows a rush. In the 1900's, Silver City capitalized on its high dry climate by becoming a treatment center for patients with respiratory problems. Today, mining and visitors like you and me provide steady revenue for the town.

Although mining ventures have created fascinating local history, one bad boy named Billy seems to have stolen the limelight. **Billy the Kid** was born in New York City in approximately 1859. His stepfather moved the family to Silver City in search of riches. By all accounts, Billy's father spent most of his time away from the family on a quest for gold and silver.

Billy got a job waiting tables at the nearby Star Hotel. He was an avid reader of dime novels and the Police Gazette. His first encounter with the law occurred when he stole several pounds of butter. Soon after, fifteen-year-old Billy robbed a Chinese laundry. The sheriff tried to teach him a lesson by putting him in jail. It didn't work.

Billy escaped from jail and moved back to New York City, where he is believed to have stabbed to death his first victim. He returned to New Mexico and Arizona, where by the age of 21 he could be linked to the death of twelve men. Finally, in 1881, he was killed in a gun battle with Sheriff Pat Garret.

Silver City has identified and restored a number of buildings that are associated with Billy the Kid. In the central **historic district** near Broadway and Highway 90, you can visit the jail site, Billy's cabin site, and the Star Hotel site.

The Chamber of Commerce at 1103 N. Hudson Street (Highway 90) should be one of your first stops. They provide excellent free publications that include maps, descriptions of sites, and interesting area history. With this information in hand, you can plan an interesting tour east and north of the city.

**Silver City Museum** is an easy walk, several blocks west at 312 W. Broadway, phone 505-538-5921. The museum is housed in the 1881 H.B. Ailman house, originally the home of a wealthy mine owner. The museum has revolving exhibits and features early Victorian furnishings.

The **WNMU Museum** sits at the south end of Alabama Street. Here you find a large collection of Mimbres pottery, dating from the eighth to twelfth century. While walking around town, you will see occasional **galleries** and a mix of shops and restaurants to poke into.

At 5:30 to 6:30, the **Copper Creek Supper and Western Show** opens their gates for cowboy food, humor, and musical entertainment. Food is served at 7:00 sharp, 505-538-2971.

**Scott Park Golf Course** has 18-holes and a driving range, 505-538-5041. As you might guess, the surrounding area is good for **hunting** and all kinds of **fishing**. Fishing licenses and regulations are available at the Silver City Wal-Mart.

The maps from the Chamber show a variety of **mines** in the area. The Santa Rita/Chino open pit copper mine, for example, is east of Silver City near milepost 6 on Highway 152. It is the oldest active mine in the Southwest, worked in 1800 by convict labor from Spain. Though profitable, it had to be abandoned to feisty Apaches. Now reopened, you can view huge 175-ton trucks move the ore to the reduction mill southwest of the pit.

The Phelps Dodge Tyrone Mine offers **free guided tours** Monday, Wednesday, and Friday at 9:00. Reservations are required, 505-538-7100. You will see 190-ton computer-routed trucks, and more. Take Highway 90 south to milepost 32, and turn right to the offices.

The **City of Rocks** is another popular stop, 30 miles south-east of Silver City at milepost 3.2 on Highway 61. These bizarre rock formations are believed by some to have been thrown 180 miles from a volcano near Albuquerque. The state of New

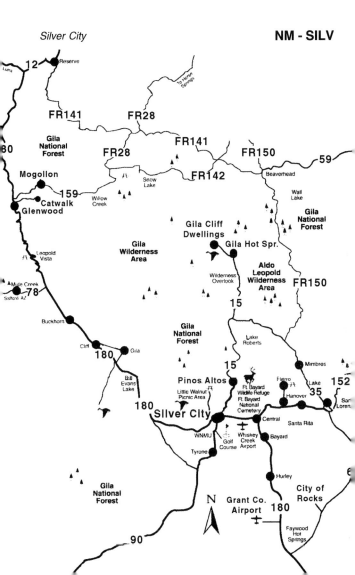

Reserve
12
Luna
To Horse Springs

FR141   FR28

**Gila National Forest**

FR28   FR141   FR150

80

FR28   FR142   59

Mogollon   Beavenead

159   Snow Lake   Wall Lake

Catwalk   Willow Creek   **Gila National Forest**

Glenwood

Leopold Vista   Gila Cliff Dwellings   Gila Hot Spr.

**Gila Wilderness Area**   **Aldo Leopold Wilderness Area**

Mule Creek   Wilderness Overlook   FR150

78

Safford AZ

Buckhorn   15

**Gila National Forest**

Lake Roberts

Cliff   Mimbres

180   Gila   152

Bill Evans Lake   Fierro   Lake   35

15   Ft. Bayard Wildlife Refuge   San Loren.

Pinos Altos   Hanover

Little Walnut Picnic Area   Ft. Bayard National Cemetery

180   **Silver City**   Central   Santa Rita

WNMU   Whiskey Creek Airport   Bayard

Tyrone   Golf Course

Hurley   **City of Rocks**

**Gila National Forest**

N   Grant Co. Airport   180

90   Faywood Hot Springs

Mexico has done a nice job of developing the site; it's a great place for kids who like to climb.  Entry is $3.00 and overnight camping is $7.00.

Just several miles southwest of the rocks and two miles from the intersection of Highways 180 and 61 is **Faywood Hot Springs**, 505-536-9663.  Facilities include public and private pools, travel trailers for lodging, tent sites, and 1200-acre ranch for recreation.  **Horseback riding** and **massage therapy** are available for a fee.  Pool rates are $7.50 per hour, and two can pitch a tent for $18.

**The Catwalk**, 65 miles northwest of Silver City, is another popular place to visit.  The Catwalk is a metal walkway that clings to the sides of riverside boulders in striking Whitewater Canyon.  Originally, this was the site of a water line that supplied water to a nearby mill.  It is a scenic spot, and there are places to branch off for hikes.  On the sectional, the Catwalk is close to the Glenwood airstrip, and about eight miles southwest of Mogollon.  To get there by car, follow Highway 180 northwest from Silver City to Glenwood and turn right.  There are a variety of sites to visit along the way.

Further northeast off 180, Mogollon is another scenic historic place to visit.  You follow a windy road up into the mountains, and then down into a valley that contains the **semi-ghost town** of Mogollon.  The town sprang to life in the 1880s, producing millions of dollars of gold and silver ore, which was pulled by 18-mule teams all the way to Silver City.  Now, Mogollon caters to tourists, offering tours, a restaurant, and art galleries.

When heading north from Silver City on Highway 15 toward the Gila Cliff Dwellings, you pass through **historic Pinos Altos**.  This town found its gold in 1859.  Like the others in the area, it quickly became a rowdy boom town, complete with Apache Indian raids. You might enjoy visiting the **Opera House**, **Judge Roy Bean Store** site, **Pinos Altos Museum**, 3/4-scale **Santa Rita trading post and fort**, **Hearst Church**, and picturesque **Buckhorn Saloon**.

Next, we head toward the Gila Cliff dwellings and hot springs. The drive goes through Gila National Forest country and near the **Gila Wilderness**.

To get to Gila from Silver City, drive north on Highway 15 or 35. Plan on driving two to four hours; the road winds through the mountains and you will want to enjoy the ride. By the Highway 35 route, you pass through Lake Roberts, a place for food, lodging, and fuel. Gila is about 15 miles north of where 15 and 35 join. The road takes you up over a 7400-foot mountain ridge with awesome panoramic views. The Visitor's Center is several miles past Gila, and the Cliff Dwellings a couple more.

The following **outfitters,** mostly near Gila, offer horseback adventures into this beautiful country. Rides range from hours to days. Although Hot Springs Vacation Center in Gila was the least expensive when I checked, query all for availability, price, and amenities.

| | | |
|---|---|---|
| Apache County Outfitters | *pack trips* | 505-536-3700 |
| Powderhorn Adventures | *pack, fish...* | 505-536-2903 |
| High-Lonesome Tours | *goat packing* | 505-388-3763 |
| Hot Springs Vacation Center | *pack trips* | 505-536-9551 |
| Wilderness Guides & Outfitters | *pack* | 505-536-2879 |

## Gila Cliff Dwellings and Hot Springs

The Gila adventure is a must for visitors who enjoy **scenery**, **Native American ruins**, and **hot springs**. Although the cliff dwellings are small compared to other well-known sites, the calm beauty and deep resonance of history left a lasting impression with me. Consequently, I wager that even the most analytical pilot will actually feel something special here. As a bonus, you won't be competing with hoards of other tourists.

Adolf Bandelier, famous for discovering a number of other Indian ruins, discovered the Gila (HEE-la) Cliff Dwellings in 1884. Deserted by the Mogollon (muggy-OWN) Indians in 1280 AD, the cliff-side structure has remnants of 42 rooms today. It is believed that the dwelling was built in times of stress, due to drought, lack of food, and population increase – probably a fortress that doubled as a home.

**Gila Cliff Dwellings**

The Visitor's Center has a quality **archeological display**, and shows an informative movie that preps you for the visit. After the Visitor's Center, you drive a couple more miles to the site. The walk to the ruins takes you through a shaded ravine along a year-round creek, and up 180 feet to the **cliff dwellings** at 5900 feet. I commented to the ranger, "I really appreciate that you allow every tax-payer to see this beautiful piece of heritage at no extra charge." He said, "That will change."

The **hot springs** are located back in the small town of Gila. On the way back, you pass a little shop that serves as post office, campground office, grocery store, gift shop, and museum. It has delicious **homemade ice-cream**!

Most of the hot springs facilities are just north of the highway off Access Road. The river is 1/4-mile from the highway. On

**Building remains from 1280 AD**

the south side of the highway, Airport Road leads to a defunct airstrip. Years ago, the owner died just after the airstrip was completed.

The Campbell family, owners of the Hot Springs Vacation Center, live to the left at the entrance of Access Road. This is where they keep the horses for their outfitting operation. It's funky, but the guest facilities, which are located elsewhere, are fine. The Campbells also own a **natural hot springs pool** by the river. The access and camping fees are reasonable. Clothing is optional, when appropriate.

David Snow showed me the various Campbell facilities within 1/4 mile radius of the house – campgrounds with soaking house and a variety of lodging. A pilot in his youth, David now looks the part of a seasoned ranch hand. His **pack trip** prices are quite reasonable, and he says the most economical group size is six.

**Wildwood Hotsprings Wilderness Retreat**

David recommends the months of May and August, though May is usually booked far in advance.

Down the Access Road, you will see a sign for Wildwood, an alternative lifestyle environment that focuses on the natural aspects of life. It's a place for individuals who are curious and tolerant. They have a nice shaded concrete soaking pool that you can use for $5. For overnight guests who camp or stay in a yert or teepee, pool access is free. Meals may be available.

Wilderness Lodge, off Access Road, will meet the needs of most guests. The building is old, but the rooms are tidy with period furniture, quilted beds, and such. Breakfast is included, and dinner is provided on request. This is not an elegant B&B operation, but the owners are non-pretentious and they have a shaded **out-door hot pool**. The river and the Campbell's natural hot pool are within walking distance.

*- RW*

**The Wilderness Lodge**

# Taos

## Taos Municipal Airport

| | |
|---|---|
| **Town** | Taos   **ID** SKX |
| **Coord** | N-36-27.49,  W-105-40.35 |
| **Elev** | 7091 feet,  0.8%, NE high |
| **Runway** | 4 - 22,  5798 x 75' asphalt |
| **Freq** | CTAF-122.8, Lights-3x7x |
| **Charts** | Denver sectional, L6, Lo10 |

*CAUTION:*  Airport information not for navigational use.  Glider activity.  Watch density altitude.

> *Taos is a center for multi-cultural art, music,*
> *and year-round outdoor recreation – a great*
> *place to shop for art and western jewelry.*
> *$150-300.  Info:  800-732-8267, www.taos.org*

## Airport Description

Taos is a high-altitude airport.  Mountains tower to the east, but airspace is obstruction-free for a ten-mile radius of the airport.  Except for possible interference from glider activity, landing is straightforward.  Depart on Runway 22 unless wind significantly favors 4.

## Services, Transportation, and Lodging

Airport phone:  505-758-4995.  Fuel:  100 octane and JetA.  A $5 fee is charged for overnight tiedown.  No restaurants are near the airport.  Oxygen, minor repairs, and rental cars are available.

Dollar Rental, 505-758-4995, has cars at the airport for $45-90 per day.  Enterprise, 737-0514, is at the south edge of Taos.  They sometimes pickup, but have spotty weekend coverage.

Many inns provide free transportation from the airport.  Verify prior to making reservations.  In town, the Taos Trolley provides transportation to all major inns and sites, including the Taos Pueblo.  The trolley operates primarily during daylight hours and dinner hours by reservation, 505-758-3873.  Conventional taxi service is provided by Faust Taxi and Shuttle, 758-3410.  Faust charges $15 per couple for rides from the airport  Bicycles can be rented next to the bus station and plaza.

Thanks to free pickup provided by most inns and the trolley, a rental car is unnecessary for visitors who plan to spend all their time in town. Chances are, however, that you will want to enjoy at least half your stay sight-seeing in the surrounding area.

Over one hundred facilities provide lodging within a 25-mile radius of Taos. Options include hotels, motels, condos, cabins, bed and breakfast units, lodges, ski dorms, and hostels. Prices range from $10 for a primitive hostel to over $200 a day for a luxury condo. The average price of a motel room falls between $60 and $130, and a good bed and breakfast inn will cost more.

Taos Central Reservation can help you find appropriate accommodations, 800-821-2437. For information about local resorts, call the Taos Valley Resort Association: in-state at 505-776-2233 or 800-992-SNOW. A sampling of Taos lodging follows:

**Features**

**B** Full breakfast
**C** Continental
**H** Historic
**P** Pets OK
**R** Restaurant
**T** Transportation

| Best Western Kachina | HT | $70-185 | 800-522-4462 |
|---|---|---|---|
| Casa de la Chimas B&B | B | $139-173 | 505-758-4777 |
| El Monte | HPT | $85-100 | 800-828-TAOS |
| Holiday Inn | PRT | $70-125 | 800 - HOLIDAY |
| | | | 505-758-4444 |
| La Fonda de Taos Hotel | CH | $72 | 800-833-2211 |
| Quail Ridge Inn | BR | $80-325 | 800-624-4448 |

The Quail Ridge Inn is a modern full-feature resort that specializes in **tennis**. Their restaurant, Carl's French Quarter, is one of Taos' best. Quail Ridge books for local activities, such as **rafting**, **jeep trips**, **horseback riding**, **balloon rides**, etc.

For a taste of old-time Taos, consider staying at the historic La Fonda de Taos hotel. Located on the south side of the square, every crack oozes of days gone by. It's worth a visit to see their exhibit of the poet D. H. Lawrence's erotic paintings (banned in London) and other works of art.

Taos has a number of beautiful, serene B&Bs. The Casa de la Chimas is a quality six-unit B&B that received rave reviews from friends who spent their honeymoon there. The fare includes fireplace, nice linens, hot tub, and a hearty breakfast. For fine dining, the honeymooners recommend the Old Taos Inn.

## Taos and Area

Although Taos has less than 5000 permanent residents, it has more art galleries than cities a hundred times its size. The local art is influenced by a blend of Anglo, Hispanic, and Indian cultures. The personal interpretation and the colors of local scenery make the resulting works mystic, warm, and pleasing.

**Taos art and jewelry store**

Art enthusiasts should reserve a full day or more for the galleries. Special tours and meetings can be arranged with local artists. Prices are negotiable.

Photo by Millicent Rogers

Second to visual arts are the performing arts. Taos attracts musicians from the world around. Check local papers for concerts and plays.

There is so much to do in the Taos area that the following is a sampling, at best. For starters, walk the square for a preview of **local art**, **jewelry**, and **crafts**. If you enjoy the shops, follow

**Taos Pueblo**

Photo by Ray Lutz

the side-streets that radiate from the square. There's a gallery around almost every corner, over 80 in all.

The **Taos Pueblo** is the area's best-known historic tourist attraction. Located three miles north of town at the base of Mt. Taos, this pueblo is said to be the oldest operating Indian village in the United States. Entry costs $5 per car plus $2 per person and $10 per still-camera. History enthusiasts will enjoy visiting others of the some twenty local historic points of interest.

On a hot day, beat the heat by driving the "Enchanted Circle." This is a **two-hour drive** that takes you up into cool green mountains, past ski valleys and shaded campsites. The loop takes you through Angel Fire, Eagle Nest, Red River, and Questa.

**Balloon rides** with amenities such as food and Champagne cost $200-250 per person: Paradise Hot Air Balloons, 505-751-6098; and Pueblo Balloon Company, 751-9877.

Those who love quiet desert heat will enjoy visiting the Rio Grande in the national park west of Questa, 505-758-6200. **Car-camping** is available at the rim or hike down 600 feet to **camp** at the river's edge.

The Taos segment of the Rio Grande, the "Taos Box," offers a full day of action-packed **whitewater adventure**. Try the following local outfitters:

Photo by Don Laine

| Big River | 800-748-3760 | 505-758-9711 |
| Native Sons Adventure | 800-753-7559 | 505-758-9342 |
| Rio Grande Rapid Transit | 800-222RAFT | 505-758-9700 |
| Rio Grande River Tours | 800-525-4966 | 505-758-0762 |

With three diverse **ski** areas, Taos becomes a center for ski enthusiasts in winter. Taos Ski Valley boasts 71 slopes and seven chairlifts. The center provides a full range of services. For information or reservations, call 800-992-SNOW or 505-776-2233. Smaller ski facilities are located nearby: Angel Fire, 800-633-7463; and Red River.

Several local streams attract **fishermen**. The Rio Hondo en route to the Taos Ski Valley is a good spot. The Rio Fernando east of Highway 60 and the Rio Grande are two other favorites.

The *Taos Outside Guide* recommends several **hikes**. The El Nogal Nature Trail is located only minutes east of Taos Plaza and is suitable for families with small children. Follow Kit Carson Road (Highway 64) east for 2.5 miles. The trail begins at a marker on the right. Further up the Kit Carson Road is the Divisadero trail, a more difficult hike of three to eight miles. The reward is a panoramic view of Taos Valley. The Wheeler Peak hike will lead you to the highest point in New Mexico, 13,161 feet. Contact the Kit Carson National Forest, 505-758-6200, for trail map and more information.

## Hot Springs

Two natural, noncommercial **hot springs** are located near Arroyo Hondo north of Taos. The Black Rock Hot Springs is a rocky, sand-bottom pool located a few feet above the river on the west bank of the Rio Grande. Temperature is 97 degrees except when high water floods the pool. Usage is light and clothing is optional. The Manby Hot Springs is similar, except that it is located on the east bank and has two pools. Both areas are clean and unmarked by commercial structures. Quality varies with the water table and time of year.

When traveling from Taos to the springs, turn left just past Arroyo Hondo's gas station. Follow the paved road west less than

2 miles as it degrades to gravel and crosses two bridges. Just after the second bridge, bear right at the "bridge intersection." Follow the dirt road west 1.1 miles as it crosses a small river and then the Rio Grande. Follow the road left along the Rio Grande one quarter mile to the first switch-back. Park at the switchback and walk 10 minutes south to the Black Rock Hot Springs.

To get to the Manby Hot Springs, bear left (southwest) at the bridge intersection mentioned above. Drive 0.4 miles until the switchback, then exit the road, heading southwest. Follow this rough 4x4 road due southwest for 1.9 miles until you reach the parking area above the Rio Grande. Park and walk ten minutes down an old stagecoach road to the hot springs.

**Santero Felix Lopez at Martinez Hacienda**

Photo by
Don Laine

# Nevada

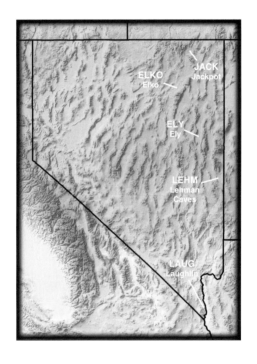

**Nevada Aeronautics**

**702-888-7440**

# Elko

## Elko Airport

| | |
|---|---|
| **Town** | Elko   **ID**  EKO |
| **Coord** | N-40-49.50, W-115-47.47 |
| **Elev** | 5135 feet, NE end high |
| **Runway** | 5rt - 23, 7211 x 150 asphalt |
| | 12rt - 30, 3330 x 60 gravel |
| **Freq** | Twr-126.5, AWOS-132.175 |
| | Lights-122.7-3x5x7x, Gnd-121.75 |
| **Charts** | Salt Lake City sect., L7, Lo2, Lo9 |

> **CAUTION:** Airport information not for navigational use. Power lines S & E. Pole near Runway 23.

> *Elko is a hub for access to hiking, hunting, and fishing in northern Nevada's beautiful mountains and plains. Cultural draws include the Basque community and yearly Cowboy Poetry Meet. $50 - $150. Info: 702-738-7135.*

## Airport Description

The airport is located at the southwest edge of town. The runway is lighted from sunset to sunrise. VASI on runway 23 is not usable beyond four miles due to obstructions. Non-precision IFR approaches are available.

## Airport Services, Transportation, and Lodging

Phone: 702-738-7123. Fuel: 100 octane andJetA. No food is served at the airport, but a restaurant is close by and there are numerous more in town. Courtesy cars are available for meal runs. A $3 fee is levied for overnight tiedown.

The airport is located virtually at the edge of town. Most destinations are within a 20-minute walk. Better yet, the casinos pick up and deliver within a moment's notice. Call directly from the FBO. A car is necessary if you plan to venture beyond city limits. Two rental agencies are located at the airport: Avis, 800-331-1212 or 702-738-4426; and Hertz, 800-654-3131 or 702-738-5620.

Due to a local gold rush, lodging can be difficult to find. Call ahead for reservations. Casinos provide lively lodging, but their prices

**Features**

B Full breakfast
C Continental
H Historic
P Pets OK
R Restaurant
T Transportation

have risen a tad above the competition.  A partial list follows.
Call the Chamber for additional help, 702-738-7135.

| Best Western Elko Inn | CPT | $60-70 | 702-738-7261 |
|---|---|---|---|
| Centre Motel | PT | $31-53 | 702-738-3226 |
| Holiday Motel | T | $39-51 | 702-738-7187 |
| Red Lion Casino | PRT | $95-105 | 800-545-0044 |
| Stockman's Casino | RT | $38-44 | 800-648-2345 |
| Thunderbird Motel | PT | $57-64 | 702-738-7115 |

## Elko

The first white men in the valley were trappers who began
their quest for beaver in 1828.  Through the 1850s, wagon trains
creaked painfully along the twisted Humboldt River until a
better route was discovered to the south.  The area remained
unpopulated until 1886 when the Central Pacific Railroad pushed
through and baptized its tent city "Elko."  As a transportation
center and mining hub, Elko grew rapidly.  Today, recent investment in local gold mining has created tremendous growth.  Housing and lodging are in short supply.

Basque culture is clearly evident in Elko.  The Basques were
sheepherders from the Pyrenees Mountains (between Spain and
France).  Their skills enabled them to dominate the sheepherding
trade in the area.  The Basque hotels overflowed with sheepherders during the slack seasons.  These hotels became known for
their multicourse, family-style meals.  Several still operate in
Elko.  The Star Hotel serves huge meals for $12-20.  The house
libation is called Picon.  Lodging costs $80 per week (if avail-
able!).  The Star and other Basque restaurants are located southeast of The Stockmen's, near Silver and Third Street.

The museum and Chamber of Commerce are located at the
northeast end of town.  The Elko Chamber is well-stocked with

information and maps, including Forest Service maps. This information is the key to the surrounding mountains and streams that are highly revered for **fishing**, **hunting**, and **hiking**. Ask the Chamber for tips. The museum next door is worth a visit if you have time to spare.

Elko supports a number of **festivals** throughout the year. Their **Cowboy Poetry Gathering** has earned itself country-wide recognition. This event includes poetry readings, music, dancing, and crafts.

| Jan, late | Cowboy Poetry | *poetry, music* | 702-738-7508 |
|-----------|---------------|-----------------|--------------|
| Mar, late | Chariot Races | | 702-738-7135 |
| May, late | Silver State Stampede | | 702-738-7135 |
| June, early | Mining Expo | | 702-738-7135 |
| July, early | Basque Festival | | 702-738-7135 |
| Sept, early | Elko County Fair | | 702-738-7135 |
| Sept, early | Festival of Planes | | 702-738-7135 |

The **casinos** operate 24 hours, 365 days per year; but they lack the glitter of Vegas establishments.

Elko's licensed **bordellos** are located southeast of The Stockmen's near 3rd and Douglas. Elko's four are: Mona Lisa Club, Mona's II, PJ's Lucky Strike Bar, and Sue's Bar.

## Lamoille Valley and Ruby Mountains

Lamoille Valley is one of the most beautiful little agricultural valleys in the state. It extends 20 miles from the Ruby Mountains to the Humboldt River and averages only three miles in width. The town of Lamoille lies about 20 miles southeast of the airport at the upper end of the valley. Lamoille is a pretty town with trees, a quaint Presbyterian church, a few rooms for travelers, and a couple of places to eat. The U.S. Forest Service station is located two blocks south of O'Carrol's Bar. Pine Lodge, 702-753-6363, allows pets and provides lodging for $45 and $65 with breakfast. The Breitenstein House, 753-6356, B&B establishment is known for excellent meals. They have rooms for $50, cabins for $100-125, allow pets, and pickup from the airport.

Southeast of town, the valley becomes Lamoille Canyon as it begins its steep ascent into the Ruby Mountains. The canyon is sheer beauty, especially in autumn when it is painted from nature's pallet of yellows, golds, reds, oranges, and greens. The Lamoille Canyon Road is open from late spring until fall. It provides access to a number of **trailheads** and Thomas Canyon Camp. The area is popular for **trout fishing** and **deer hunting**.

The drive from the airport, past Lamoille, up through the canyon, and to the trailheads is about 30 miles. The road dead-

**Ruby Mountains' Dollar Lakes**

ends at about 8600 feet elevation. This is the gateway to the Ruby Mountain wilderness, where you can enjoy a two-hour **hike** or a two-week backpack. I recommend a hike at least as far as Dollar Lakes. The elevation gain is 1000 feet. The round-trip hike requires 100 minutes to three hours, depending upon fitness and breaks. Carry water. Potable water may not be available at the trailhead in colder seasons.

## Elko Area Outfitters

The mountains around Elko are a great resource for the sportsman. A number of outfitters are licensed to help visitors pack into the best spots for **fishing**, **hunting**, or simply enjoying the **scenery**. The Elko Chamber of Commerce or Nevada Outfitters Association can help you pick an outfitter that meets your needs. A sampling of outfitters follows:

| | | |
|---|---|---|
| Prunty Ranch Outfitters | *Charleston* | 702-758-7882 |
| Hidden Lake Outfitters | *Ruby Valley* | 702-779-2268 |
| Humboldt Outfitters | *Wells* | 702-752-3714 |
| Nevada High Country Outfitters | *Wells* | 702-752-3809 |
| Ruby Marsh Guide Service | *Elko* | 702-738-7847 |

The **Ruby Marsh** is located on the other side of the mountains. This unusual 26,000-acre maze is known for trout fishing and waterfowl hunting.

## Northern Drive

This loop takes you through the inhabited **ghost town** of Tuscorora, into the Wild Horse Mountains, and past the Wild Horse Reservoir. Obtain a National Forest map from the Chamber of Commerce before venturing into the mountains. The loop offers scenic variety and can be easily driven in one day.

Take Highway 225 north from Elko. About 26 miles north of Elko, turn left onto Highway 226; continue for 18 miles. You pass Taylor's Canyon Resort, the last opportunity for food and restrooms before Tuscorora. The "resort" is closed on Tuesdays – somewhat run down, but not without personality. Turn left one-half mile further and head west seven miles to Tuscorora. Just before entering town, you pass a classic old cemetery.

Tuscorora is a working **ghost town** with lots of opportunities for exploration and photography. One building has a sign "Tuscorora Hotel and **Pottery School**." It's not really a hotel, but it is a school and they gladly give tours of the facility.

On the way out of town, stop at the cemetery and take a moment to reflect. The desert mountain terrain looks barren. On closer inspection, the foliage has a quiet beauty. The plants

**Farm land north of Elko**

iridesce in golds and pastels as the sun works its way between afternoon thunderclouds. Your next destination is the mountains of brown velvet that rise to the northeast. Drive back to Highway 226 and head north to the Independence Mountains.

Jack Creek Resort is 15 miles north of Taylor's Canyon. It offers a substandard motel, RV park, bar, bait, snacks, ice, and information. A Forest Service campground is located four miles to the right. You can follow the road to the right, drive through the mountains, and head back to Elko if you are ready to call it a day. Otherwise, bear left and follow the signs another 32 miles to Mountain City. The road becomes dirt as it ascends into the mountains. It intersects paved Highway 225 five miles south of Mountain City. Mountain City is not attractive, but it is a source of food and fuel.

**Tuscorora gas station**

The drive along Highway 225 back to Elko takes less than two hours. You can extend your drive another day by looping northeast through the old mining town of **Jarbidge**.

The Jarbidge loop begins at Wild Horse Reservoir. Head northeast through Gold Creek and past the Big Bend Forest Service campground. Picturesque undeveloped campsites are available in the ten-mile stretch beyond Big Bend.

Eventually you intersect the Jarbidge River. Follow it left to Murphys Hot Springs (see **ID-MURP**) or right into Jarbidge. The Outdoor Inn, 702-488-2311, allows pets and has simple, clean rooms for $30-60. An improved campground is located just south of Jarbidge. The drive from Jarbidge to Elko requires several hours. You rejoin Highway 225 six miles south of the Wild Horse Reservoir.

**Tuscorora graveyard**

**Jarbidge neighborhood**

# Ely

## Ely Airport

| | |
|---|---|
| **Town** | Ely **ID** ELY |
| **Coord** | N-39-17.98, W-114-50.51 |
| **Elev** | 6255 feet, S end high |
| **Runway** | 18 - 36, 5998 x 150' asphalt |
| | 12 - 30, 4944 x 60' asphalt |
| **Freq** | CTAF-122.8, Lights-5x, ASOS-120.65 |
| **Charts** | Las Vegas sect., L5, Lo2, Lo3, Lo9 |

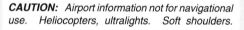

*CAUTION:* Airport information not for navigational use. Heliocopters, ultralights. Soft shoulders.

*Ely is known for its steam train museum and
railroad museum. Sportsmen will enjoy local
hiking, hunting, and fishing.
$75-200. Info: 702-289-8877.*

## Airport Description

Ely airport is easy to spot – a large asphalt V four miles north
of the city. The local mountains do not interfere with daytime
operations in good weather. An IFR VOR approach is available
for use in foul weather via on-field ELY 110.6 VOR. Do not
count on UNICOM response for airport advisories.

## Airport Services, Transportation, and Lodging

Airport phone: 702-289-8804. Fuel: 100LL and JetA. No
food services. Tiedown is $3. FBO hours fluctuate, so call
ahead. If fuel is purchased, a couple hours of courtesy car use is
free; otherwise $10. Full winter service is available.

There are no taxis in town, but all casinos with lodging
pickup from the airport. Avis is at the airport, 702-289-8972;
and National is close by, 289-3058. Agencies play hard-to-get
on weekends, so call in advance for rates and reservations.

Lodging is not a problem, as Ely seems to have an excess of
old motels. Casinos have the advantage of
free airport transportation and on-site entertainment. The Copper Queen is the newest
casino/motel, featuring swimming pool, hot
tubs, and the closest walking distance to the
railroad museum.

**Features**

B Full breakfast
C Continental
H Historic
P Pets OK
R Restaurant
T Transportation

| Copper Queen Casino | **RPT** | $65-135 | 800-851-9526 |
| Hotel Nevada Casino | **RHPT** | $22-52 | 888-406-3055 |
| Jail House Casino | **RPT** | $51-65 | 800-841-5430 |
| Steptoe Valley Inn | **BHT** | $91-97 | 702-289-8687 |

## Ely

Ely is known to tourists and railroad enthusiasts for its **railroad museum** and the **Ghost Train of Old Ely**. A 105-minute round trip ride behind old #40, a 1910 Baldwin steam locomotive, costs $16 for adults and $8 for children. Schedules for steam train rides vary from year to year, so call for dates and reservations at 702-289-2085. The museum is open for visits from May to early October. You can touch and smell the mammoth machinery as you walk through the blacksmith shop, machine shop, roundhouse, and among the cars. The railroad depot and museum are at the foot of 11th Street East in east Ely.

Full-service **gambling** is available at the Copper Queen, Jail House, and Hotel Nevada casinos. Ely's three licensed **brothels** are located at the western edge of Ely, one block north of Highway 50: Stardust, Big 4, and Green Lantern.

## Surrounding Area

The Ely area is known for hunting, fishing, backpacking, and ghost towns. **Hunting** and **fishing** are superb. The following can help sportsmen score: Sports World, 702-289-8886; Nevada Division of State Parks, 728-4467; Nevada Department of Wildlife, 289-1655; and Humboldt National Forest, 289-3031.

The local mountains offer scenic **backpacking**. Topo maps and advice are available from Sports World on Highway 50, west of town. The Great Basin National Park near Baker is a beautiful, high-elevation (cool) place to hike and camp. The park and its Lehman Caves are a fun day-visit; see **NV-LEHM**.

Eight **ghost towns** are located within a 45-mile radius of Ely. The sites will be of interest to people who study Nevada history, but in most cases, very little actually remains intact. Entry into most of these towns is seasonal and limited due to road conditions and location. The Chamber can provide an update.

*- RW*

# Jackpot

## Jackpot Airport

| | |
|---|---|
| **Town** | Jackpot **ID** 06U (zero-6U) |
| **Coord** | N-41-58.56, W-114-39.49 |
| **Elev** | 5213 feet |
| **Runway** | 15 - 33, 6500 x 60' asphalt |
| **Freq** | CTAF-122.8, Lights-122.8-3x |
| **Charts** | Salt Lake City sect., L7, Lo2 |

*CAUTION:* Airport information not for navigational use. Bluff, Runway 33. Ultralights.

> *Jackpot is a small Nevada border town, designed from ground up for gambling and recreation – a worthy overnight stop with good accommodations, entertainment, and reasonable prices. $25 - $175. Casino: 800-821-1103. Info: 702-755-2653*

## Airport Description

Jackpot's prominent black runway is located just east of the complex of casinos and recreational facilities that make up Jackpot. Approach and landing are straightforward. The runway is plowed during winter months. If lights are off at night, activate by clicking 122.8.

## Airport Services, Transportation, and Lodging

Phone: 702-755-2448. Fuel: 100 octane, on request. Fuel service is available from Cactus Pete's RV park operator, adjacent to the tiedown area. Call 122.8 to get the combination to the pilot's john.

Though nearly all destinations are within 15 minutes walking distance, there is no need to walk. Cactus Pete's Casino provides free taxi service between all points in Jackpot. Simply call from the airport or ask for a taxi at any casino or restaurant.

Lodging and restaurants are provided at four casinos. The facilities are clean and look new. Total capacity is about five hundred rooms, which are often filled to near

**Features**

B Full breakfast
C Continental
H Historic
P Pets OK
R Restaurant
T Transportation

capacity. Call in advance to guarantee a room at the casino of your choice. Low-end lodging prices fluctuate from $25 on a winter weekday to $50 on a summer weekend. Cactus Pete's and the Horseshu offer slightly higher quality than the others.

| | | | |
|---|---|---|---|
| Cactus Pete's | **RT** | $25-100 | 800-821-1103 |
| Horseshu | **PRT** | $25-75 | same as above |
| Four Jacks | **R** | $32-49 | 800-251-6313 |
| Ninety-Three Club | **PRT** | $38-108 | 800-258-2937 |

Campers may pitch a tent for $6 per night at the RV park adjacent to the tiedown area.

**Horseshu Casino**

# Jackpot

Back in 1954, Jackpot consisted of the original Horseshu Bar, with a barn sheltering a jackass and a pair of snarling mountain lions in a cage. Since then, gambling and the tourist trade have been good to Jackpot. Today, the border town boasts a good complement of modern, well-run facilities dedicated to Nevada-style recreation.

Facilities include full-scale **gambling casinos**, a variety of **restaurants**, **swimming**, **tennis courts**, **golf**, and outdoor recreation.

Cactus Pete's has the best (and most expensive) gourmet restaurant in Jackpot, and was one of nine Nevada properties to be awarded the prestigious Four Diamond rating. Cactus Pete's provides a mix of **entertainment**, from big names to fascinating, obscure acts like hypnotism. The Horseshu, a Western-decor casino, has the best deals in steak dinners.

The Red Barn is Jackpot's center for outdoor activities. The owners specialize in **rock-hound trips**, but also provide **fishing** and **hunting excursions**. The Red Barn avoids the intrusion of phone service. You can write them at Box 574, Jackpot, NV 89825.

Private individuals in the area provide **hunting**, **fishing**, and **scenic tours**. Ask for names at the Jackpot information services.

In summary, Jackpot is a great overnight stop with easy transportation, evening entertainment, above-average facilities, and good food – all at below-average cost.

*- RW*

# Laughlin

## Bullhead City AZ Airport

| | |
|---|---|
| **Town** | Bullhead City AZ **ID** IFP |
| **Coord** | N-35-09.44, W-114-33.57 |
| **Elev** | 692 feet |
| **Runway** | 16rt - 34, 7500 x 150' asphalt |
| **Freq** | Twr-123.9, Lights-3x5x7x, Gnd-118.25 |
| **Charts** | Phoenix sectional, L3, L5, Lo10 |

> ***CAUTION:*** *Airport information not for navigational use. Ultralights. Hills and mountains near. Avoid power station .5 mi W due to possible turbulence. Don't land at the old runway!*

> *Laughlin is a prosperous gambling town, de-*
> *signed exclusively for that purpose.  Rates are*
> *reasonable at this riverside location, and you can*
> *drive or boat to places of interest outside of town.*
> *$50 - $125.  Info:  800-4-LAUGHLIN.*

## Airport Description

The airport parallels the east bank of the Colorado River.  It lies across from the west-bank strip of casinos in Laughlin. Several IFR approaches are available.  The new runway can handle large aircraft.  (Don't land on the old runway.)

## Airport Services, Transportation, and Lodging

Bullhead Laughlin Aviation:  520-752-3922.  Fuel:  100LL and JetA.  Charter flights, instruction, and aircraft rental are available.

Rental car rates are competitive at the airport.  Avis had the best price when I visited, but check all three for the best deal:

| | | |
|---|---|---|
| Avis | 800-331-1212 | 520-754-4686 |
| Enterprise | 800-325-8007 | 520-754-2700 |
| Hertz | 800-654-3131 | 520-754-4111 |

Unless you plan to visit the outlying areas, a car is not needed at Laughlin.  Free transportation from airport to casinos is provided by a riverboat transit system.  Casino-to-casino transportation up and down the Colorado River is provided by the same free service.  Usage of the system is not intuitively obvious;  ask your first riverboat captain for an explanation. The airport boat dock is located several hundred feet to the west of the terminal.

Lodging and food are plentiful and affordable. Casinos lure gamblers with seductive prices and a variety of entertainment. Rooms can be had for $25 to $50. Full-course meals for less than $8 are common. See "Laughlin Casinos" below.

## Bullhead City

Bullhead City is the support city for Laughlin. Traffic is a nightmare, but work is in process to improve the situation. The Bullhead Chamber of Commerce, 520-754-3891, a good source of information, is located on the west side of Highway 93 between the airport and Bullhead City.

## Laughlin Casinos

Laughlin is essentially a strip of high-rise casinos. Decor is thematic, and the atmosphere is generally of medium- to high-quality. The Colorado Belle is the most photogenic; it looks like a huge riverboat, complete with stacks and water-wheel. Other themes include Old West, trains, and mining.

In my opinion, the Riverside Hotel has a touch of class above the others. It offers amenities such as a phone next to the toilet, a table to write on, remote-control TV, a quiet ventilating system, and rooms for nonsmokers. Its worst defect was the long wait in lines for check-in, eating, and checkout. The food is excellent, with options from inexpensive buffets to gourmet dining. One of their best deals is a full-course roast beef dinner for $8, including dessert and beverage. On-site entertainment includes **gambling**, **big-name performers**, **inexpensive movies**, **swimming**, **tea dances**, free **country and western dance lessons**, and more. Advance reservations are advised.

**Features**

B Full breakfast
C Continental
H Historic
P Pets OK
R Restaurant
T Transportation

Weekday rates are considerably cheaper. A list of Laughlin hotel/casinos follows:

| | | | |
|---|---|---|---|
| Colorado Belle | RT | $20-130 | 800-458-9500 |
| Edgewater Hotel | RT | $20-125 | 800-257-0300 |
| Golden Nugget | RT | $20-70 | 800-237-1739 |
| Harrah's Del Rio | RT | $23-55 | 800-447-8700 |
| Pioneer Hotel | RT | $25-85 | 800-634-3469 |
| Ramada Express | RT | $25-75 | 800-243-6846 |
| Riverside Hotel | PRT | $25-90 | 800-227-3849 |
| River Palms Resort | RT | $22-55 | 800-835-7903 |

Laughlin is one of the fastest-growing gaming towns in the world. In the 60's, Laughlin consisted of not much more than a gas station, bait shop, and the Bobcat Gambling Club. In the late 60's, Don Laughlin (Riverside) and Oddie Lopp (Nevada Club) purchased properties and began development. Over a twenty-year period, Las Vegas investors helped expand the facilities to nine major casinos with thousands of rooms and four area golf courses. Laughlin's enclosed Horizon Outlet Center now houses 65 "factory outlet" stores.

## Surrounding Area

**River trips** are a pleasant way to see more without a rental car. The Little Belle, a scaled-down riverboat replica, gives two-hour cruises up and down the Colorado for $10. The boat has an air conditioned salon, cocktail bar, snack bar, and entertainment. The Little Belle docks at the Edgewater Casino.

The **Lake Havasu London Bridge tour** is a day-long cruise south to the London Bridge (imported from London) at Lake Havasu. The $50 cruise includes lunch and departs from the Pioneer Casino, 702-298-5498. Blue River Safaris provides a 45-minute speedboat trip from the Riverside to the Davis Dam for $10. Reservations can be made at the casinos listed above.

Desert River Outfitters will take you down the Colorado River in a **kayak** or **canoe**, 888 KAYAK33. The following rent **motorized watercraft**, including **jet-skis**: Riverfront Watersports, 520-763-5333; and RiverJetz, 754-1222.

A rental car extends access to the desert, mountains, and **ghost towns**. Oatman, once a gold-mining center, is now a working ghost town that thrives on the tourist dollar. Oatman merchants take pride in keeping their town as authentic as possible. Wild burros leisurely cruise the main street waiting for a handout of alfalfa pellets, on sale at most Oatman shops.  On weekends, the town comes to life.  **Shoot-outs** are staged and **western music** is provided for **dancing**.  Oatman is located southeast of the casinos.  Follow Highway 95 and historical Route 66 approximately 30 miles to Oatman.

You can take a self-guided tour of the **Davis hydroelectric dam** north of Laughlin between 9:00 and 4:00.  Or, visit Grape-vine Canyon, ten miles further north on Highway 163.  Turn right at Christmas Tree Pass.  A short hike is required on a clearly marked trail to view the canyon, **Indian petroglyphs**, and stream. The Davis Dam creates Lake Mohave. At Katherine's Landing, the Lake Mohave Resort and Marina provides restaurant, lodge, picnic areas, and **boat rentals**, 520-754-3245.

**Oatman's resident burros wait for a tourist with alfalfa pellets**

# Lehman Caves

## Baker Airport

| | | | |
|---|---|---|---|
| **Town** | Baker | **ID** | none |
| **Coord** | N-39-00.0, W-113-52.4 | | |
| **Elev** | 5340 feet est., S end high | | |
| **Runway** | 15 - 33, 3000 x 20 dirt | | |
| **Freq** | CTAF-122.9 | | |
| **Charts** | Las Vegas sectional (not listed) | | |

> **CAUTION:** Airport information not for navigational use. Surface marginally maintained and may not be safe for landing. Strip may be muddy after rain. Watch density altitude. Crosswinds out of west in summer.

> *Lehman Caves (at Baker) have natural beauty and aesthetic lighting that leave lasting impressions. Great Basin National Park is another of Nevada's best kept secrets. $60-100. Park Service: 702-234-7331.*

## Airport Description

Baker airport, one mile south of Baker, is not listed in airport reference books and is not shown on the Las Vegas sectional. Do not confuse it with the closed BLM strip further south. The Baker airport looks like a dirt road from the air. Its surface is rough, sandy dirt, but contained no large rocks when I landed. Look for one or more planes parked near the strip's wind-T.

The surface is smooth, but rolls up and down. Depart north, as land is lower in this direction. Due to density altitude, early morning departure is recommended.

If terrain is wet, consider landing at the Baker Ranch, two miles east of Baker. Call Dean Baker for runway condition, 702-234-7316. The Baker's two runways are longer, and more likely to be firm when wet. The runways can be mistaken for roads because they are used as roads. One or more airplanes are typically parked near the intersection of the runways.

## Services and Lodging

The landing strips have no services, no water, and no phone. Chances are, no one will care if you pitch a tent at the strip.

The only motel in town is the Silver Jack at 702-234-7323. Reservations are advised for this eight-unit motel. Rooms are modest and clean, and cost about $39-92. The Border Inn is owned by Denise Baker and is located several miles east of the Baker ranch airstrip. Call 702-234-7300. The Border Inn costs $32-41. They pickup from the airstrips and allow pets.

The Great Basin National Park has four pleasant campgrounds. Two are located within several miles of the caves, a transportation problem if you have no car.

## Transportation

The act of acquiring transportation will test your creative skills. The basic dilemma is: no rental cars, no public transportation, and the caves are five miles from town. Baker is small, but business operators are often willing to drive a visitor to the caves, providing they have someone to man the store. Buzz the town and chances are someone will meet you at the airstrip. If nobody shows, it's only a 20-minute walk north to town.

In town, try soliciting a ride from one of the following businesses: Outlaw Bar, 702-234-7302; gas station, 234-7264; or food store. I suggest offering a fair price for the ride, say $10-20. For additional ideas and help, call the National Park Service at 234-7331. Rangers have been known to give rides.

If all this sounds like too much hassle, consider landing at Ely and renting a car at the Ely airport. See **NV-ELY**.

The proprietor of the Silver Jack motel, Bill Roundtree, will pick up customers from the airport. Call Bill at 702-234-7323 to make advance arrangements.

## Lehman Caves

Lehman Caves are located five miles west of Baker at the end of Highway 488, the main entrance to the Great Basin National Park. The park's Visitor's Center is located at the caves.

Absalom S. Lehman is credited with bringing the caves to the attention of white men. He moved to the area in the late 1860s and discovered the caves on his property somewhat later. Taking time off from ranching, he explored the cave and guided parties through its underground galleries from 1885 until his death in 1891. Access to the caves has been improved over the years. Today, the caverns are easy to tour and artfully lighted.

The tour through the caves covers 2/3 mile and requires 90 minutes. The stalactite and stalagmite formations are beautiful.

Flash cameras are permitted, but for safety reasons, tripods are not. The guide did not object, however, to the six-inch tripod that I used for one-second time exposures. Tours are given at frequent intervals, seven days a week 8:00 to 5:00. The cost is $4 for adults and $3 for children and seniors. Check for other special activities.

## Great Basin National Park

Established in 1986, Great Basin is one of America's newest national parks. Its 76,800 acres includes Lehman Caves and 13,063-foot Mt. Wheeler. The Park Service information phone is 702-234-7331. See their web site at *www.nps.gov/grba*.

A number of scenic hiking trails are situated just northeast of the peak. Topo maps are available from the Visitor's Center. Trailheads are accessible from the Wheeler Peak Campground.

To get to the trailheads, follow the paved road 12 miles northwest from the Visitor's Center. You pass Lower and Upper Lehman Creek Campgrounds as you climb in elevation. Just before Wheeler Peak Campground, look for a parking lot on the left and two trailheads on the right. Camping at the camp-

ground costs $5. The trailheads begin at approximately 10,000 feet elevation.

The trails offer a number of options, from a one-hour loop to the five-mile ascent of Wheeler Peak. Trails are well marked and pass by a wide variety of terrain and foliage. You can visit lakes, streams, forests, and an ice field. In summer, this is a refreshing way to beat the Nevada heat. In autumn, the colors are outstanding.

*- RW*

**Mt. Wheeler at Great Basin National Park**

# Utah

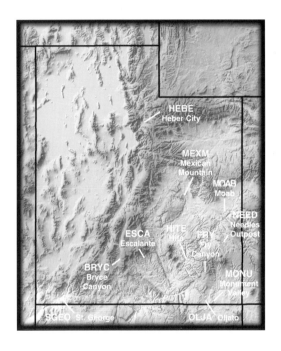

**HEBE**
Heber City

**MEXM**
Mexican
Mountain

**MOAB**
Moab

**NEED**
Needles
Outpost

**ESCA**
Escalante

**HITE**
Hite

**FRY**
Fry
Canyon

**BRYC**
Bryce
Canyon

**MONU**
Monument
Valley

**SGEO** St. George

**OLJA** Oljato

**Utah Aeronautics**

**801-715-2260**

# Bryce Canyon

## Bryce Canyon Airport

| | |
|---|---|
| **Town** | Bryce Canyon   **ID** BCE |
| **Coord** | N-37-42.38,  W-112-08.73 |
| **Elev** | 7586', 0.5%, SW end high |
| **Runway** | 3 - 21, 7400 x 75' asphalt |
| **Freq** | CTAF-122.8,  Lights-122.8 |
| **Charts** | Las Vegas, SLC sect, L5, Lo9 |

> ***CAUTION:*** *Airport information not for navigational use. Helicopters. Power lines SW. Lights 75' from runway edge. Watch density altitude.*

> **Bryce Canyon is one of America's most photoge-**
> **nic wonders. Hike and camp, or just stay at a**
> **lodge and enjoy the views from the rim. $30-250.**
> **Info:  435-834-5322, www.nps.gov/brca**

## Airport Description

The airport is located in a high valley.  Head toward Bryce
BCE VOR and look for a gigantic runway; you can't miss it.  The
runway is large enough for emergency commercial jet landings.

Before landing, consider a scenic flight over Bryce Canyon,
south of the airport.  Before departing in summer, carefully
calculate density altitude.  The runway is open during winter.

## Airport Services, Transportation, and Lodging

Airport phone: 435-834-5239.  Fuel: 100LL and JetA.
Tiedown costs $3.  Snacks are available from vending machines.
Or, walk 10 minutes south to a highway restaurant for a meal.

Taxis are not available, but an airport shuttle will take you to
the park for $5 per person or less.  The FBO rents cars for $55-65
per day, 834-5200.  Two inns provide free transportation.  The
trip takes about ten minutes by car, or two hours on foot.

Camping at the airport is discouraged.  Camping in the park
near the rim costs $10.  Lodging is sometimes fully booked
during tourist season.  Make advance reservations if you prefer
the bed to the bag.  The Bryce Canyon Lodge serves reasonably-
priced meals and has the most idyllic setting.  It is located in the
park near the canyon rim, about five miles from the airport.  Call
the lodge at 435-834-5361 for information or reservations.

| Best Western Ruby's | PR | $50-100 | 800-468-8660 |
|---|---|---|---|
| Bryce Canyon Lodge | HRT | $96-131 | 435-834-5361 |
| Bryce Canyon Pines | R | $35-80 | 800-892-7923 |
| Fosters | | $66 | 435-834-5227 |

My favorite campsites are inside the canyon. They offer advantages of being free, more picturesque, and miles from "RV City." Permits are required. Either way (rim or canyon), make your camping arrangements at the Visitor's Center.

## Overview

Bryce Canyon looks good from the air, looks better from the canyon rim, and is absolutely overwhelming when viewed amongst the multi-colored, unearthly, towering structures. My first impression was that this natural burst of color must be one

**Cabins at Bryce Canyon National Park**

of America's best kept secrets. I was wrong. Foreign visitors seem to be well aware of Bryce; about half of the visitors come from other continents.

Chances are, you will want to shoot pictures of everything you see. The best photographic conditions occur with partial cloud cover or near sunset. The serious photographer will make full use of tripod and exotic lenses.

Due to its high elevation of 8000 feet, Bryce Canyon facilities are operated only during summer months: mid-May or June until the first of October. For cooler temperatures and less people, visit Bryce at either end of the season. This, however, introduces the possibility of snow. Snow provides a beautiful touch to an environment that seems to be beyond improvement. In mid-season, note that camping areas at the rim fill quickly.

During operating season, the park provides a number of useful services. The Visitor's Center is a good source for tips and printed information, most of which are free. Located near

the rim are the park-operated grocery store, laundromat, showers, and lodge. The lodge serves tasty meals and provides entertainment such as **movies at night**. Reservations are advised for evening meals. During the day you can take **hikes** with a park naturalist, or **ride a horse or mule** into the canyon for $10-25 dollars. The $25, three-hour ride might be the most beautiful horseback ride you ever take.

The Visitor's Center is usually open from 8:00 to 19:00, depending on season. At the Center, load up on maps and information. Pick a campsite, and get a permit for the canyon or pay a fee for camping at the rim. The ranger can help you select a hike that matches your interests, capabilities, and schedule. Carry adequate water when heading into the canyon.

During the winter, most of the facilities are closed. However, park and Visitor's Center remain open. **Cross-country skiing** is excellent. **Snowshoes** are loaned out on a first-come, first-served basis. Winter lodging is available at the local motels listed above.

## Bryce Canyon Loop

This stunning 2.6 mile hike begins at Sunrise Point on the canyon rim. Take Queen's Garden trail down into the canyon. Follow the Navaho Loop Trail back to Sunset Point on the rim. With time for a seven mile hike, you can extend the experience by walking a figure-eight down to and including Peekaboo Loop Trail. Though these trails require some climbing, they are easy to follow and are clearly marked on the park's free maps.

## Rim Hike To Airport

You can return to the airport on foot by walking the scenic rim. Start from the campground near the lodge. Follow the Rim Trail north for 15 minutes to Fairyland Point. The views are spectacular.  At Fairyland Point, the official trail veers off to the right and descends into the canyon.  Instead, follow the rim northeast.

The park's perimeter fence is 30 minutes from Fairyland. Cross the fence and join the horse trail that follows the rim north.  Within 10 minutes after crossing the fence, the trail bends left, leaving the rim.  Follow it until the fence ends on the right. Take the horse trail that bends right through a stand of fir trees. Continue heading 340 degrees, with a small stream at the right. You emerge at Highway 63 and Ruby's 15 minutes past the rim.

Follow 63 north toward the airport.  At Highways 63 and 12, head directly across the field to the airport.  The segment between Ruby's and the airport takes 35 minutes and is the only non-scenic leg of the hike.  Time from campground to airport is two hours.

# Escalante

## Escalante Municipal Airport

| | |
|---|---|
| **Town** | Escalante **ID** 1L7 |
| **Coord** | N-37-44.70, W-111-34.21 |
| **Elev** | 5740 feet, dip in middle |
| **Runway** | 12rt - 30, 5025 x 60' asphalt |
| **Freq** | CTAF-122.8 |
| **Charts** | Las Vegas sectional, L5, Lo9 |

> ***CAUTION:*** *Airport information not for navigational use. Mountain ridge near field. Do not mistake closed strip for runway. Midfield dip in runway.*

12rt

30

---

*Escalante, gateway to Escalante Grand
Stairway National Monument. Small town
with lodging that provides access to scenic
drives, hikes, and packtrips.
$50 - $250. Chamber: 435-826-4810.*

---

## Airport, Services, and Transportation

Escalante Airport is 60 miles northwest of Lake Powell. From
almost any direction, you fly over beautiful terrain when destined
for Escalante. The airport is an asphalt runway, two miles southeast of town. Do not mistake the nearby closed airstrip for the
proper runway. Although pilot's guides list pilot controlled lighting, be forewarned that the runway lights are non-functional.

Airport Phone: 435-826-4644. Fuel: None. Although the
airport is unattended and without services, a public phone is
available. Walking distance to the center of town is about 2.5
miles. Retired pilot Bill Bowmar is a good source of airport and
local information, 826-4662. Bill monitors 121.5 and 122.8.

Once in town, bikes can be rented, and Bronco 4x4s are
available from the Prospector Inn at $80 per day, 435-826-4653.
The Rainbow Country B&B provides tours of the backcountry and
shuttles to trailheads. Tours cost $40 per person for a half day, and
$80 for a full day. Shuttles to trailheads cost $1 per mile for the
round trip ($2 per mile for the distance you travel).

## Escalante

Escalante lies in the heart of colorful canyon and mountain
country. With a half dozen motels and as many arts-and-crafts

shops, Escalante caters to the escalating flow of tourists who are attracted by the newly designated national monument – **Escalante Grand Staircase National Monument**. Information is available from the BLM at 435-826-5499.

After a month of intensive flying, I planned to stay one night in Escalante before heading home. The flight from Page to Escalante revealed fascinating terrain. Next time, I promised myself, I will spend the better part of a week trekking the land below.

Gene, owner of Rainbow Country B&B, was waiting as promised at the Escalante airport. We drove to his inn, which is just northwest of the airport. Shortly after dropping the bags, we hopped in Gene's car for a tour of the mountain ridges. The scenery was even more captivating than what I saw from the air. At dusk, we returned for dinner and a soak in the hot tub.

**View from Rainbow Country B&B**

Escalante has four restaurants and a variety of lodging. The best **restaurant** is the Pondorosa, which has a Hungarian chef who supplements the menu with Hungarian and European specialties. The town has a half dozen **arts and crafts shops,** and interestingly, a Native American-style **drum factory**, 435-826-4700.

**Features**

B Full breakfast
C Continental
H Historic
P Pets OK
R Restaurant
T Transportation

| | | | |
|---|---|---|---|
| Bunkhouse Motel | | $28 | 435-826-4266 |
| Circle D Motel | PT | $33-44 | 435-826-4297 |
| Moqui Motel | HT | $28-55 | 435-826-4210 |
| Padre Motel | | $33-66 | 435-826-4276 |
| Prospector Inn | T | $55 | 435-826-4653 |
| Quiet Falls Motel | HPT | $33-66 | 435-826-4250 |
| Rainbow Country B&B | BPT | $50-66 | 800-252-8824 |

**Bunkhouse Motel, bargain price – but no pilot pickup**

Escalante and surrounding area were one of the last frontiers explored in the continental U.S. Explorer John Wesley Powell named the town and river in honor of Father Escalante, an adventuresome priest who explored the area around 1776. The Mormons eventually began settling the land in 1876.

Today, Escalante is visited by **hikers**, **mountain bikers**, **fishermen**, and by families who simply appreciate a **scenic drive**. Within 30 miles of Escalante, you can drive to the following: **Escalante Petrified Forest**, 826-4466; **Escalante Canyons**; **Call Creek Recreation Area**; and an **Anasazi Indian Village** near Boulder, 435-355-7308.

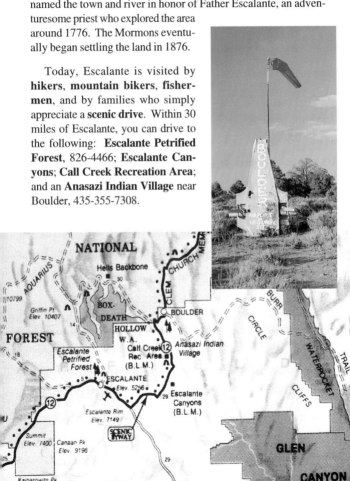

**Boulder** is 29 miles north of Escalante via a **scenic highway** that explores canyons and panoramic ridges. On the way, you pass unmarked **Boulder Airport** at 6700 feet. Assuming its runway is dry, the airport is suited for Super Cubs and serious STOL aircraft. A sign at the windsock reads, "Airport and UFO Landing Site."

Boulder has additional lodging, restaurants, and the International Boulder **Outdoor Survival School**, 800-335-7404. The Boulder Mountain Ranch provides **horseback rides** and offers a cabin and breakfast for $65, 435-335-7480. The fare for a two-person pack trip is $250 total per day. Coincidentally, owner Bob Cochran maintains the Boulder airstrip. If you stay at his ranch, he will pick you up from the Escalante Airport.

Escalante has two summer events worthy of note. Their Escalante **Mountain Man Rendezvous** occurs in June. A big celebration commemorating Mormon entry to the area occurs in late July. Call the Chamber at 435-826-4810 for details.

# Fry Canyon

## Mexican Mountain

| | |
|---|---|
| **Town** | Fry Canyon   **ID**   none |
| **Coord** | N-37-39.0,  W-110.09.5 est. |
| **Elev** | 5325 feet est, NW end high |
| **Runway** | 13 - 31,  3000+ x 75' dirt |
| **Freq** | CTAF-122.9 |
| **Charts** | Denver sectional (uncharted) |

> *CAUTION:*  Airport information not for naviga-
> tional use.  Tall weeds. Soft dirt. Not maintained.

> *Fry Canyon is within walking distance of*
> *the Fry Canyon Lodge and remants of a*
> *little-known Native American cliff dwelling.*
> *$0-120.   Lodge: 435-259-5334*

## Airport

The runway runs parallel to and between a blacktop highway to the south, and a canyon to the north.  Note the dirt road that crosses the runway, and connects the highway with the canyon.  The northwest end is high, but you can safely land in either direction.  There is no windsock.  The surface is soft dirt with clumps of grass and weeds.  When landing, take care to avoid the larger weeds.

## Fry Canyon Lodge and Canyon Cliff Dwelling

Within a minute of leaving the airplane, I spotted a beat up pickup truck heading in my direction.  The driver asked if I needed help.  I discovered that he was headed for nearby cliff dwellings, which he visits whenever in the area.  I asked if I could join him, and he said, "hop in."  He made room in the cab, which was cluttered with stuff like boots and empty Marlboro packs.  Although he introduced himself as Bonny, a plaque on the weathered dash board read "Crazy Man."  We drove a half mile to the canyon's edge.

The **cliff dwelling** is in the northeast wall of the narrow canyon.  It is unmarked and not known by tourists.  If restored, this site would be of Mesa Verde class.  I had difficulty visualizing how the inhabitants got to their dwellings – probably with a series of very long ladders. Although the site has likely been looted of artifacts, its inaccessibility has protected the building structure from vandals. Bonny said that he had tried a dozen times to find an access from different directions, without success.

As we drove away, Bonny related how he found his first arrowhead in the area. He stopped to relieve himself, looked down, and saw that his stream had exposed a shiny arrowhead. He wiped it off and stuffed it in his pocket. Later, he showed it to his buddy who immediately stuck it into his mouth, wetting it to enhance the colors. Bonny didn't have the heart to fully disclose the details of his find, a temptation that would have been difficult for lesser men to resist.

**Little-known cliff dwelling near the air strip**

Finding an arrowhead is like identifying a distant airport. I have never found an arrowhead, but I can sense a distant airport, minutes before I can actually put my finger on it. Bonny says finding arrowheads is like that. He looked 12 years before finding his memorable first. Since then, he has found dozens.

The **Fry Canyon Lodge** is a mile southeast. The lodge has pleasant, clean units for $50-80. The facilities include a restaurant and a store. The store is limited to providing drinks and snacks. If you land and walk to the lodge, the owner will drive back and pick up luggage at his convenience. When I visited, they had a satellite phone with marginal reliability that cost the owner a staggering $500 per month. Their reservation phone number is 435-259-5334 in Moab.

**Fry Canyon Lodge**

# Heber City
# Park City

## Heber Valley Airport

| | | | |
|---|---|---|---|
| **Town** | Heber City | **ID** | 36U |
| **Coord** | N-40-29.08, W-111-25.54 | | |
| **Elev** | 5632 feet, 1%, NE end high | | |
| **Runway** | 3 - 21, 6900 x 75' asphalt | | |
| **Freq** | CTAF-122.8, Lights-3x5x7x | | |
| **Charts** | Salt Lake City, L7, L8, Lo7, Lo9 | | |

> **CAUTION:** Airport information not for navigational use. Power lines SE. Soaring.

*Heber City, home of steam train and hot springs resorts. Park City caters to skiers in winter, and outdoor enthusiasts in summer. $50-250.*
*Heber: 801-654-3666, www.hebervalleycc.org*
*Park: 800-453-1360, www.parkcityinfo.com*

## Airport Description

Heber City airport is located one mile south of the city. Though high mountains are located in the area, they do not influence airport operations during daylight in good weather.

## Airport Services, Transportation, Lodging

Airport phone: 435-654-3962. Fuel: 100LL and JetA. Wasatch Aero provides fuel, tiedown for $5, winter services, maintenance, flying instruction, airplane rental, and car rental for $50-90. Call 654-3962 for rental car reservations.

The best (and most expensive) lodging near Heber City is The Homestead. They are four miles west of Heber City and pickup from the airport. To get there, drive west from Heber's only traffic light on Midway Lane.

The Homestead, 800-327-7220, is a classic country resort that features a number of recreational activities: **swimming**, **horseback riding**, **golf**, **cross-country skiing**, **sleigh rides**, **snowmobile rides**, and **hot springs soaking**. You can even **scuba dive** in their 90-degree hot springs crater to a depth of over 40 feet! The spa includes a small, natural **hot springs pool**. The overall charm and quality of the resort is high. Food is very good to excellent. Room prices are $125-400.

A second **hot springs** resort, the Mountain Spa, 435-654-0721, is three miles west of Heber City in Midway. It has a 1930s flavor and is rustic, almost primitive, in comparison to The Homestead. Room prices are $45-72 for two, and they offer free pickup from the airport. Family accommodations are available. Activities include **swimming** and **horseback riding**.

A number of medium- and low-quality motels are located in Heber City. Most pilots will find acceptable the $44-100 Danish Viking Lodge, 800-544-4066, and $43-74 High Country Inn, 800-345-9198. Nearby Park City has over fifty high-quality lodges and condos, primarily rented by skiers in winter. Call the Visitors' centers for additional recommendations.

The Wasatch Mountain State Park has a scenic campground. It is located five miles west of Heber City and north of Midway. The cost is $10 per night and reservations are advised. The

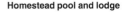

**Homestead pool and lodge**

reservation service is undergoing changes, but you can try calling 800-284-CAMP. The nearby Wasatch Mountain Golf course charges a reasonable fee for nine and eighteen holes. Numerous unimproved (free) campsites can be found in and around the area's mountains.

## Heber City

Heber City is known primarily for the Heber Valley Historic Railroad and its **coal-fired steam locomotives**. During summer, the railroad offers trips through Heber Valley, past Deer Creek Reservoir, and into Provo Canyon's Vivian Park near Bridal Veil Falls. Steam and diesel service varies from season to season, so call 435-654-5601 to verify operation. Costs for standard runs are $10-17 for adults. Specialty rides are offered at less frequent intervals: a Bluegrass Ride, and the Murder Mystery Train

**Heber Valley Historic  Railroad**

(rolling theater). The depot is located six blocks west of Main Street, across from the fair grounds.

## Park City

Park city was established as a mining camp in the late 1860s. The town enjoyed great prosperity as its mountains surrendered $400 million in silver. As prices fell in the 1930s, enterprising Park City survivalists began turning their attention to the white stuff on the slopes. Ski jumpers from around the world started competing at Ecker Hill in 1930. Snow Park **ski resort** opened in 1946, and others followed: Park City Ski Area, Park West Ski Area, and Deer Valley Resort.

Although Park City is known primarily as a lively Utah ski center, its year-round activities qualify it as a four-season recreation area. You can enjoy a pleasant stroll past **interesting**

**Park City**

**shops** and restaurants any time of year. Mountains rise above colored store fronts, skiers and tourists bustle in their colorful costumes, delightful aromas from restaurants tempt you, and happy sounds of music and laughter drift through the crisp mountain air.

**Golfers** have a choice of four courses: Park City Golf Course, 435-649-8701; Park Meadows Country Club, 649-2460; Wasatch Mountain State Park, 654-0532; and Mountain Dell Golf Course, 582-3812. You'll be surprised how far your balls will fly in thin air at 6900 feet.

Kids and adults can enjoy the **Alpine Slide** at the Resort Center, 435-649-8111, in summer. For $6.25, ride up the mountain in a chair lift, and down in a specially designed sled.

Feel like a **balloon ride** in mountain country? Call ABC Ballooning, 800-820-ABCD; or, Park City Balloon Adventures, 800-396-8787 Flights usually include transportation, champagne, and silver service.

Park City is a center for mountain recreational activities. Local outfitters offer access to **fishing**, **hunting**, **horseback riding**, **pack trips**, **backpacking**, **gentle hiking**, **wildflower treks**, **ca-**

**noeing**, **raft trips**, and even **llama leasing**. For information, about activities or events, call the Visitor Information Center.

Park City attracts summer vacationers by offering a full calendar of special events. Their typical year includes:

> Mountain Man Rendezvous
> State Muzzle Loading Championships
> Third Annual Festival of the Fifties
> Highland Games
> Bicycle tours and festivals
> Rodeo
> Utah Symphony and other music
> Shakespeare Festival and other theater
> Championship Sheep Dog Trials
> Bluegrass Festival
> Hot air balloon festivals

Many of the above are yearly events. Call Park City Chamber of Commerce at 800-453-1360 for dates and details.

## Timpanogos Drive

The surrounding area offers a wealth of **scenic opportunities** – too many to cover in detail. The following drive can be done in less than a day and provides a sampling of interesting activities. In fall, autumn colors can cause sensory overload. The drive takes you south, past the Deer Creek Reservoir, Timpanogos Wilderness, Timpanogos Caves, and Bridal Veil Falls.

Drive 14 miles south of Heber City past the Deer Creek Reservoir on Highway 189. Turn right at the Sundance turnoff to Highway 92. Follow 92 past Robert Redford's Sundance Ski Resort and into the mountains for five miles. The Theater in the Pines on the left has a trailhead that leads up Mt. Timpanogos. The trail winds its way up the mountain past several waterfalls, with con-

tinuous exposure to views of the area.  The first usable campsite is
a one-hour walk to a flat rock that overlooks the valley.

Continue driving on Highway 92 up the mountain.  You pass
several tempting trailheads.  Six miles past Theater in the Pines,
bear left at the Y toward **Timpanogos Cave**.  Still on Hwy 92,
you descend to the canyon floor after four miles.  Follow the
canyon south two more miles past a beautiful campground until
you reach the cave.

The cave's Visitor's Center includes nature displays, videos ,
and a snack bar.  Literature and topo maps are available at the
information desk.  The cave is located 1000 feet above.  The
ascent is pleasant and guaranteed to use up excess energy in
children.  An average person can make the climb in one hour.
The round trip requires 2.5 hours.  If you like caves, you're
bound to enjoy the experience.  I rank it slightly below Lehman
Caves (see **NV-LEHM**) in overall quality.

Continue south three miles.  Turn left on Highway 146.  After
five miles join the main thoroughfare east.  Follow it into Orem
and turn left onto Highway 152, and left again onto Highway 180
toward Heber City.  After four miles on 180, you arrive at the
Bridal Veil Falls Sky Tram.

The **Sky Tram** rises 1228 feet to a vantage point above
**Bridal Veil Falls** and is claimed to be the steepest passenger
tram in the world.  The tram was the lifelong dream of an old
gentleman who struggled to see his project to completion.  He
met his goal in 1962 and died one year later.  The site includes
hiking trails, food, gift shop, ducks, fish, and other natural amusements.  The round-trip ride costs $5.

Follow the highway back to Heber.  Two miles northeast of
the falls, you pass a steam train station on your right.

*- RW*

# Hite

## Hite Airport

| | |
|---|---|
| **Town** | none **ID** UT03 |
| **Coord** | N-37-53.65, W-110-22.58 |
| **Elev** | 3840 feet, 9%, E end high |
| **Runway** | 9 - 27, 2200 x 40' asphalt |
| **Freq** | CTAF-122.8 |
| **Charts** | Denver sectional |

> **CAUTION:** Airport information not for navigational use. Steep runway. Listed as hazardous on the sectional. Quartering winds.

> *Hite is suitable as an overnight campsite, or a stop for a refreshing swim in Lake Powell. Perched above the lake, campers enjoy a great view of the beautiful lake.  No amenities.  $0.*

## Airport

Hite sits at northern tip of Lake Powell, surrounded by towering canyon bluffs to the north and lake water in remaining quadrants.  The runway lies at the south edge of the only blacktop highway that cuts clear through the rugged Canyonlands. The sectional lists the strip as "hazardous," possibly because the

runway has a 9% grade (unofficial source) and winds are not uncommon. You can see the bright windsocks for miles, and the steep grade can work to advantage.

Given low winds, bleed altitude over Lake Powell, followed by an up-hill landing on Runway 9. Depart downhill on 27. Using this procedure, you conveniently face away from the sun for both afternoon arrival and morning departure.

## Near the Airport

There are no services, amenities, or phone at Hite. There is, however, a barren shade pavilion without walls, tables, or benches. This is probably for rafters who pull out near Hite and wait for pickup. You can easily pitch a tent within feet of your airplane – a scenic and convenient spot for an overnight. The panoramic

view of lake and canyon bluffs is awe-inspiring at sunset and sunrise.

Private, unofficial campsites are available down by the lake. To get to the lake, walk southeast from the tiedown area and plot a zigzag path down the rock ledge. It is not as bad as it looks. I'm not a rock climber and I clocked my trips at 15 minutes down, and 10 minutes up. The terrain includes multicolored rock outcroppings with curious cavities and holes.

By the lake, there are flat areas where a camp can be setup, and plenty of driftwood for a campfire. A dip in the lake water can be most refreshing. Keep in mind that the lake is a man-made reservoir, so take care not to jump onto submerged remnants of foliage that remain below the surface.

**Camp near the lake  –  plenty of driftwood for a camp fire**

# Mexican Mountain

## Mexican Mountain

| | |
|---|---|
| **Town** | none **ID** none |
| **Coord** | N-39-01.1, W-110-26.6 est. |
| **Elev** | 4465 feet |
| **Runway** | 10 - 28, 1325+ x 40' dirt |
| **Freq** | CTAF-122.9 |
| **Charts** | Denver sectional (uncharted) |

*CAUTION:* Airport information not for navigational use. Towering bluffs, all quadrants. STOL runway. Marginal 200-500 foot overrun. Not maintained.

> *Mexican Mountain is a picturesque get-away
> below towering red-rock bluffs on the San
> Rafael River.  A site for camping, hikes,
> petroglyphs.  The site is inaccessible by land
> vehicle – a good site for STOL pilots  $0.*

## Airport

The airport is nearly hidden between towering red-rock bluffs,
10 miles west Green River Airport.  Look for the strip northeast
of the river.  Most pilots land east and depart east.  When
landing, come in low and slow with wheels just above the bush at
the west end.  Plan an efficient stop, as the runway becomes
marginal past 1325 feet.  Past this point, an additional 200-500
feet may be usable for overrun or aborted take-off.  The runway
is surrounded with cottonwood trees within 40-50 feet of both
sides.  In the airport drawing, note the stump at 1900 feet.

In view of the runway's short length and high elevation, this
strip is for experienced backcountry pilots in calm air.  When
visiting Mexican Mountain, your best insurance is experience,
good judgment, power, low stalling speed, and light loading.
With those prerequisites, the safety margin becomes acceptable.

The runway surface is dirt, inadequately drained in at least
one spot.  Sections can become unusable after a downpour or
after the river has flooded.  Visitors tend to keep the weeds at
bay.  When I landed, they were generally less than one foot tall,
and I removed any taller than six inches before departing.

The Utah Back Country Pilots have installed a windsock west of midfield. Several areas are adequately clear of the runway for safe tiedown. Bring your own ropes and stakes. The strip is not accessible by road.

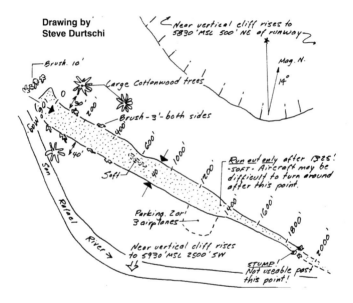

**Drawing by Steve Durtschi**

Near vertical cliff rises to 5830'MSL 500'NE of runway

Mag. N. 14°

Brush. 10'

Large Cottonwood trees

Brush - 3' - both sides

Run out only after 1325' - SOFT - Aircraft may be difficult to turn around after this point.

Soft

Parking. 2 or 3 airplanes

San Rafael River →

Near vertical cliff rises to 5930'MSL 2500'SW

STUMP! Not useable past this point!

## History, Hikes, and Camping

According to a former BLM field man, the runway and a now-defunct dirt road from Buck Horn Wash were built in the mid-60s to support gas and oil exploration. The survey was unsuccessful, but you can still see the plug for a dry hole one-quarter mile east of the strip.  Judging from runway surface condition, the strip has been in light continuous use since that time.

Prior to men and their flying machines, the country enjoyed interesting history.  Fortunately, Pearl Baker documented Green River in her books – in particular, **The Wild Bunch at Robber's Roost**.  A pilot herself, Pearl also documented pilot Him Hurst's experiences as a back country pilot in **Rim Flying Canyonlands**. I purchased the book from Redtail Aviation in Moab and read it while kicked back at Mexican Mountain.  The following excerpt tells about an event that occurred at the Lower Box, within walking distance downstream:

"The San Rafael River cuts down through the Reef in a narrow chasm with its overhanging sides almost touching at the top.  In fact the narrowest place is called Swasey's Leap because Sid Swasey actually jumped his horse across it.

"The Swaseys had a cattle and horse empire in the Sinbad and surrounding country about 1880 to the turn of the century.  They were fine horsemen, with Sid being about the pick of the family in that line.  One time they were camped by this crack in the rock, and got to arguing whether or not a horse could actually leap across it.  Sid said he had a horse that could do it, and the other boys finally bet him ten head of yearling heifers that he couldn't do it.

"The gap was about 11 feet, it was later bridged by a 12-foot wagon box so that sheep could be trailed across the river during high water and not have to swim.  The south side was about two feet higher than the north side from which he was jumping, and there wasn't room for a run.  Actually, he had to ride up to it and turn sharply into the jump.

"It was an absolutely crazy thing to do; Sid was a big man. Any horse would have all it could do to make such a jump, and if it faltered, both it and the rider would fall over 200 feet to their certain death.

"But Sid was no ordinary horseman, and he and his mount trusted each other. He brought the horse up on a dead run, whirled and as the horse jumped, he lifted it with both bridle and spurs, swing his weight in perfect rhythm with the straining animal, and they soared across to a perfect landing on the sloping slick-rock of the other side."

Besides interesting history, Utah is home to some of the most beautiful flying country in the world. The abandoned uranium mining strips in Canyonlands are great fun to visit, but few places

in the area have the solitude, beauty, and camp worthiness of Mexican Mountain. The green cottonwood trees and towering red and orange bluffs have etched a permanent image in my mind.

The area between the runway and San Rafael river has trees for shade and soft ground for **camping**. Fire wood is within easy reach. Other than the windsock, there are no improvements at the site. Because visitors have taken care to remove trash and fire rings, you may wonder if you are the first to arrive in years. Come prepared for protection from sun and insects.

**Petroglyphs** can be found on large boulders with dark brown surfaces. Walk roughly 50 degrees from the windsock, and within 300 yards you will find some. The most prolific includes a picture of a large figure with some sort of headdress, a smaller femine figure, and a still smaller figure - all holding hands. It

appears to be somewhat crudely pecked, almost like someone's first attempt. Steve Durtschi of the Utah Back Country Pilots told me he felt the artist to be a young boy or girl. He visualized the child willing away the hours in the shade of that big rock, sketching a picture of his family while hiding from chores.

The **San Rafael River** was, no doubt, another popular escape for the young ones. The most convenient river access can be found at the west end of the runway. The water was most refreshing, but too cool for total immersion of my tender hide.

The **Upper Box** and **Lower Box** are walled sections of canyon, revered by hikers who frequent the area. You can get to either by **hiking** upstream or downstream, respectively.

**Petroglyphs embellish rocks northeast of the windsock**

Mexican Mountain and surrounding 65,000 acres are currently in a "Wilderness Study Area," or WSA. Because current representatives of the federal government claim to have been unaware of the runway's history, Mexican Mountain is in jeopardy. If government closure of yet another back country airstrip is of concern to you, write to the local BLM office. If you write, consider that BLM folks, like most of us, are doing the best they can. You can help them make the best decision by cordially providing them with awareness and new information.

> San Rafael Area Manager
> Bureau of Land Management
> 900 North 700 East
> Price, UT 84501

# Moab and Canyonlands

## Canyonlands Airport

| | |
|---|---|
| **Town** | Moab **ID** CNY |
| **Coord** | N-38-45.30, W-109-45.28 |
| **Elev** | 4553 feet |
| **Runway** | 3 - 21, 7100 x 75' asphalt |
| **Freq** | CTAF-122.8, Lights-122.8-5x |
| **Charts** | Denver sectional, L5, Lo9 |

*CAUTION:* Airport information not for navigational use. Pole and power lines near the airport. Extreme heat in summer; watch density altitude.

> *Moab and Canyonlands, beautiful flying-scenery –*
> *getting there is half the fun. Rugged redrock*
> *topography, Arches National Park, ancient Indian*
> *artifacts, and whitewater recreation. $100-250.*
> *Info: 800-635-6622, www.canyonlands-utah.com.*

## Airport Description

Canyonlands airport is located near some of the most scenic
flying country in the U.S. – incredible color and rugged terrain.
VOR reception is spotty at lower AGLs, but the on-field OAB
VOR will guide you in if you are near the field. OAB can be used
for non-precision IFR approaches.

If unfamiliar with the area, plan arrival to avoid afternoon
cloud buildups, which can push you below VOR reception altitude. Look for the airport 15 miles northwest of Moab. The
airport is unobstructed by bluffs or mountains.

## Airport Services and Transportation

Airport phone: 435-259-7421 at Redtail Aviation. Fuel:
100LL and JetA. Tiedown is $2.50. Redtail Aviation provides
Thrifty rental cars and informal tourist information. Camping at
the airport is allowed.

Funpigs Shuttle, 435-259-9402, charges $20 for one or $22
for two for a ride to Moab. Coyote Shuttle, 259-8656, charges
$12 for one or $24 per couple. Thrifty and Budget routinely
deliver cars to the airport. The 4x4 agencies deliver, as well.

| Budget | | 800-527-0700 | 435-259-7494 |
|---|---|---|---|
| Farabee Rentals 4x4s | | 800-806-5337 | 435-259-7474 |
| Thrifty | | 800-367-2277 | 435-259-7317 |
| Slick Rock 4x4s | | | 435-259-5678 |

## Lodging

| | | | |
|---|---|---|---|
| Best Western Greenwell | R | $45-112 | 435-259-6151 |
| Blue Heron B&B | B | $56-100 | 800-870-6537 |
| Canyon Country B&B | B | $63-111 | 800-435-0284 |
| Castle Valley Inn | B | $90-170 | 435-259-6012 |
| Cedar Breaks | P | $67-90 | 888-272-8181 |
| Dark Canyon Recreation | T | $50-130 | 435-259-8389 |
| DeLong B&B | B | $60 | 435-259-7651 |
| Desert Chalet | B | $56-84 | 800-549-8504 |
| Lazy Lizard Hostel | T | $13-30 | 435-259-6057 |
| Big Horn Lodge | PR | $55-85 | 800-325-6171 |
| Pack Creek Guest Ranch | BP | $89-170 | 435-259-5505 |
| Sunflower Hill B&B | BH | $95-170 | 800-MOABSUN |
| Super 8 | | $80-100 | 435-259-8868 |
| Virginian Motel | P | $30-80 | 800-261-2063 |
| Whitehouse Bed & Bath | | $45-56 | 435-259-6318 |

For a low-cost, rustic alternative without meals, consider Dark Canyon Recreation's log cabins. Located at 10,000 feet, this facility is snowed in through winter. Snowmobile transportation costs for $30 per couple each way; you must bring your own food.

### Features

- **B** Full breakfast
- **C** Continental
- **H** Historic
- **P** Pets OK
- **R** Restaurant
- **T** Transportation

Located a 20-minute drive south of Moab at the base of the LaSal Mountains, the Pack Creek Ranch is an upscale **dude ranch** that offers western **gourmet meals** and **horseback rides**

as part of their package deal.  From the ranch you can follow
horse trails that wind through stands of pine and aspen into
12,000-foot mountains.  Pack Creek also provides three- and
four-day **pack trips** into Grand Gulch or the LaSals.

## Moab

Moab is best known for its colorful rock formations.  Four
**national and state parks** surround Moab within sixty miles:
Arches National, Canyonlands National, Dead Horse Point State,
and Newspaper Rock State Parks.  The topography is dramatic, a
special treat for pilots and passengers who fly into the area.

The Canyonlands have a tremendous Native American heritage.  Moab sits on the border between the lands of the ancient
Fremont and Anasazi, two very diverse cultures.  The early
history of man in Moab can be traced back 10,000 years and is
still visible in the ancient petroglyphs found in the area.

Today, you can go most anywhere around Moab and find
**petroglyphs** and **pictographs** that have been in place for over a
thousand years.  Ruins and artifacts are still being found.  Local
4x4 guides can take you to ancient sites of interest.

Moab is like a double-dip ice cream cone with two distinctly
different flavors.  The top dip is pure western:  movie-quality
scenery, rich Native American heritage, western art, and a touch
of cowboy culture.  The bottom dip is pure outdoor recreation:
rafting, fishing, riding, hiking, mountain biking, and four-wheel-
ing.  The density of river operators and out-back tour guides per
square mile is among the highest in the world.

Whether seeking a laid-back visit or outdoor adventure, you
can find things to do in Moab.  First, locate the **Travel Council**

in the plaza next to Eddie McStiff's **micro brewery**. Ask lots of questions, grab a handful of brochures, and trot over to Eddie McStiff's for a cold one. A second alternative is the Poplar Place Pub on First North and Main, listed in Toby Thompson's "100 Best Saloons in the U.S."

Art enthusiasts will enjoy browsing the **galleries** up and down Main street. You will find a wide variety of art, jewelry, and clothing – from tacky souvenirs to quality art. Wine connoisseurs can visit the Arches Vineyards **tasting room**, 435-259-5397, a couple miles south of town on Highway 191 at the innocent looking white building across from DAR/C Truck Plaza.

There are several **museums** in the area. The **Dan O'Laurie Museum**, 435-259-7985, tells the story of the Moab valley, both prehistoric and contemporary. The new **John Wesley Powell**

**Grand Old Ranch House restaurant**

**River History Museum**, 564-3526, is located in Green River and serves as the river runner's "Hall of Fame." Other attractions, the Stuntman's Hall of Fame and the Canyon Field Institute's multimedia show, have come and gone. Although this is a loss, it is also an opportunity for visitors to spend more time enjoying Canyonland's natural treasures, Arches and Canyonlands National Parks.

Moab's bright green **golf course** is set at the edge of town with a backdrop of red rock and blue sky. The fee for 18 holes is $18, 435-259-6488. Or, walk the town for free with the aid of an official Moab **Walking Tour** Guide. The guide pamphlet is available from the Travel Counsel or from the Dan O'Laurie Museum, in town at 259-7985.

Although Moab is a small town, it offers diversity in **dining** that is typically unavailable in western towns twice its size. Options range from soda fountain to Chinese, from chuck wagon BBQ to western gourmet meals. The Grand Old Ranch House on North Highway 191 serves German dishes, prime rib, seafood, and steaks. The Bar M Chuckwagon, 800-214-2085, four miles north of Arches Park provides a chuckwagon dinner and western entertainment for $16. Be there at 7:00 sharp.

The second option is a unique **sound and light show** called **Canyonlands By Night**, 800-294-9978. Cultured visitors will turn up their noses at this unusual experience, but I thought it was great! Imagine anyone dreaming up a concept like this:

"How about hitching a 40,000 watt generator to a truck, attaching some search lights to shine at the canyon walls, and driving the truck down the canyon while a bunch of tourists view the spectacle from a boat floating down the Colorado River? Yea, and let's add stereo sound, some narrative about the faces you can imagine in the canyon walls, a few corny jokes, and a story or two about how the God-fearing settlers took the land from the Indians."

This conversation (or one like it) took place some 25 years ago, and the show has been running summer evenings at dusk ever since. More than a roadside attraction you can't miss, this show is an expression of folk art and a living monument to fundamental American ingenuity. The experience can be yours for $20, the cost of a couple touch and gos.

## Canyonlands Area

**Scenic drives** radiate from Moab. Just five miles north of town is a drive that takes you through the **Arches National Park,** 435-259-8161. Wind, water, extreme temperatures, and underground salt movement are responsible for the sculptured rock you see as you drive. The park boasts the world's largest concentration of stone arches, over 2000 of which fill the 73,000-acre park. The park is open year-round, and has numerous hiking opportunities. Campsites may be available at Devil's Garden Campground, 259-4351.

You can take several hours or a full day to see the arches. It's a pretty drive, but it fell short of my expectations. If squeezed for time, consider taking a flight over the Canyonlands area between Moab and Page instead. If you have time, find a way to experience **Canyonlands National Park**, 435-259-7164. The park is a great expanse of primitive beauty centered around the Green and Colorado Rivers.

The "**LaSal Loop**" is a scenic drive that offers continual changes in scenery, elevation, vegetation, and terrain. It takes you along the Colorado River and into the LaSal Mountains, from red rock and sage to aspens and conifers. There are plenty of views, including an expansive 270-degree view near the top of the LaSals.

You can drive the loop in two hours if pressed for time, but why not allow for three or four. Avoid driving after dusk, as portions of the road contain no white line or markers and are extremely dangerous at night. The 60-mile route begins as you drive north on Highway 191 and turn right onto Scenic Byway 128 just before the Moab bridge.

The drive follows the Colorado River northeast. Negro Bill Canyon, a good stop for hikers, is three miles past the bridge. Turn right on Castle Valley Road. If the rock formations look familiar, it is because you have seen them in numerous movies and TV commercials.

**Arches National Park**

After traveling 11 miles on Castle Valley Road, turn right on LaSal Mountain Loop Road. Now you really begin to climb. Notice how the vegetation changes with the elevation. Pinyon and juniper trees give way to oak, then to pines, aspen, spruce and fir. Take time to enjoy the views. A five-mile road branches off to Warner Lake Campground. The loop road dips into Mill Creek Canyon and rises before descending down past Pack Creek Ranch to Highway 191, eight miles south of Moab.

Moab has a number of **hiking** options close to town. The Negro Bill Canyon hike is a local favorite. Find the canyon as described above and park at the marked parking lot. A noteworthy feature of this hike is Morning Glory Bridge, two miles up the trail. This 243-foot bridge is the sixth largest foot bridge in the U.S. Allow three or four hours for the round trip.

View from "LaSal Loop" drive

Although Moab and the Canyonlands are primarily known for colorful rock formations, river recreation is the largest tourist industry in Moab. Drive through Moab, and you see a large variety of signs and advertisements about **river running**. Trips leave almost daily for **multi-day floats** down Cataract Canyon of the Colorado River, as well as shorter but equally exciting floats down the Westwater section of the Colorado. Half- and full-day trips, including lunch, are offered for beginners. The following is a partial list of area operators:

| | | |
|---|---:|---|
| Adrift Adventures | *bike, 4x4, river* | 800-874-4483 |
| Adventure River Exp. | *river* | 800-331-3324 |
| Canyon Voyages | *hikes, 4x4, river* | 800-733-6007 |
| Canyonlands Field Inst. | *hiking, river* | 435-259-7750 |
| Holiday River Expeditions | *river* | 800-624-6323 |
| Moab Rafting | *river* | 800-RIOMOAB |
| Moki-Mac River Expeditions | *river* | 800-284-7280 |
| Navtec Expeditions | *4x4, river* | 800-833-1278 |
| Nichols Expeditions | *bike, river* | 800-648-8488 |
| N. American River Exp. | *4x4, river* | 800-342-5938 |
| Sheri Griffith River Exp. | *river* | 800-332-2439 |
| Tag-A-Long Exp. | *bike, 4x4, hike, river* | 800-453-3292 |
| Tex's Riverways | *river shuttle, river* | 435-259-5101 |
| Western River Exp. | *river* | 800-453-7450 |
| World Wide River Exp. | *river* | 800-231-2769 |

If cool spray and frantic paddling are more than you care to handle, kick back and enjoy a **jet-boat ride**. These safe and sturdy vehicles provide a speedy way to enjoy the river canyons. Most of the river-boat operators offer motorized river trips.

Many visitors prefer to enjoy the rugged Canyonlands from the perspective of solid ground. The following offer land-based adventures:

| Cowboy Trails | *trail rides* | 435-259-8053 |
| Dan Mick's Guided Tours | *4x4 tours* | 435-259-4567 |
| Desert Highlights | *bicycle, 4x4* | 800-747-1342 |
| Dreamrides | *bicycle, climbing* | 435-259-4619 |
| Gnarley Photo Adventures | *photo* | 435-259-9076 |
| Lin Ottinger Tours | *4x4 tours* | 435-259-7312 |
| Pack Creek Ranch | *hike, trail, pack* | 435-259-5505 |
| Rim Tours | *bicycle* | 800-626-7335 |

## Festivals and Events

Moab's big **summer event** is Butch Cassidy Days. Running early- to mid-June, the celebration includes several days of rodeo performances, square dances, music, food, ropers, autograph parties, stunts, fiddlers, and more. Contact the Visitor Center at 800-635-6622 for dates and details.

*- RW*

**Pack Creek Ranch trail ride photo, next page . . .**

# Monument Valley

## Monument Valley Airport

| | | | |
|---|---|---|---|
| **Town** | Monument Valley | **ID** | 71V |
| **Coord** | N-37-01, W-110-12 approx. | | |
| **Elev** | 5192 feet est, S end high | | |
| **Runway** | 16 - 34, 4000 x 75' dirt/asphalt | | |
| **Freq** | CTAF-122.9 | | |
| **Charts** | Denver sectional | | |

> **CAUTION:** *Airport information not for navigational use. Land 16. No go-around, due to nearby mesa. Soft when wet. Commercial sight-seeing traffic.*

**34**              **16**

> *Gouldings Lodge sits below a bluff at the heart*
> *of Monument Valley. Founded as a trading*
> *post in the 1920's, later a site for western*
> *films, and now a polular stop for tourists.*
> *Horseback and motor tours are their specialty.*
> *$70 - 330. Goulding's: 801-727-3231.*

## Airport

The airport is typically not listed in pilot's guides. Even so, the dusty strip gets a good deal of use from commercial sight-seeing aircraft. Listen and announce intentions on 122.9.

Runway 16 points toward the lodge, which sits at the base of a high bluff. You make an up-hill landing on Runway 16. This is considered a no-go-around approach. The last 800 feet and a tiedown area are paved. The tiedown area is sloped, but tiedowns

are scarce. Bring ropes and stakes. Significant winds are not uncommon, so do what you can to make your bird secure.

Depart on Runway 34. Winds were unfavorable and variable when I visited. I had to wait for five to ten minutes for better conditions before departure.

There are no aviation services at the strip. Call 801-727-3231 or 727-3225 for information.

## Goulding's Lodge

Harry Leone "Mike Goulding" built his home at the site in 1924. By 1928, and for 40 years thereafter, he and his family were traders and friends of the Navajos. As the West matured, the Gouldings were gracious hosts to famous writers, archeologists, anthropologists, and film crews.

A number of John Ford westerns were filmed in the valley between 1946 and 1960. Stars who kicked back their heals at

Goulding's Trading Post include the likes of John Wayne, Henry Fonda, and Shirley Temple.

Today, Goulding's hosts visitors who come to see the **classic western scenery**. When arriving by air, you can't miss the valley's famous 1000-foot monoliths. For a different perspective, take one of the ground tours offered by Navajo guides. The Navajo Tribal Park is part of the Navajoland, a 30,000 square mile reservation that spans four states. Tribal Park Supervisor: 801-727-3287.

**Horseback**, **4x4**, and **truck tours** cost $25-100 per person. Full-day tours usually include lunch. Overnight camping trips are available. Call Ed Black at 800-551-4039 to find out more about horseback and 4x4 trail rides. Call Goulding's at 801-727-3231 for information about covered truck rides into the valley.

At the lodge, you will find an interesting **museum**, **multimedia presentation**, **swimming pool**, **restaurant**, and **grocery shop**. All is within walking distance of the tiedown area.

# Needles Outpost

## Needles Outpost Airport

| | |
|---|---|
| **Town** | Monticello    **ID** UT59 |
| **Coord** | N-38-10.4, W-109-44.5 est |
| **Elev** | 4950 feet, E end high |
| **Runway** | 7 - 25, 4500 x 30' dirt |
| **Freq** | CTAF-122.9 |
| **Charts** | Denver sectional |

> *CAUTION:* Airport information not for navigational use. Verify runway condition, especially after thaw or rain. Watch density altitude.

25      7

**Needles Outpost, a dirt strip and small store at
the edge of Canyonlands National Park. Campsites, and trails into colorful canyon country.
$0 - 30. Cell phone: 435-979-4007.**

The airport is located at the edge of Canyonlands National
Park in the Needles District, 34 miles south of Canyonlands
airport and 10 miles east of the junction of the Colorado and
Green Rivers. A number of years ago, the airport was known as
"Canyonlands National Park" and was marked as *closed* on the
Utah Aeronautical Chart. It now appears as *Needles Outpost,
Restricted* on FAA charts. Although the airstrip is officially
restricted, owners Tracy and Gary monitor 122.9, periodically
drag the airstrip, and welcome fly-in visitors. "Restricted" seems
to mean "Land at your own risk (no insurance)."

The dirt runway was in good condition when I visited, but abnormally heavy rains could damage it at any time. Tiedown ropes are not available, so bring your own.

Cell phone: 435-979-4007. No fuel or shelter is available. A small restaurant and general store provides food, maps, and some camping supplies, open 365 days per year. Campsites with shower cost $15. Without the campsite, a shower costs $3. Primitive campsites are available several miles below in the park, but these have no showers and no water in winter. You can sleep under the wing for free.

This country is just southeast of an area called "The Maze." The Maze gained national notoriety in Edward Abby's humorous book, *The Monkey Wrench Gang* (on sale at the Needles Outpost store). The district got its name from the beautiful towering rock formations that catch the eye from air and ground.

alike. Some of the local rock surfaces are decorated by **Native American petroglyphs**.

A number of **trails** radiate from the park campground, meander amongst the rock formations, and interconnect to form a grid. Always carry plenty of water on these trails! Because flash floods can be deadly and often occur without warning, never camp in a dry-wash.

The Outpost store stocks a selection of interesting books on the area. The owners can arrange for **jeep tours** of the district. Some tours take you to remote Indian ruins with petroglyphs. Ask the store owners for a description of available tours and make reservations in advance. For general park information, call Moab Ranger Station, 435-259-7164.

*- RW*

Turquoise-sapphire blue industrial ponds surrounded by nature's reds and golds, a visual treat for flyers, between Moab and Needles airports

# Oljato

## Oljato Airport

| | |
|---|---|
| **Town** | Oljato **ID** 73V |
| **Coord** | N-37-02, W-110-19 est. |
| **Elev** | 4838 feet est. |
| **Runway** | 14 - 32, 3950 x 75' old asph. |
| **Freq** | CTAF-122.8 |
| **Charts** | Denver sectional |

> *CAUTION:* Airport information not for navigational use. Runway deteriorating; ruts and potholes. Prarie dog holes/mounds at runway edge.

> *Oljato, a Navajo airstrip and trading post that lost track of time. Funky but friendly, a tourist-free place to stay the night and take a trail ride. $0 - 275. Trading Post: 801-727-3210.*

## Airport Description

The Oljato airport is located in a little valley, not far from some low bluffs. A stream bed meanders just west of the runway. Unlike Monument Valley Airport seven miles east, Oljato has negligible air traffic. In fact, you are probably *it* for the month.

The asphalt runway has deteriated to the point where it has mild pot holes and ruts. The runway condition was not a problem for my Cessna 172. I was concerned, but managed to stay clear of

**Dean shows lights that once lined the runway**

serious roughness at touchdown and departure. An airplane with small wheels would certainly feel the ruts.

The Trading Post is next to runway; you can tie down just a stone's throw away. There are no tiedowns provided, so bring your own. If you forget, the guys at the Trading Post will give you a hand. Camping is allowed at the airport, and limited food and lodging are available. Call 801-727-3210 for information.

## Oljato

The Trading Post was built on Navajo land in 1921. In its early days, the place was quite alive. At one point after a generator was brought in, a complete set of military surplus landing lights were installed. Ed and Virginia Smith operated the Trading Post and airport from 1956 to 1988. They put the site on the National Register of Historical Places in 1980. Today, the runway lights are corraled near a shed, and the runway is in need of repair.

**Gunner tends the store**

Within the limits of a modest budget, the three residents are leisurely rejuvinating the facilities. Gunner mans the **store**. He has a small selection of basic food, supplies, and ice. He can warm up sandwiches or burritos for visitors who want a **quick meal**.

Dean Lewis plans to convert some of the old buildings into **lodging** – an ambitious project. At present, he has a double-wide trailer with rooms he can rent. He charges $55 for a room. The facilities are rather basic, compared to the standards to which most pilots are accustomed. If you arrive un-announced, Dean may have some chores to do before the room is ready for visitors.

Evelyn Jensen owns Navajo Country Guided **Trail Rides**. She keeps her horses primarily at Kayenta, Arizona. During the summer, she moves some some of them to Oljato. Trail rides cost between $25 for one hour, to $100 for a full day. Overnight trips cost $125 per person. Food is provided for full-day and overnight rides. Make arangements by calling 801-727-3210.

**Out-buildings, planned for conversion to guest cabins**

# St. George
## and Zion Park

## St. George Municipal

| | | | |
|---|---|---|---|
| **Town** | St. George | **ID** | SGU |
| **Coord** | N-37-05.48,  W-113-35.58 | | |
| **Elev** | 2938 feet, 1.1%, N end high | | |
| **Runway** | 16 - 34, 6101 x 100' asphalt | | |
| **Freq** | CTAF-122.8, Lights-3x5x7x | | |
| | AWOS-135.075 | | |
| **Charts** | Las Vegas sectional,  L5, Lo9 | | |

> **CAUTION:**   Airport information not for navigational use. Elevated runway can cause mis-judgment in approach. No line of sight between ends.   Strong cross-winds possible.

16

34

> *St. George, a clean, quiet town.  Gateway to*
> *picturesque rock, desert, and mountains.  Near*
> *ghost towns, and Zion National Park.  $100-200.*
> *Info:   435-628-1658, www.stgeorgechamber.com*

## Airport Description

St. George airport is located on a mesa, several hundred feet above the  surrounding city to the east. UNICOM is active.

## Airport Services, Transportation, and Lodging

Airport phone: 435-634-5822.  Fuel: 100LL, JetA, and auto fuel.  No tiedown fee.  Aero West, 774-1000, is a full-service FBO with oxygen and courtesy car.

Taxi services are provided by Auto Bus, 435-628-2287; Quality Cab, 656-5222; and St. George Taxi, 628-8320.  Rentals:

| | | |
|---|---|---|
| Avis, *airport* | 800-331-1212 | 435-634-3940 |
| Budget | 800-527-0700 | 435-673-6825 |
| National, *airport* | 800-CARRENT | 435-673-5098 |
| Quality, *airport* | | 435-634-0090 |
| Thrifty | 800-367-2277 | 435-674-2234 |

Lodging in St. George is clean and reasonably priced, often with amenities like swimming pool, Jacuzzi, and sauna.  Travelers favoring bed and breakfast environments will enjoy the Green Gate Village Bed and Breakfast Inn.  The Victorian units were built in the mid to late 1800s.  The historic Seven Wives

### Features

**B** Full  breakfast
**C** Continental
**H** Historic
**P** Pets  OK
**R** Restaurant
**T** Transportation

Inn is said to have gotten its name from the seven wives of the owner's great great grandfather. It includes two century-old buildings decorated with period furnishings. Ask for pilots discounts at the following:

| | | | |
|---|---|---|---|
| Green Gate B&B | **BHPT** | $60-140 | 800-350-6999 |
| Hilton | **PRT** | $41-145 | 800-662-2525 |
| Holiday Resort Inn | **PRT** | $76 | 800-457-9800 |
| Ranch Inn | **PT** | $44-72 | 435-628-8000 |
| Rococo, *airport* | **CRT** | $34-66 | 888-626-3671 |
| Seven Wives Inn | **BHT** | $66-140 | 800-600-3737 |

Lodging for Zion Park, Hurricane, and Springfield is listed later in this chapter.

## St. George

St. George is one of many Utah towns first colonized by the Mormons. Its temple was the first Mormon temple completed west of Ohio, and is the oldest in use today. The temple's construction has an interesting history. Because they were laying the foundation in mud, builders used one of Napoleon's 1000-pound cannons to cram volcanic rock deep into the earth. Not surprisingly, the huge white limestone structure is a prominent landmark from air or ground.

St. George presents a spotless first impression and sustains its personality with a number of old, well-preserved buildings, several **golf courses**, and a tidy college community. In wintertime, St. George becomes a mecca for golfers. Its greatest asset, however, is its close proximity to the **scenic wonders** of southwestern Utah.

# Pine Valley

"There stretching before me was the most beautiful sight I had ever beheld on God's green earth," Isaac Riddle said as he discovered Pine Valley. Today, as you drive through this charming little alpine community, Heidi skipping with her goats would not seem out of place.

Pine Valley's chapel has been an object of much folklore. Built by a ship builder in 1868, some old-timers claim the builder built the structure watertight, and that it would actually float. It is believed to be the **oldest Mormon chapel** still in use.

To get to Pine Valley from St. George, take Highway U-18 twenty-five miles north. Turn right and drive seven miles east into town. Pine Valley is located in a segment of the Dixie National Forest and is surrounded by mountains peaking at 10,000 feet.

The Pine Valley Lodge, 435-574-2544, rents cabins for $33. They offer **horseback riding**, **pack trips**, **hunt trips**, and **cross-country skiing**; but availability may be spotty, as the lodge is for sale. Two miles north is the **national park** with a reservoir and three secluded **campgrounds**. The park is said to be the greenest area in southern Utah, and its trails take you past lush vines, flowers, towering conifers, and crystal clear creeks. The reservoir is an excellent hole for **trout**.

# Snow Canyon State Park

Five miles northwest of St. George, Snow Canyon reveals a diverse display of **geological sights.** Hollywood discovered this photogenic locale in the 50s. Since then the canyon has hosted the likes of John Wayne, Susan Hayward, and Clark Gable. Robert Redford guided his horse along a parched streambed, flanked by desert-varnished cliffs in *The Electric Horseman.*

The drive into the canyon takes you between huge monolithic sandstone walls of red, standing above puddles of once-molten lava. Like layered biscuits, massive steps of stratified sandstone reach toward the sky. The vastness of the park is deceiving when judged from this beautiful three-mile drive. Off-road, one can hike one-half to three miles to **pictographs**, **desert tanks** (potholes filled with water), **lava-cone overlooks**, **lava caves**, and **sand dunes**.

To get to **Snow Canyon**, drive approximately five miles north on Highway U-18. Turn left and drive about two miles to the Shivwits Campground. Park information and trail maps are available at the campground. If you plan to camp at this nicely laid-out oasis, it is wise to call 800-322-3770 for information and reservations.

**Snow Canyon State Park campground**

## Ghost Towns

With an awesome Zion horizon towering in the background, Grafton has been the site of many famous Western movies (including *Butch Cassidy and the Sundance Kid*). Follow the route to Zion National Park as far as Rockville. Then cross the Virgin river and follow the dirt road for about three miles.

Silver Reef sprang into existence in 1866 after a mother lode of silver was discovered in the sandstone reefs of Pine Valley mountains. Once the largest town in southern Utah, Silver Reef was unique among Utah settlements in that saloons far outnumbered churches. Much of the original town was looted or moved to St. George. To see the restored version, drive north on I-5 and exit through Leeds. Follow the Silver Reef sign at the edge of Leeds.

## Hurricane Area and Pah Tempe Hot Springs

Hurricane is home of **Pah Tempe Hot Springs**. The springs are set beside the turquoise Virgin River that flows through a canyon of towering red limestone cliffs. The naturally heated water flows through a stream of beautiful cascaded pools. Temperatures range from 100 to 107 degrees Fahrenheit. The content is mild mineral and sulfur, reputed to be very healing.

The river adjacent to the pools is special. It is warm, with hot water bubbling through the sand at the river's bottom and burping through the mud at the river's edge. Wallow in the warm mud or let the bubbles find themselves between your toes in the sand. Rules at the pools are no nudity, drugs, alcohol, or smoking.

Due to earthquake damage in 1992, flow to the pools had been compromised. The pools are now back in full operation, 9:00 to

22:00. Day use fees are $10 per person. For an additional $10 per car, you can camp on site. Lodging at the B&B costs $60-71, including a vegetarian breakfast. In addition to the spa's outdoor pools, lodgers have private Jacuzzis in their rooms.

Ken Anderson purchased the springs in 1985 after a 15-year search. A landscape architect by trade, he has spent years restoring the property and fathering plant life in the canyon.

Ken is a good source of information for local hikes. One such hike is the flume-walk. Climb the canyon wall via the Rain Forest Trail. Continue climbing several hundred feet to the flume that is carved into the canyon wall. It was built one hundred years ago and is still in great shape, but has been retired and replaced by a 60-inch pipe. You can walk through the

**Pah Tempe Hot Springs**

tunnels, and you are treated to beautiful views of the canyon as you follow the flume up to the dam.

Pah Tempe Hot Springs is just northeast of Hurricane (pronounced "HER-a-kin"). When driving from St. George, follow Highway 9 several miles through Hurricane toward La Verkin. Just before crossing the Virgin River, turn right on the Enchanted Way. Don't be put off by the approach. Pah Tempe is several hundred feet below. Phone: 888-726-8367.

Quail Creek Reservoir, southwest of Hurricane on Highway 9, can provide refreshing relief from summer heat. Bass **fishing** is best in June, October, and April. Unfortunately,this resource became somewhat disabled on New Years Day 1989 when the reservoir dam broke. Facilities were available for **camping**, **boating**, **water skiing**, **sail boarding**, and **jet skiing**. Hopefully, all these options will be restored soon.

**A soak in warm, bubbling sand in the Virgin River**

## Zion National Park

The most famous local scenic attraction is Zion National Park. Known for its towering majesty of weather-honed cliffs of white and red, the canyon provides an awesome visual experience to those who fly over the park.

Zion National Park is a geological paradise of lush riverbeds, shimmering pools of clear water, veiled waterfalls, and soaring painted rock cliffs. The park's canyon has been carved from a 7000 foot high plateau that can be reached from Highways I-15, 9, or 17. Highway 9 bisects the park from east to west. The gorge is over 2000 feet deep and narrows in places to less than 100 feet across.

Inside the park are **camping** facilities, networks of **hiking** trails, **horse rentals**, a lodge, and a restaurant. The Zion Visitor's

**Zion National Park cabins**

Center is located at the Springdale entrance. It is open year-round and provides an abundance of information about hiking, geology, and folklore. Call the Center at 435-772-3256 for information. You can stay in the park at the park's lodge, 772-3213; or campground, 772-3256. The Bin-N-Spur Restaurant in nearby Springdale is a hot spot for evening action.

Camping and lodging are available in Hurricane and Springdale. For lodging in Hurricane, try Motel 6, $33-88, 435-635-4010; or the Best Western Lamplighter, $50-100, 435-635-4647. Both allow pets. Limited lodging and camping are also available just northeast of Hurricane at the Pah Tempe Hot Springs, 888-726-8367. Additional lodging is located 23 miles northeast of Hurricane at Springdale, the gateway to Zion National Park:

| | | | |
|---|---|---|---|
| Bumbleberry Inn | PR | $68-84 | 800-828-1534 |
| Canyon Ranch Motel | P | $63-86 | 435-772-3357 |
| Driftwood Lodge | CP | $66-88 | 888-801-8811 |
| El Rio Lodge | P | $52-60 | 888-772-3205 |
| Pioneer Lodge | | $48-87 | 888-772-3233 |
| Zion House B&B | B | $63-86 | 435-772-3281 |
| Zion Park Lodge | HR | $90-130 | 435-772-3213 |
| Zion Park Lodge, *reservations* | | | 303-297-2757 |

*- RW*

# Index

*Special thanks to pilot Dr. Sandra Brown
for her valuable contributions of research,
critique, and copy editing.*

# Lava Hot Springs Airpark Project

*A recreational residential airpark at the western edge of the Rockies, eastern Idaho.*

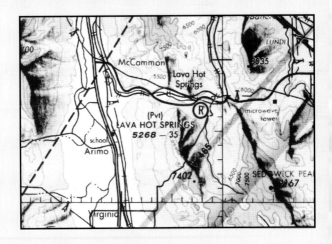

For information about residential lots and business opportunities, contact:

**Alta Research**
131 NW 4th Street #290, Corvallis, OR 97330
Corvallis: 541-929-5738, Roaming: 500-288-2582
alta@alta-research.com, www.alta-research.com

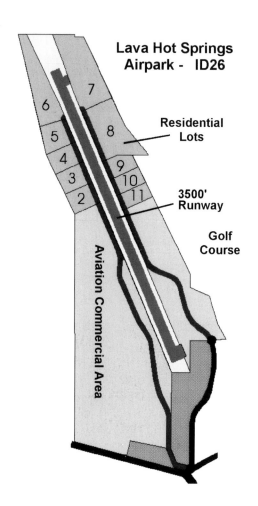

# Lava Hot Springs
# Airpark - ID26

**Residential Lots**

**3500' Runway**

**Golf Course**

Aviation Commercial Area

7
6
5
4
3
2
8
9
10
11

**Coordinates: N-42-36.5, W-112-1.9, Elevation: 5268 feet**

© 1998 by ALTA Research

Lava Hot Springs Airpark is located 1.5 miles southwest of Lava Hot Springs, a small town with a variety of hot springs facilities. The airpark sits on a mesa, 200 feet above the valley floor, surrounded by mountains.

The area has the following recreational opportunities: hot springs, golf, Pebble Creek Ski Facility, hiking, horseback riding, snow-mobiling, hunting, and fishing. Pocatello, the county seat, has an IFR airport, ample shopping, and a university. Pocatello is a 45-minute drive east from Lava, and Salt Lake City is a two hour drive south. Jackson Hole and many other interesting fly-in sites are within an hour or two of the airpark.

Residential lots range in size from 1.5 to 8 acres. All lots have access to the runway and a spectacular view of the valley and surrounding mountains. Because the airpark is an aviation community, all purchasers must be (or have been) pilots or students in pursuit of a license. If you would like to join this community, give us a call. Come visit whenever conditions permit.